True Life in God

Vassula

Volume Four

(Notebooks 42-53)

Published by

Trinitas™

Declaration

The decree of the Congregation for the Propagation of the Faith, A.A.S. 58, 1186 (approved by Pope Paul VI on October 14, 1966) states that the Nihil Obstat and Imprimatur are no longer required on publications that deal with private revelations, provided they contain nothing contrary to faith and morals.

The publisher wishes to manifest unconditional submission to the final and official judgement of the Magisterium of the Church.

True Life in God

Vassula

Volume Four

(Notebooks 42-53)

Second printing Aug. 1992

Published by

Trinitas™

P.O. Box 475
Independence, Missouri, USA 64051
Phone (816) 254-4489

For further information direct all inquires to **Trinitas**™

Cover photo: Agamian Portrait, courtesy of Holy Shroud Guild.

Printed in United States of America.

Also available in Spanish, French, Italian, German. Translations in progress include Greek, Danish, Russian, Portuguese, and Japanese. For information contact Trinitas.

Table of Contents

Introduction, *Fr. Michael O'Carroll* .... Page I

Prayers Given to Vassula by Jesus and Mary .... Page XI

Notebook 42 .... Page 1

Notebook 43 .... Page 17

Notebook 44 .... Page 33

Notebook 45 .... Page 49

Notebook 46 .... Page 65

Notebook 47 .... Page 81

Notebook 48 .... Page 97

Notebook 49 .... Page 112

Notebook 50 .... Page 128

Notebook 51 .... Page 144

Notebook 52 .... Page 160

Notebook 53 .... Page 176

Note from the Publisher

As you read **<u>True Life in God</u>** you will notice pages on which a portion of the message has been removed. Vassula, in discernment with her Spiritual Director, has decided to omit certain sections from the handwritten messages. These are of a personal nature and were not intended for public distribution.

Trinitas™

Welcome

To the praise of Jesus and Mary

In reading the messages, always read Volume One first and follow the order of the books so that you become immersed in God's Love for you.

Jesus asked me to tell you to always take my name, Vassula, out of the messages and replace it with your own name.

I really must express here my gratitude to my family, my spiritual director, and all my faithful friends who have made the preparation of this book possible.

I want to mention Father René Laurentin, Sr. Lucy Rooney, Father Bob Faricy, Father Michael O'Carroll, Tony Hickey, Pat Callahan, Tom Austin, and everyone who promotes and helps distribute these messages. I bless the Lord and thank Him for the ears that heard His Cry of Love from His Cross and now, touched, become His mouthpieces broadcasting this Cry of Love.

The text presented in this volume is the original English. At my request, there have been some abbreviations and additions which were necessary either due to the personal nature of a message or to clarify the sense of certain passages.

Vassula

Previous Volume Synopsis

True Life In God
Volume One

1) **Notebooks 1-16**
2) *A Note to the Reader* by Lucy Rooney, SND and Robert Faricy, SJ
3) *Foreword* by Patrick de Laubier, Professor, University of Geneva; University of Fribourg, Switzerland
4) *Introduction* by Fr. René Laurentin
    - Nine pages of interviews with Vassula.
    - A graphological analysis by handwriting expert J.A. Munier.
    - Excerpts from a speech by Fr. Don Gobbi, of the Marian Movement.
5) *A Book of Prayer* by Vladimir Zielinski, Russian Orthodox Theologian

True Life In God
Volume Two

1) **Notebooks 17-28**
2) *Introduction* by Fr. James Fannan, Vassula's Spiritual Director through April, 1991
3) *Foreword* by Fr. Michael O'Carroll, Vassula's Spiritual Director
4) *Presentation* by Fr. René Laurentin

True Life In God
Volume Three

1) **Notebooks 29-41**
2) *Introduction* by Tony Hickey, Director, Manchester Medjugorje Center, Manchester England

Introduction

Fr. Michael O'Carroll
Vassula's Spiritual Director

This interview was recorded at the home of Lord John Eldon in London, England, in November 1991.

Fr. O'Carroll: Vassula, fortunately there is no need to introduce you. You and your means of expression are now well known to us. You are the bearer of very important messages from Our Lord Jesus Christ to our time. I am most impressed by the amazing rapidity with which your writings have been diffused. Within less than two years, apart from the English edition, translations are available in Spanish, French, Italian, German, Greek, Danish, Russian, Portuguese, and Japanese, with others promised in the near future. I also noted recently that the Canadian Catholic periodical L'Informateur Catholique published a nine page feature about you and your message. It sold out immediately, and for the first time in the history of this publication, they had to reprint twice - a print order in each case of 15,000 copies. Does this surprise you or did the Lord give you some intimation that this was how things would work out, Vassula?

Vassula: Yes, one day, in 1987, when He was dictating to me He said, *"My Word will be like a cedar spreading out its branches like arms, healing your wickedness, feeding your misery and delivering you from evil."* (NB 8, P 19-20) And again in that same year, He spoke again about the messages: *"My Word will be like a rivulet, flowing, then rushing, until it pours out and turns into an ocean, an ocean of Peace and Love."* (NB 9, P 31)

The Two Hearts

Fr. O'Carroll: Now, the heart of your message is unquestionably the heart of Christ, of Jesus Christ. This devotion was approved and supported by the Catholic Church from medieval times, and became prominent in the 17th century through the revelations of St. Margaret Mary which were approved and supported by Church authority. It was a very powerful insight into the whole meaning of Jesus Christ for each individual's soul. Unfortunately it had lapsed to some extent, indeed, in places, it almost died out. Could you state briefly what the Heart of Jesus means for you, what it means to have Him speak to you?

Vassula: I'll quote His words to me directly, *"Love Me and I shall continue to pour out to you the Riches of My Sacred Heart, all this Wealth that had been reserved for your times. I had once said that from My Sacred Heart I will perform at the End of Times, works as never before, works that will marvel you to show the radiant glory of My Sacred Heart. I had promised that I would expose My Sacred Heart entirely and wholeheartedly to entice hearts, because My Words are sweeter than honey."* (NB 53, P 47-48)

Fr. O'Carroll: This is indeed very moving, very consoling, and will be, I think, a very great help to many Catholics. Now along with this I have noted that you have likewise a profound sense of the meaning of the Immaculate Heart of the Mother of Jesus in our lives. I should perhaps say in parenthesis, Vassula, that not only is this both enlightening and helpful to many Catholics I am quite sure, but it is most unusual in the great tradition to which you belong. You are a member of the Greek Orthodox Church and I think it is wonderful that there is this innovation, I do not think "innovation" is too strong a word, and that from this innovation there will be, as it were, an extra strong argument for the importance, the urgency as well as the validity of this appeal, that you make on behalf of the Heart of Jesus.

Would you say something about the Immaculate Heart of Mary as she has come to be expressed and to express herself in the messages which you receive. Would you concentrate particularly on the union, or, to borrow the words of both the present Pope and the Great Prelate of the Far East, Cardinal Sin, the "Alliance of the Hearts of Jesus and Mary."

Vassula: Well, first, before I read these messages to you, I want to explain that I have never been trained in any catechism, especially, as I am a Greek Orthodox, a Catholic catechism, so I would never have guessed that the Sacred Heart, as such, existed, or the words Immaculate Heart were in the Catholic tradition. I am taking only what Jesus dictates to me and when He comes as the Sacred Heart, I take down the Sacred Heart; when He tells me about the Immaculate Heart, I take down what He says. Then it comes to me that this terminology did not exist in the Orthodox tradition. I am being used as an instrument; I am taking down the dictation of Jesus. In reference to the Alliance of the Two Hearts, of which you speak now, I had no idea that this also existed. But I want to read a little prayer that Jesus told me to write down in His own words: *"My child, to the Father, repeat after Me this prayer; 'Father, blessed be Your Name; since Your Beloved Son Jesus Christ came to the world, not to condemn it, but to save the world, have Mercy upon us, look at Your Son's Holy Wounds, that are wide open now and remember the price He has payed for us, to redeem all of us, remember His Sacred Wounds, and the two Hearts You Yourself united in Love and who suffered together, this One of the Immaculate Conception and Your Beloved Son, O Father, remember His Promise now and send us the Advocate, in full force, the Holy Spirit of Truth, to remind the world of the Truth and of Your Son's docility, humbleness, obedience and great Love, Father, the time has come, when the reign of division cries out for Peace and Unity, the time has come that Your Son's wounded Body cries out for Righteousness, that of which the world has not known yet, but through the Immaculate Heart of Mary, and the Sacred Heart of Jesus, give us, Precious Father, this Peace in our hearts, and fulfill the Scriptures by fulfilling Your Beloved Son's*

Prayer to You: that we may all be one, one in the Divine Holy Trinity, so that we worship and praise You all, around one single Tabernacle." (NB 50, P 52-56)

Fr. O'Carroll: This is very inspiring indeed, Vassula, it is very inspiring to me, because I labored with a number of others to put together all the data available on the history of the Two Hearts through the ages. This information was presented at the symposium organized by Cardinal Sin and powerfully supported by the present Pope, in Fatima, in 1986.

Christian Unity

Fr. O'Carroll: Now you have had very broad experience of the world. You know Third World countries, especially Africa, and Bangladesh in Asia, very well. You have had a very distinguished career as a painter and you know the realities of modern life. This must give a certain sense of poignancy to the appeal which Jesus makes to you for unity. Would you like to say something now about the pressing nature of His prayer to us to unite, to end division, to be one, and to have this unity primarily from the heart?

Vassula: Yes, Jesus has been dictating to me, I would say, many messages for unity. He is putting it quite strongly, because, to me, it seems as if He cannot wait any more, He is too wounded. I am going to read these very recent messages directly from what is written here: *"Daughter, for My sake, take My Cross of unity and carry it across the world. Go from country to country and tell those who speak of unity, yet never cease to think the contrary and continue to live the contrary, that their division has separated My Heart from theirs. Shout, and eventually My Voice will break through their deafness. Be My Echo. Be the defender of the truth and of the one Church I Myself had established. Go to every nation and present yourself to them. Tell them that I want peace and one church under My Holy Name. Tell them that he who maintains to be just, yet remains divided, will eat from the fruit he has sown and will perish. Tell them* also how I abhor insincere hearts; their solemnities and their discourses weary Me. Tell them how I turn away from their loftiness and their rigidity. Their judgement appears, indeed, great and impressive to man but not to Me. I cannot congratulate a dying church nearing putrefaction. Tell those who want to hear that, unless they lower their voices, they will never hear Mine. Should they lower their voices then they will begin to hear Mine and thus do My Will. I am One, yet each of them made a Christ of their own, I am the Head of My Body yet all I see are their heads, not Mine. Tell them to lower their heads and they will see Mine. Tell them to lower themselves so that I may be able to lift them to Me. Tell everyone that I shall establish My Kingdom in the midst of poverty. Those very ones who have time to hear My Spirit adore Me and do My Will. In these My Soul rejoices." (NB 55, P 2-7)

Fr. O'Carroll: Vassula, there exists in the Catholic Church, since the late sixties, an Ecumenical Society of the Blessed Virgin Mary. This is, in a sense, a challenge to the assumption that the Mother of the Savior, Mother of Unity as St. Augustine called her, could be an obstacle to the true profound unity for which we long. This Society has had considerable success, if I may be allowed that word, within the Catholic and other Christian churches. Of course, we should have known, and it is wonderful that we are getting confirmation of this from one of the Orthodox communion, that there can be complete unity with the Orthodox as well as with the other Christian churches of the West. The Orthodox have profound, tenacious, inspiring, enlightening, and splendid traditions both of doctrine and devotion to the Mother of God. Their ancestors in the East continued to keep all her early feasts. They still use the Great Akathistos Hymn, the most beautiful ever composed in honor of Our Lady - which, of course, is used also by the Eastern Rite Catholics. They, too, use the "Sub Tuum," ("We fly to thy patronage"), the oldest prayer to Our Lady in Christendom, dated at the fourth, possibly third century, preserved in Greek on papyrus in the John Rylands Library in Manchester. In the light of all of this and all that Our Lady means to many within the varied Christian traditions,

we cherish her as being our powerful advocate for unity. How would you see this and how would the words you have received from on high concur with what I have just said?

Vassula: Well, there is Mary's very strong call for unity. Before I read that message I want to say that I do not agree with the common interpretation of "unity." The Greek Orthodox sometimes say that when our brothers, the Roman Catholics, will become Greek Orthodox, then there will be unity. And the Catholics sometimes expect everyone to become Roman Catholics. This is how man thinks. Heaven does not think that way. Heaven sees unity built inside each one's heart. I am still a Greek Orthodox. I remain a Greek Orthodox. I am practising as a Greek Orthodox but I do not make any difference in going to my brothers who are Catholics. I go to their church. Jesus is sending me everywhere. He does not send me only to the Greek Orthodox. We should unite in the heart and with the heart.

As to the new church that Jesus is talking about building from the church which is in ruins now, He does not mean to build a new church completely different, like a sect, if you will, but He says: *"I will make it resemble the primitive church, one and united, built with the foundations that are love and humility"* - accepting each other and praying to Jesus together.

So I will read what Mary is saying to me: *"Treason barricades unity among brothers. Insincerity of heart induces God's cup to augment. They wrenched the body of my Son, divided it, mutilated it, and paralyzed it. I am reminding you all that through Him all of you have, in the one Spirit, your way to come to the Father, yet you remain divided under my Son's name. You speak of unity and peace and yet stretch a net for those who practice it. God cannot be deceived nor is He convinced by your arguments.*

The Kingdom of God is not just words on the lips. The Kingdom of God is love, peace, unity and faith in the heart. The Lord's Church united in one inside your heart. The keys to unity are love and humility. Jesus never urged you to divide yourselves. This division in His Church was no desire of His. I implore my children to unite in heart and voice and rebuild my Son's primitive Church in their heart. I am saying my Son's primitive Church since that Church was constructed on love, simplicity, humility, and faith. I do not mean you to reconstruct a new edifice, I mean you to reconstruct an edifice inside your heart. I mean you to knock down the old bricks inside your heart; bricks of disunion, intolerance, unfaithfulness, unforgiveness, lack of love, and reconstruct my Son's church by reconciling. You need intense poverty of the spirit and an overflow of wealth of generosity and not until you understand that you will have to bend, will you be able to unite." (NB 54, P 44-47)

Fr. O'Carroll: This is very wonderful, Vassula, I remind you, and our readers, that according to the Code of Canon Law promulgated by Pope John Paul II, you, as a member of the Greek Orthodox Church, are now entitled to receive the sacraments within the Catholic body from Catholic priests. I am aware of the immense quality, nobility, and dedication of your Catholic friends who see in you a true witness to the love of Jesus - to His caring, saving power in our midst. I am thinking of people like Fr. Gobbi, the founder of the Marian Movement of Priests; Fr. Faricy; John Eldon; and above all, the giant of Catholic scholarship, Fr. René Laurentin. Fr. René is the specialist in Charismatic phenomena charisms which have been proclaimed as valid and as continuing by the Second Vatican Council. Fr. Laurentin was one of the first Catholics to welcome your message and to support you with his expertise, sincerity, and courage. It is wonderful that we should already have in your own person, your own life, and your own friendships, a beginning, a nucleus of the Christian Unity for which you work so courageously and so faithfully.

The Conversion of Russia

Fr. O'Carroll: Now, may I turn to a different subject? The issue of Russia, its upheavals inside the country itself as well as in those countries annexed since the Second World War is a burning one. There is a more profound concern

about which I want you to speak. That is: What is going to happen to the soul of Russia? Will Russia come back to its ancient Christian allegiance? Will the prayers offered incessantly by so many faithful devout souls, the sacrifices that have been heroically offered to God for Russia, will they bear fruit? Certainly, we know they will bear fruit but will this be delayed? Or will it take place, do you think, in the near future? Will the consecration of Russia to the Immaculate Heart of Mary by one Pope after the other, from Pius XII to Pope John Paul II, bear its fruit? When will the words of Our Lady of Medjugorje "In Russia my Son will be glorified as no where else" come true? I think Jesus has spoken to you very often about Russia. Would you like to communicate some of that precious message to us, Vassula?

Vassula: Yes. Since the beginning, in 1988, I have received seven long prophecies about Russia, her condition, the way she has abandoned Jesus, and her resurrection. He promised me that Russia will be one of the nations that will glorify Him the most, and while saying these words to me He seemed to rejoice already in seeing the glory that she will give Him.

In the first messages in January He showed me Russia as a woman lying dead in a desert, telling me: *"Vassula! O Vassula! I have one of My beloved daughters lying dead! a sister of yours! My well-beloved daughter Russia. come! come and I will show her to you, look!"* (NB 20, P 12) Then I started to weep because it was really very sad to see that scene. I felt as if I were present there seeing another person who is dead. I felt Him so sad that I could not stop my crying. Jesus said: *"O do not weep, I will resurrect her Vassula, I will resurrect her for My Glory, I will revive her as I have revived Lazarus."* (NB 20, P 13) He told me He is close to her, warming her cold heart and very, very soon she will change. This was three years before the recent fall of communism.

In a more recent message, on the 30th of August, 1991, Jesus stated, *"your Holy One is resurrecting Russia to be a noble nation; Russia will be perfected in the Arms of her Spouse. I the Lord shall perfect her; have I not said to you My child, that I have My Hand on her cold heart warming it?* (A prophecy received on the 11th of March, 1988, NB 22, P 26) *and the day My bride will open her eyes and see Me her Spouse standing beside her, she shall see and understand what My Hands have done in her midst and from thereon, Russia, My bride shall openly hold My Name Holy; and all erring evil spirits within her will flee; I had told you all these things before they happened so that you may believe that it is I, the Almighty, who is guiding you; hear Me: I shall not conceal My Plans; if men are tempted to conceal My Plans, I, with My Own Hand shall unveil everything to you all before they happen. The Holy One has been warning you, I had not been menacing anyone of you - A Ray of Light from Heaven shall come in the midst of My Body and change the face of this earth and bring peace among brothers; this will be the reward of the martyr saint's prayers, sacrifices, penances, constancy and faith; - do not be afraid when the <u>hour of great distress</u> comes if you were constant and kept your faith, for this <u>Hour</u> has to come to change the face of this earth; thus everything said at Fatima's will be accomplished.*

. . .not long ago, most of the nations of the world never believed that the enemy, the Red Dragon, would lose its power, in Russia, so suddenly; Vassula, if your sister Russia rebelled against Me, it came through the sins of the world and its crimes; tyranny comes from below." (NB 53, P 56-59)

I asked, "But how did her children feel, those martyrs who belong to you, because we know well that there are also very faithful people in Russia?" And He answered, *"How can I describe what her children suffered, to what can I compare them, daughter? all Heaven mourned for her children; her sons laid helpless, but who was there around them to mourn for them? was there anyone strong enough among them to pierce the Dragon through? not when their skins were shrunken against their bones; her children went begging for Bread, oppressed by the enemy, they collapsed under their burden, if they left in secrecy to take refuge in My Arms, they would be punished severely; they were not allowed to show their zeal for Me; their pursuers were swifter than vipers, eyeing each step they took, and had they any suspicions that The Book of Life would be hidden under their mattress, My children would be harassed, tracked, then*

captured; ah, daughter, My Eyes wept ceaselessly to see this nation reduced to silence by the sword; priests and prophets were made prisoners and were forced to dwell in darkness; many of them were slaughtered pitilessly before My very Eyes; - this nation who at one time honored Me and praised Me openly, radiant as a sapphire, a Citadel of delights, was reduced into a waterless country of drought, by the sins and crimes of the world; I tell you, daughter, Russia, your sister, has not yet shown you what she will accomplish in My Name; the <u>Day of Festival has yet to come and how I wish it were here already!</u> pray, pray for this Glorious Day." (NB 53, P 56-59) And by that He made me feel that in spite of the fall of communism itself in Russia He is still hiding from us something far, far stronger and much, much better and fantastic because, He says, the Day of Festival has yet to come; and when He was saying this He was so pleased, it was like, you know, something very nice that will really come out from Russia. So, it's very promising.

<u>Fr. O'Carroll</u>: It certainly is very promising, Vassula, and it will be a wonderful fulfillment for the faithful Russians whom we have known. I think of the great Russian teachers, who adorned the Saint Serge Institute in Paris: people like Serge Bulgakov or his very great disciple Paul Evdokimov. Or I think of a great, deported Christian, Solzhenitsyn, who witnessed inside and outside Russia. And I think, also, of a remarkable young lady, Tatiana Govitcheva, another great witness to Christ, whose life mirrors this wonderful change that has already begun, and which, no doubt will come, as I say, to a still greater fulfillment, and will reach much greater heights. Tatiana is a university professor who was converted from the worldly life that she led. She joined the Clandestine feminist Christian movement in her country, called "Maria," suffered persecution, harassment, and deprivation of her occupation, loss of her social status, finally being forced to make a choice between banishment or prison. Fortunately for us, she chose exile and wrote of her experiences. It is very precious. Since the great change which you have already outlined, Tatiana has gone back to her country and has

already found this very revival immensely impressive.

The thirst for God is strong in Russia. The Mass celebrated in public after the young men were killed during the Coup was televised. We have seen the head of Russia, the lineal successor of Stalin, go twice to Rome to speak to the Pope, to invite the Pope to Russia. He promised a charter of religious freedom which has already been enacted, and he has expressed his wish to inaugurate an era of freedom, of good relationships with the church.

This, in a certain sense, is a facet, I suppose, Vassula, of the whole unity for which the Lord is sighing, for which He is praying before the Father as He prayed on earth. He has chosen this theme of urgency in His recent messages to you. With so much around us that discourages our search for unity and our feeble efforts to obtain unity, it is very uplifting to know that the Lord is not abandoning us, that He is still desirous to help us and that He will bring the eventual blessing of one true church of Jesus Christ in our midst. Would you like to read some of these messages?

Vassula: Yes, first I will read what I have asked the Lord so that you understand how the Lord discusses these things with me. I said, "Lord, I feel content to know that we will be united, although no one yet really knows how. The problems are apparently great and the schisms greater still. As You say, the staff of the shepherd has been broken; not only in half but in splinters; and Your body has been mutilated, wrenched, and paralyzed. You ask us all to bend. How? What is to be done? Which is the first step? I'm a Greek Orthodox and I am sharing everything with my Roman Catholic brothers. I do not differentiate myself under Your name when I am with them nor do they treat me any differently from their own. I also know that many of them go to the Greek or Russian Orthodox churches." After I discussed more, the Lord said, "_The day will come when they will break bread together on one altar and no one will stop My Children coming to Me. This fortress they have built to divide you is already condemned by Me. You are all brothers in Me. This_

is what you are to teach them to believe and persuade them to do. As for those who remain divided in body and spirit, differentiating themselves under My Holy Name, I tell them as I have told the Church in Sardis; you are reputed to be alive in the eyes of the world but not in your Maker's eyes. Revive what little you have left, - it is dying fast - and wherever the corpse is, there will the vultures gather. Unite, assemble, invoke My Name together, consecrate My Body and My Blood together. Do not persecute the Way. Humble yourselves and bend to be able to unite and glorify Me. You speak of the Spirit but do not act in the Spirit. You speak of the Way but you rank first to obstruct it. How little do you know Me. You call out My Name, yet you murder My Children between the sanctuary and the altar. I tell you solemnly, all of this will be brought to you in the day of judgment. Can you face Me and truly say 'I am reconciled with my brothers?' Can you truly say, I have not differentiated myself among brothers under Your Holy Name? I have treated them as my equal. When you present your case before Me, I shall then say to your face, 'Away with you, you have not treated your brothers as your equal. You have massacred daily My Body - where is your triumph? While I was building, you were tearing down; while I was reassembling, you were scattering; while I was uniting, you were dividing; yet, even today, if you come to Me as you are, I can heal you. I can transfigure you and you will glorify Me. Alas for those with child or with babies at the breast when My day comes.' Jesus told me to write the explanation of this verse - "_Alas for those I find with sin coiled in them as with child and with adepts formed by them and of their own kind, but it has been said that from your own ranks there will be men coming forward with a travesty of truth on the lips to induce the disciples to follow them. I am shouting and I am trying to break through your deafness to save you and if I reproach you, it is because of the greatness of the love I have for you. But I tell you truly, I shall assemble one day all the separated parts of My Body together into one assembly._" (NB 55, P 23-32)

Then He speaks for those who are really sincere and trying to unite - who love Him, He tells these people, "_Do not weep, My Friends, you who love Me. Endure what I endure, however, console Me and have faith in Me. You will achieve great works in My Name. Be tolerant as I am_

tolerant. I have been hungry, thirsty and often starving and you came to My help, carry on your good works and I shall reward you. I tell truly you are not alone; I am with you. Be united in Me and live in peace. You are the posterity of My Blood and the heir of My Kingdom. Tell them that the Heart of the Lord is Love and that the heart of the Law is based on Love. Tell My People that I do not want administrators in My House. They will not be justified in My Day because it is these very ones who have industrialized My House. I have sent you My Spirit to live in your hearts. This is why the Spirit Who lives in you will show you that My Church will be rebuilt inside your hearts, and you will acknowledge each other as your brothers in your heart."
(NB 55, P 23-32)

First I want to describe the vision He has given me of Himself. Jesus, in saying all this, had taken the voice of a victim, weary, begging, as though He depended on us like a prisoner in a cell going to the little window in the cell door asking the guard how much longer until the day of his liberation. He was saying it in this attitude, *"Will I, brother, one more season, go through the pain I have been going through year after year, or will you give Me rest this time? Am I going to drink one more season the cup of your division? Or will you rest My Body and unify, for My Sake, the feast of Easter? In unifying the date of Easter you will alleviate My Pain, brother, and you will rejoice in Me, and I in you, and I will have the sight of many restored. My Beloved, My Creator, He Who is my Husband has revealed to us things that no human hand could have performed. This is what you would cry out once your sight is restored in My Name and I will come to you. I solemnly tell you, assemble all of you and listen, this time, to your Shepherd. I will lead you in the way that you must go. Send My Message to the ends of the earth."* (NB 55, P 23-32)

The Holy Spirit

Fr. O'Carroll: Well, Vassula, there is another mighty theme about which you have much to say. We are, under the inspiration of the present Pope, recovering the sense of the Holy Spirit not only theoretically, as an act of faith, as an article of our Creed, but as *the* vital, dominant force even in the life of Jesus Christ Himself as Man. This was so from the moment of the baptism to His Resurrection and to the sending of the Spirit in the life of the church after Pentecost; it must continue in the life of each individual person. This recovery, begun with the Second Vatican Council, and at the popular level, with the help of the Charismatic movement has done such wonders. In France, through one of its principal, best known representatives, Frére Ephraim, of the Lion de Juda, supports your mission very, very, strongly.

A book titled The Forgotten Paraclete published in France in 1921, was rather challenging. The Spirit was being forgotten and the great spiritual author, Dom Columba Marmion, used to recall the episode of the neophytes in the Acts of the Apostles who said to St. Paul that they had not even heard if there were a Holy Spirit. The position of some Christians is, perhaps, not quite that severe, but not very far from it.

Now, at the Second Vatican Council, and this is very relevant to your status as an Orthodox Christian, Vassula, certain of the Orthodox theologians were admitted to the Council as observers and encouraged to express their opinions. They were disappointed and were quite frank; disappointed at the lack of a vital, enlarged, meaningful teaching about the Holy Spirit in the Council documents. One of them, a Greek theologian, one of your fellow countrymen, Nicos Nisciotis, said in a remarkable essay which had quite an impact at the end of the third session of the Council, "If there is not more about the Holy Spirit in your Council documents they will not have great influence in the Orthodox world." As a result of that, there was a considerable effort, in the last session of the Council, to formulate teaching on the Holy Spirit. This was continued by Pope Paul VI and has been amplified by the present Pope. He has done so in a lengthy series of Catecheses, in his great encyclical on the Holy Spirit "Dominum et Vivificantem," in some of the marvelous addresses he gave at the time of the sixteenth centenary of the Council of Constantinople which proclaimed the divinity of the Holy Spirit. The wonderful passage he has in his recent encyclical, <u>Redemptoris Missio</u>, on the mission on the Holy Spirit, establishes the Holy Spirit as the principal agent of mission.

It is in the light of that theological and historical background, some of which is rather sad, that I would ask you, Vassula, to speak to us about the words Jesus gives you on His Spirit. I know these have been frequent, meaningful, and can have very, very, great influence on your listeners.

<u>Vassula</u>: Yes, Jesus often speaks about the Holy Spirit, but first I will give you a prelude to what He says: *"beloved ones; indeed, the devil's smoke has penetrated into My Sanctuary, but what smoke lasts forever? I shall, with the Breath of My Holy Spirit, dissipate and blow away this smoke and no authority nor any power from beneath will be able to intervene. I am coming to bring Fire to the earth and purify nation after nation."* (NB 51, P 14) And I said to Jesus, "Lord, come to us in full force with Your Holy Spirit, for, most Tender Abba, as You glorified Your Son and Your Son glorified You, the hour has come that Your Holy Spirit of Truth glorifies Your Son. Prove to the world that Your Word is something alive and active, and not just printed words on paper. Let Your Holy Spirit turn the hearts of fathers toward their children, and the hearts of children toward their fathers."

And He replied: *"peace be with you, Vassula. Scriptures never lie; it has been said that in the last days to come, people will keep up the outward appearance of religion but will have rejected <u>the inner power</u> of it; ah! my beloved, will there be any faith left on My Return? . . .*

the inner power of My Church is My Holy Spirit in it, alive and active; like a heart in a body, My Holy Spirit is the Heart of My Body which is the Church; the inner power of My Church is My Holy Spirit who gives freely and distributes its gifts and its graces, so that the Church gets some benefit; - the inner power of My Church is My Holy Spirit, the Reminder of My Word, revealing nothing new, but the same instructions given by the same Spirit, - the inner power of My Church is My Holy Spirit, that transfigures, uplifts and turns you into real copies

of Myself; - the inner power of My Church is My Holy Spirit, this Fire which enlivens you, purifies you and makes out of your spirit columns of fire, ardent braziers of love, living torches of light, to proclaim without fear My Word, becoming witnesses of the Most High and teaching others to look only for Heavenly things - the inner power of My Church is My Holy Spirit, the Life and the Breath that keeps you alive and makes your spirit desire Me, calling Me: Abba; if you refuse, My child, and suppress the gifts of My Holy Spirit, <u>what services will you be able to do and offer Me</u>? do not be like corpses that keep up the outward appearance of religion but reject the inner power of it, with futile speculations thus limiting Me in My Divinity; do not stop those who come, as children, to Me, living a life of devotion to the Holy Spirit; it is I, who calls them to the wedding of My Holy Spirit; <u>the secret of holiness is</u>: devotion to Me Your God, and you can do nothing of yourselves, unless My Spirit living in you guides you and teaches you Heavenly things; I tell you truly, whoever fears Me will accept My correction; so do not sleep now, for these <u>are</u> the Times when one should be awake and vigilant, more than ever; these are the Times to open your ears and listen to My Spirit and not disregard it; do not play the sage at the wrong moment by pushing the Breath of My Holy Spirit aside and suppressing the inner power that activates My Church; you want to be prudent? open your eyes then; you want to be prudent? open your heart and your ears, My friend, not your mind; a prudent person never scorns a warning from the Spirit, only the proud do not know anything about fear; the fear of the Lord is the beginning of Wisdom; you want to be prudent? look for the Truth that desperately leans over your misery to save you! look Who is bending towards your wretchedness and your wickedness to pull you to Him and lift you from your graves to breathe Life into you again! O come! do not misunderstand Me, <u>I am not forcing you nor am I trying to violate your liberty</u>! I have taken pity on you generation; do not say that all I had to say has been said; why limit Me as yourself? I am the <u>Reminder of My Word</u>, yes, <u>the inner power of My Church</u> and I am <u>free</u> to send you new portents and do fresh wonders; I am free to raise you generation and pour healing ointment on you from the Riches of My Sacred Heart, when I wish and on whom I wish; I am building, yes, re-building

My Church that lies now in ruins, so do not let Me face you, generation, in the Day of Judgement and be obliged to tell you: you, you were one of My persecutors, who pulled down while I used to build; Mercy is at your doors now, and My Compassion knocks on your doors in your times of tribulations, you say yourselves holy? prove yourselves holy by showing Me your adoration to Me; prove your-selves holy by showing Me the souls you are con-verting and bringing to Me, for My Kingdom consists not in spoken words, nor of <u>an outward appearance of religion</u>, but in an inner power that only <u>I</u> can give you through My Holy Spirit, if you seek it; feel My Presence and My Love I have for each one of you; I, Jesus Christ, am present and bless you all out of the depths of My Sacred Heart, leaving My Sigh of Love on your forehead; be one; ecclesia shall revive." (NB 51, P 15-22)

The Rosary

<u>Fr. O'Carroll</u>: Perhaps by way of conclusion, Vassula, we should turn our thoughts to a form of prayer that has a very profound and, I would say, creative history in the Catholic Church, which in its formulas is known in your Ortho-dox world. We are very edified to see you recite the Rosary with us when you attend the meet-ings. It seems to be a bond of unity, a chain of love between us.

The Rosary has a wonderful history since medieval times. It has been said by those of the greatest wisdom and scientific achievement like Pascal, the French genius, who was once asked if he said the Rosary. He responded: "Of course, I do and my housekeeper says it as well." Or, the great Marshal Foch, Generalis-simo of the allied armies in the First World War, who was seen with the Rosary by one of his agnostic friends who made fun of him. Foch said, "Don't do that. I prize it as the eyes in my head." Cardinal Newman prayed the Rosary in his last weeks as he had done all through his life. And we know that Our Lady, in the 300 or more apparitions in this century with which she has graced her Catholic and her Orthodox children, has frequently recommended the Rosary as a form of prayer. Because of its im-

portant biblical content, it has the capacity to meet the needs of every possible spiritual and intellectual culture. So now, would you like to tell us what the Rosary means to you in light of the messages you receive from Jesus.

<u>Vassula</u>: Yes, it was Jesus who came once and asked me, "*Vassula, for My sake, will you learn the Rosary?*" (NB 20, P 3) I did not know it then. I find in the Rosary a beautiful prayer in which to meditate on the whole life of Jesus. These prayers in the Rosary do exist in Orthodoxy. We don't have the chain as you have it, but we put it into different prayers which I learned from some religious nuns in a monastery with whom I stayed. They were saying these prayers along with the Hail Mary. I was a bit surprised when I heard them but this does show that we cannot say that this is a Catholic prayer nor an Orthodox prayer exclusively. On the other hand, before I say something more about the Catholic Rosary there is the other Rosary we have in Orthodoxy which is the monk's prayer. We also call it a Rosary and it is like this, "Jesus Christ, Son of God, have mercy on me, the sinner."

<u>Fr. O'Carroll</u>: The Jesus Prayer.

<u>Vassula</u>: Yes, the Jesus Prayer. Later on in the messages Jesus asks everybody to pray this to show that for Him it doesn't make any differ-ence, Orthodox or Catholic. They are all beau-tiful prayers. Jesus said, "*adore Me then in the splendor of My Holiness; be constant with your prayers; Satan will be chained by the Rosary; - be constant in your confessions, little children.*" (NB 53, P 21-22) Satan will be chained by the Rosary. It is a chain, it looks like a fragile, frail little chain, yet it has so much power that it can chain Satan.

<u>Fr. O'Carroll</u>: And I will remind you that, at Medjugorje, as elsewhere, Our Lady said that it is a powerful weapon against the evil one.

<u>Vassula</u>: Well, you see that it is such a nice prayer, a delightful prayer. Today many, many Greek Orthodox young people of the Univer-

Page X

sity gather in Athens and recite the Rosary there; the one you are reciting and they like it.

Fr. O'Carroll: So, Vassula, we end our conversation about these wonderful experiences that you are so generously sharing with us.

For the benefit of those who may have heard of the unique means by which you receive your messages, the manner of your writing, I perhaps would wish to quote an expert in graphology, that is, the study of handwriting, who works for the Court of Appeals of Paris, Monsieur J.R. Munier. When the manuscripts were submitted to him by Fr. René Laurentin your identity was not disclosed. He said, "There is an extraordinary telluric force, a controlled enthusiasm with a touch of delight that is, it seems to be, the source of some kind of well-being. She is filled with a force that goes beyond her normal self. She is filled with invisible forces to which she reacts with a kind of primitive simplicity. Whereas, there is also in other areas a refined element." And he continued in that laudatory style though he did not know your identity. "She has the faith of a mystic," he said. I would ask you, dear reader, not to misunderstand the word 'mystic.' It is a genuinely, scientifically established concept which is a very great service to us in our theological studies.

Perhaps I should also quote a word from Sister Lucy Rooney and Fr. Robert Faricy who are on the teaching staff of the Jesuit Gregorian University in Rome. "We believe that Vassula's experience is authentic, that is our personal discernment. We do not, of course, nor could we, make any kind of official recognition or pronouncement of validity. On the contrary, we submit our judgment to the judgment of legitimate church authority. Read the book and share in Vassula's experience of the Lord." Therefore, the mode of transmission, along with the contents, is very special. No one except one who is from God could speak with such clarity, such power and such enlightenment on essential, totally orthodox doctrine of our faith so utterly relevant and so powerfully helpful and comforting to us at the present time.

So now, Vassula, perhaps you will conclude this brief conversation with a prayer given to you by Jesus.

Vassula: *"Father, come to our help and guide our steps to perfection, bring back our divinity and make us the perfect dwelling of Your Holiness."* (NB 53, P 2)

1

recognized Me as the Messiah! they provoke Me, they do not exult Me, they block My way with thorns and briars, promoting impurity and promiscuity in this godless and senseless generation; feel My Agony, feel My Sorrow... My Eyes grew dim and are wasting away with weeping; I come all the way to you with great love to offer you the gift of My Love, the gift of My Spirit, the gift of My Divinity, I come to remind you of My Holiness, tell Me then, let Me hear you, you whom My Sacred Heart loves and throbs

2

for you; will I ever see you coming from this desert? return to Me so that I may no longer lie in agony in wait for the sound of your step ♡ I shall not reprove you, no, I shall only let you thrust yourself on My Bosom and I shall cradle you with Tears of Joy My child, I shall wrap you with the flow of My Love leaving your soul in My Peace... I will take care of you, am I not your Shepherd? see, you are living in the beginning of those days promised you, I have said that My Spirit of Grace shall breathe on

3

your dead, I mean to raise you from your graves and lead you back to your domain:
                    My Sacred Heart;
and I shall fill you with My Spirit, healing you and you will acknowledge Me your God; you on the other hand open your eyes and your heart, abandon yourself to Me, offer Me your will, and I shall do the rest ♡ remember My Holy Presence, be My vessels of Light carrying My Word and diffuse My Messages; I the Lord bless each one of you, leaving My Sigh of Love on your forehead;

4

be one IΧΘΥΣ ⊃⊂—————

peace be with you; I am   For Paris & Italy 12.4.90
the Resurrection, if anyone believes in Me even though he dies he will live ♡ I am the Holy Spirit of Truth, I am ♡ the Reminder of My Word who comes to you and stirs you up from your deep sleep; it has been said that My Spirit of Grace shall be poured out lavishly on all mankind and that your sons and daughters shall prophesy, all that Scripture says is being fulfilled; I am preparing you from Heaven to acknowledge the Truth; I

5

am encouraging you by displaying portents in heaven and on earth, I am giving to the poor and the small visions, I am sending you My Mother to instruct you as a teacher in different nations, I am displaying My Infinite Mercy like a banner above your heads generation to educate you and bring you back to divinity; if you would listen to Me today I shall lift your soul and you will reach the place of rest; generation! you have been worshipping long enough unnamed idols, lifeless idols, inventions that harm

6

you to death; you accorded divine honours to these, corrupting your life; for years I have not heard the sound of your voice, nor of your step, you have not invoked Me nor praised My marvels; ah generation why have you rejected Me your Holy One? come and listen to Me again: Love will be coming back to you as Love ♡ this is My Promise, so be prepared to receive Me and I shall give you the gift of My Love and the gift of My Holiness ♡ beloved ones you who are gathered here ♡ today learn that it is I,

7

Jesus who sought you and called you all the way from the desert to enter My delight-ful Garden: <u>My Assembly</u>; ♡ I am the Sacred Heart ever so sensitive who asks you to make peace with Me and reconcile with Me, let those thorns encircling My Sacred Heart bloom into a wreath of flowers; open your heart to Me and welcome Me, offer Me your heart and I shall ravish you to delight My Heart; speak to Me with your heart and I shall not remain unresponsive ♡ realize that I who am your King and

8

Sovereign of all, descend all the way to you in this world drenched with sin to seek you My friend, how much longer do I have to seek? My Eyes are worn out looking for your welcoming response to My Spirit of Grace, I open My Mouth panting eagerly for your response but the word is not even on your tongue... My Spirit of Grace cries out to you to lead you in the depths of My Sacred Heart, but today My Spirit of Grace gets no gratitude for Its Mercy... I bend all the way down to you from My Throne to your door, I come to

9

you weary and as a Beggar in rags, wounded
beyond recognition, barefoot and forlorn;
hear My laments: it is I, the Christ ...
I am thirsty ... I am thirsty for lack of
love ... My Lips are parched for thirst of
love ... My Mouth drier than parchment
from repeating My pleas ... My Heart is sick
with love ... I love you to distraction in spite
of your awesome pride and wickedness ♡ I
come to you My little ones with My ♡ Heart
in My Hand, I know how poor you are
but can I share your meal with you? will

10

you quench My thirst? will you appease My
Wounds? no, you have not sought Me,
it is I who sought you and found you naked
in this desert you are living in, allow Me to
enter your heart and I shall adorn you majestically ♡ if you allow Me to enter your heart I
shall make you see My Wounds given to Me in the
house of My best friends, you shall be awed
by their depth and struck by the numerous
marks savagely inflicted on My Body, the
Wounds of My Body are such that they left
Me, maimed in their battle; I tell you

11

solemnly, anyone who does not welcome the
kingdom of God like a little child will never
enter it, seek Me in simplicity of heart and
you shall find Me; do not put Me to the
test and you will see Me recognizing My Omni-
potency; do not stay aloof and cold to Our
Calls, do not be deaf to Our Calls, hear
Our supplications, open your ears and recognize
the Shepherd's Call; if you are weak I shall
lift you and I shall carry you on My
Shoulders; I am ready to blot out every sin of
yours in My Purity and My Light, O friend!

12

why do you still waver with hesitation? your
navel-string is still attached to Me, I am
the Source of your breath, I am the Bountiful
all-nourishing Source and it is with My Word
that I give you life and preserve you from
death, it is not the various crops you eat
My friend that gives you life, it is I who
gives you life; lift then your eyes to Me and
treasure My Word in your heart and you shall
live! come and ask Me to open your eyes and
I shall come eagerly and pull away your veil
My friend, come and ask Me to bring you

13

back from your exile, where many of you
strayed, and I shall come flying to you,
even if you have built a wall across My
Path in the time of your wickedness, to di-
vorce Me from you, I shall with one blow
of My Breath pull down that wall, then
I shall remind you of My Love, I shall
remind you that I am He who loves you
most, and that your abode is My Sacred
Heart, I shall remind you not to differentiate
yourselves in Me; I shall remind you to be
united in heart and soul and love one another

14

as I love you; yes, it is I, the Constant
Reminder of My Word who speaks to you
to refreshen your memories ♡ receive My
Holy Spirit ... I bless each one of you and
at this very instant I shall leave on your
forehead the Sign of My Love; be one;

ΙΧΘΥΣ 🐟 ─▷   Message for all those who work
and diffuse these messages. Holy Friday   13. 4. 90
peace be with you, I am
the One who stimulates My instruments;
cease worrying, I am beside you My child;
Lord? invade me.
I shall, if you let Me; ♡ make space

15

for Me; I love you, do you realize that
through Me My Message shall be known;
I hold the keys to all doors; if there is
any hindrance remember that I allowed it
for My Glory; be subtle with My Work
and this I say to everyone whom I have
chosen to spread My grains, those that fail
Me shall be replaced; be clever as snakes
but harmless as doves; fear no one; be alert
to the dangers; confide to each other, share
with each other; remain all of you in My
Love; remember you have not sought Me, it

16

is I who chose you and it is I who formed you,
transfigured you and made you zealous; I
have given each one of you a task so that
you go out and bear fruit; it is I who
have commissioned you for this work ♡
I love you and I shall guide you till the
end; persevere until the end; do not sleep
to give Satan a foothold, stay awake; rest
when you must but do not neglect My Work,
do everything you can and I shall do the
rest; I am the Door and no one can
enter into My Kingdom unless he passes through

17

Me; please Lord, name these people you are talking to;

Vassula, everyone who carries My Word carries My Light, I have chosen them and they know themselves ♡ I bless you all, all you who diffuse My Message; Vassula, My lamb, I always knew you weak and this is why I have chosen you, weakness attracts Me; ♡ My Power is at its best in weakness; trials you shall always have, but these are for your growth, I want you strong, I want you to be able to face difficulties with prudence; I want you to glorify Me ♡ so My Vassula, do not allow the

---

18

serpent to tempt you, he is prowling near you and trying desperately to make you fall; be alert always; I am with you and I shall sustain your falls; pray without cease so that the tempter has no opportunity to approach you, this is My recommendation: pray, pray, pray and remember always My Presence; fast, confess and adore Me, eat Me and drink Me, repay evil with love and rejoice for all I am giving you; ahh Vassula... delight Me and stay small Lord, crush me if you must but keep me small.

19

I shall keep you small... take now My Hand and let us climb ♡ I Jesus love you all, remember I am the Resurrection; IΧΘΥΣ ⫸

22.4.90

« It was the stone rejected by the builders that proved to be the keystone, » Ps. 118:22. My Lord Jesus, You were rejected then as the Messiah, because their spirit was not prepared, their hearts were closed and hard, yet You proved to be The Keystone. In our generation my Lord, the effusion of Your Holy Spirit is also rejected by the 'builders' and yet one day Your Holy Spirit will prove to all of us that He was the Keystone. By denying and suppressing Your Holy Spirit, that comes to us as the Reminder, 'the builders' are preparing again their own downfall.

see how former predictions have come true?

indeed, I have said that 'the Advocate,

20

the Holy Spirit whom the Father will send in My Name will teach you everything, and remind you of all I have said to you', but I knew all along that only a remnant would listen and return to Me; on these very ones who would listen to Me I shall invest with My Holy Spirit of Wisdom and Insight, yes, I shall invest them with My Spirit of Counsel and Knowledge; and the flickering light that now is left in this world will become a vivid fire; I repeat, that My Holy Spirit of Grace is being sent out to the four corners of

21

the earth to teach you to be holy and raise you up again into divine beings; the earth shall turn into a copy of heaven and thus My Will will be done, the prayer I have taught you to pray shall be fulfilled;

Lord! Turn then all of us away and quick from the path of delusion, may we be one, united, and live holy as your angels in heaven, like all souls who live in heaven and undivided in Your Love may we too share like them, Your Love in unity, so that the earth becomes a reflection of heaven, let Your Kingdom come and renew the earth with fresh things, let Your Holy Spirit in this second Pentecost come quick to renew us with a new spirit of love and transfigure us all into divine beings! Maranatha!

peace be with you; I tell you truly that the

22

days are coming when My Kingdom on earth shall be as it is in Heaven; you shall not remain divided for long now under these skies, soon you shall all be one, and Love will be dwelling among you: this is My Promise, but My beloved ones, this renewal shall not come without tribulations; like any birth, this renewal will have its birth-pangs too, but the pains will also be quickly overtaken by joy; I am pouring out My Spirit on your generation, to water your desert and to make rivers out of your dry soil, yes! I shall water your

23

desert and turn it into a Garden, eventually you will see the force of My Words and the splendour of My Beauty, I intend to bring you all back to divinity one after the other; I am your Hope, I am your Refuge I am your Consoler; Almighty, I Am ♡ recognize the Times, recognize the gentle ♡ Breath of My Holy Spirit of Grace upon you; I am blowing now on your nations rising up with My Breath your dead, turning them into a reflection of My Image; I am rising new disciples every single day to glorify My Name

24

again and evangelize with love for Love; I ask you then My beloved ones to pray daily for My second Coming which is the second Pentecost, pray for the conversion of souls that they may convert before My Coming, ♡ come to Me as you are and lean on Me, as John, My beloved one, leaned on Me, you too, place your head on My Bosom and listen to Love's Heartbeats, every heartbeat is a call for Love, all I ask from you is a return of love; love Me, adore Me, rejoice Me your Lord; I bless you, leaving

25

My Sign of Love on your forehead; be one;

IXΘYΣ 🐟

Message for prayer meeting for Lens. From our Holy
Mother. Also Message for Italy & Paris,

peace be with you, little children, I am
your Holy Mother of Love, the Mother of the
Word made flesh; I come to you in these
days of darkness to educate you in the path
of divinity; be vigilant and fully aware
because Satan, the enemy, prowls around you
like a roaring lion and seeks any opportunity
to make you fall; stand up to him and
combat him together with Me: combat him

26

with your prayers; your prayers are the most
powerful weapon against him; obedience and
humbleness makes the demon flee; God is
offering you the gift of His Love; respond to
his Merciful calls; God is speaking, and Me
and I call you from the four corners of the
earth for your conversion because time is
pressing; My little children, stay small
and simple, be the salt of the earth by
remaining small for you are the light of
the world, you are the predilected souls
of Our Heart... and the Kingdom of Heaven

27

belongs to the children and to the very
little ones; I appear today in various nations
to turn your heart towards the Divine Light;
I want to restore your soul, I want to
remind you that you all belong to the Father
and the Father is Holy so you ought to live
holy too; but do not get discouraged because
I am here with you to teach you step by
step and I can assure you of Our blessings,
every step you take We Bless; I want to,
if you allow Me, make you a reflection of
the Eternal Light so that when you meet

28

God you would look like an untarnished
mirror of God's active power and an image
of His Holiness and His Goodness; today I
invite you all to pray with fervour for
the renewal of the Church, for the second
Coming of the Lord: for the second Pentecost;
this is why Jesus and I come today in various
countries to prepare you all for this Coming;
pray and lead a life of adoration, pray for
the conversion of souls so that everyone may
be ready for the Lord's Return ♡ Love is
on the Way of Return, listen and you will

29

already hear His Footsteps ♡ this is why I
implore you to change your lives and live
only for God and in God; remember, Scripture says: " Anyone who claims to be in

the Light but hates his brother

is still living in the dark " (1 John 2:9)
reconcile with your brother, reconcile with God,
make Peace with God; beloved ones: remember
Our Presence; I bless each one of you; be in
Peace ♡

24. 4. 90

I rely on Your Love, let Your love rest on us,
let it live in us as never before.

30

beloved one, all that I have given you
was to draw you closer to Me and adapt
you to being with Me; I have given you
this grace because it pleases Me; I wanted
to comfort you; this My child is for your
salvation and I shall remain near you in
this way till the end; you are My altar
and I want My altar pure, I want to fill
you with My ardent flame: My Fire: My
Holy Spirit ♡ it was, daughter, only
yesterday that I had found you caught
and ensnared by the evil one, and today

31

see? you are free ♡ I your Saviour freed
you and not only have I freed you, I
have also given you Life; you were im-
prisoned and I have liberated you, you
were naked but I have adorned you majestically,
you were barren but I have prospered you
and flourished you; your knee had never
bent to praise Me nor worship Me your
Lord, yet I bent all the way to you to
reach you and anoint you blessing you;
I had never heard your voice acclaim Me
nor had I seen you in My House coming

32

consciously for Me, yet I came all the way
to your house, in your room, to let you
hear My Voice, I sang a song of love to
you, so that you in your turn go out to
the nations and teach them My Song;
I have dispelled your faults like a cloud,
your sins like mist, rejoice then in My
Presence soul! I shall continue to show
to humanity, My great Love and Mercy
through you so that they may at last
believe that it is I, I am LOVE; this is
how I shall summon My people and surround

33

them with My Love - I shall be to them like a wall of Fire surrounding them and I will be their glory in their midst; come My Vassula ... O God how I love You!

these words are like flashing jewels of a diadem ... yes, love Me your God, follow My first commandment without nevertheless neglecting the others; rest now, without forgetting My Presence, we, us? Yes my Lord, we, us, forever and ever. I bless you, bless Me too; I bless You my Lord, and I thank You for all that You are giving me.

34

(This was a message given to a Russian orthodox friend of mine, concerning Russia.)

(...) I will give Russia My Restoring Peace, an everlasting covenant shall be sealed by Me; like a shepherd rescuing his lambs from the wolves' mouth, so will the sons of Russia be rescued by Me, I intend to rise her and make her holy, and make out of her sons, holy men, who will teach incorruptibility, for within her My Spirit shall be living and shall govern her with holiness and justice ♡ (...)

35

30. 4. 90

Lord, my God, save us in Your Love, raise us in Your Light and with Your Infinite Mercy forgive us; make us strong in faith, unite us to be one, so that we may say together, around one Holy Tabernacle: ' There is one Lord, one faith, one baptism, and one God who is Father of all, over all, through all and within all': *

try then to imitate Me ♡ give us the Wisdom then to imitate You. Wisdom is given to mere children, unless they seek Me in simplicity of heart, Wisdom shall not be given to them ♡ and as long as their intellect is at work, Wisdom will remain hidden and as a riddle to them, tear away Lord their intellect so that they may at last see with their

* Ref. Eph. 4 : 5-6

36

eyes Your Beauty and Your Splendour! little heart, pray for them then, pray in these godless times, let your prayers be like blended incense ♡ pray that I may give them back their sight ♡ pray that I may go over to them and wake them up from their everlasting sleep, pray My little one, you who had the Law brought to you by Me, and directed by My Holy Spirit, pray that they die to their sin and resurrect to Holiness, Love and Faith, and if there are any wise men, let them show their wisdom by their

37

simplicity of heart towards Me, their zeal to all that is holy, and by their ardour to draw souls to Me, may all these things be done with humility and love, remember that if you do not get what you ask it is because you do not pray hard enough and with your heart ♡ come now, never forget My Presence, ⁜ I am your Holy One and the One who loves you most; * Lord, You are Good, Patient and Forgiving most loving to all who invoke You, hear our prayers my Lord, although they may be of extreme poverty, have mercy upon us and open Your Ear, we are sinners and not saints, but You were known to

* I insist

38

go to the sick and heal them with Your Love, we are all sick, a sickly generation drenched in sin, come to us and heal us helping us to believe in our unbelievable unbelief!

My Righteousness is eternal, My Love I have for you all is Infinite, My Compassion for the wretched and the sick is Great and beyond human understanding, ask and it shall be given to you, I open My Mouth panting eagerly for your prayers, ⁜ I ask and on behalf of my brothers too, that You come and save us Lord in Your Love, return to us, purify us!

I shall return to you as Love, and My Fire shall purify you all, You have promised us a

39

New Heaven and a New Earth Lord, I have promised you more than that little one, I have promised you a new Jerusalem, and I have promised you that I shall be living among you; I will make My Home among you, see? very soon now, I shall be with you; then

hurry Lord, hurry, we are all waiting eagerly for the 2nd Pentecost and the outpouring of Your Holy Spirit, the 2nd Coming.

are you all prepared to receive Me?... why are you silent? * Because my Lord it is difficult to say these words: ' many are not prepared to receive You ...'

* Timidly & sad I said:

40

pray then for those who ignore Me, pray for the godless, pray for those who are not ready to receive Me, prepare yourselves! the fig tree is ripe and soon you shall be eating its fruit ♡ come, we, us? Yes my Lord, we, us.

12.5.90

Jesus? I am, peace be with you, Vassula, let Me hear the sound of your step tomorrow in My Church; I shall be waiting for you impatiently; ... are you as impatient as Me for this hour when I shall be united to you? Vassula, * leave Me

* Jesus said, 'I love you' and I stopped Him from writing it.

41

write it, I love you; are you still willing to answer Me?   Yes Lord. I shall go
to the Greek Church but I always have a problem
of language, I can hardly follow what the priest
says.
        but I am there and I do listen to
your heart; speak to Me ... come, listen to
this: suppose you go and visit a friend of
yours who eagerly is waiting to see you,
would you, upon meeting your friend, remain
erect and distant? or would you go towards
her and warmly greet her with a kiss?
then, would you not sit together and

42

talk? or would you sit and keep silent?
you would talk of course! this is the way
I want you to be with Me when you come
and visit Me in My House; I want to feel
your heart rejoicing every time you meet Me, I
want to hear your heart talking to Me,
to talk to Me, your God, is praying,; My
Ear then shall be stuck on your lips and
I shall receive each word as drops of honey;
daughter, then comes My great moment,
the moment I am so much looking forward
too, the moment I had given Myself to you

43

on Golgotha, the Holy Hour of My Sacrifice,
the Holy Hour of your redemption, the Holy
Hour when I unite Myself to you; I shall
wait for both of you*to eat Me and drink
Me; I bless you My child; do not deny
Me these moments of love, these moments of
Holy Communion ♡

My Lord, praised be the Lord, glory be to
God, blessed be the Lord!
peace be with you little one, please Me
and discern Me, these very minutes you
are with Me are a delight to Me, they

* My Russian friend and I.

44

are like a welcomed rain on a thirsty soil;
I delight to hear you;*... take and read
what I have given you; ... tell Me, are you
happy inspite of all these trials? yes!
flower, when one of your petals is torn out
I make sure that another petal takes its
place; with My light I reinforce your stem,
if you only knew how I guard you,
and with what care I treat you ... lean
on Me when you are weary and I shall
rest you ♡ come ΙΧΘΥΣ 〜◁

* Jesus was silent for a while, He then asked me,
' would you like to write?' I said yes.

45

12. 5. 90

Message for Lens, above Sion.

peace be with you, beloved children My
Heart sings with joy to have you all
united here in My Love; your prayers are
like music in My Ears; come to Me and
I shall fill your spirit with My Spirit;
come to Me as you are and I shall lift
you to make you holy, beloved ones;
My Cross today calls out for Holiness, My
Voice resounds in the four corners of this
earth to remind you all that I am Holy
and that you should be living holy;

46

O generation ... do I not know how weak
you are? your era has created images unpleasing
in My Eyes and not according to My Mind,
and in this Babylon you have created I
descend to find most of My creation impris-
oned, yes, captive, by the evil one who feeds
them godlessness, rationalism and iniquity,
do I not see all these things? the supplications of the saints have reached My Ears,
I tell you that I am now like on Fire and
I shall not wait much longer, I shall not
leave you much longer in this darkness,

47

I will come back to you, in a short time
the world will see Me again, yes, Love shall
descend on you and live among you; but
before your trees start blooming with noble
branches, thick-set leaves and lofty trunks,
and before the birds of heaven start nesting
in their branches, and before I spread rivers
to water your thirsty soil, I shall send from
heaven Columns of My Purifying Fire, I
intend to purify you all; dead will be
the days when the dead rejoiced in the
presence of the dead ... you shall, after this

48

purification be talking one language, My Own
language, called : LOVE; DIVINE LOVE
♡ I mean to extinguish all evil and
wickedness; this is why in these days, My
Veil will be thrown over the sun, the moon
and the stars; I will cover the sun with
dark clouds and the moon will not be giving
you its light; I will dim every luminary in
heaven for you and I will cover your
countries in darkness, so that Babylon will
cease intermarrying with sin, she shall
then adopt My Law of Love, because her

49

renegades I shall put up in flames ; if your era has failed to appreciate My great love and has defiled My Holy Name, it is because of the great apostasy that penetrated in the core of My Sanctuary ; today generation My Spirit of Grace comes to help you more lavishly than ever before, see? I am rising in each corner of the earth new altars to sanctify your lands and sanctify you all ; it is by Grace that I intend to raise you and make out of you living altars carrying My Flame for within you will be

50

living My Spirit of Holiness, a Spirit unique, subtle, unsullied and Pure, then I shall send you out throughout the earth and your message will be to proclaim My Infinite Love, and I promise you, you who love Me, that in those days of darkness which will come on the whole world, I will keep you safe and I will lock you in the depths of My Sacred Heart ; I shall be with you ; but alas for all those who spend their time breaking down and trampling on My altars ! alas for those who kill My prophets ! alas for these souls !

51

alas for those who follow the black beast! alas for all those who reject My warnings, spurn and ignore them ! they shall in these days of darkness call to Me, but I will not answer ... five of My Wounds are wide open and My Blood is gushing out all over again, repent generation, repent ... think twice before you open your lips to speak ; seek Me with your heart and not with your mind, imitate Me your God, follow Me in My Footprints ; ask your-selves this before you speak : " what would have Christ said in this situation ? " or :

52

" what would have Christ done in this situation ? " think twice before opening your lips, do not let your lips be the cause of your downfall, do not let your spirit err you, imitate Me and be the perfect reflection of My Image ; even if you are unable to pray properly, My Spirit will pray for you, see? I never abandon you ... even when you fail to appreciate My great Love, for the sake of My Holy Name I stoop even more towards you to lift you to Me, and in My loving kindness I forgive your

53

sins; the minute you open your mouth to invoke Me, I come flying to you and place My Ear on your lips ... and every word you utter consoles My Heart and rejoices Me; come back to Me with all your heart and let your prayers reach Me, because it is not those who say to Me: "Lord, Lord, who will enter the kingdom of heaven, but the person who does the will of My Father in heaven"*, so speak with love, and I shall hear you, give with love, and I shall know you, pray with love,

* Matth: 7:21

54

and the doors of My Kingdom shall open for you to receive you, act with love, so that I may say to you: "you are Mine, you are My seed, come to your Father!" I am Love and anyone who lives in love lives in Me and I live in him ♡ do the Will of My Father in heaven so that you enter My Kingdom; remember that the Root of the Tree of Life is Love; pray more with your heart My children and feel confident that My Ear is near your lips; I bless you and bless every step

55

you take; Love loves you; remember My Presence; I leave My Sigh of Love on your forehead; be one ΙΧΘΥΣ 🐟

Later on: men have lessened and have degenerated ... if only they renounce their folly ... pray daughter, nevertheless even in your state of degeneration I love you and I weep on your atrophy ...

I had been with Jesus in dictation. When He had finished dictating, I hurried up to do other things without blessing Him or praising Him; in my wickedness I treated Him as if He was any human being who dictates a message, somehow forgetting His Divinity. I felt very ashamed and so I came flying back

56

to Him and I asked Him to forgive me. When He told me all this, He was like someone not surprised, calm but sad.

14.5.90

Lord and Redeemer, hear my prayer, listen Lord all Merciful, my prayers indeed are atrophic, I am poor and needy but I am here and from this desert I call for Your help, You know our needs and You have surely heard the supplications of the dying, with just one Blessing coming from You Lord and they shall be healed!

I who brought you out of Egypt, you have only to open your mouth for Me to fill it, and I shall do the same to all of your brethren; ΙΧΘΥΣ 🐟

57

15.5.90

Our Holy Mother's Message for Lens/Sion

peace be with you children; I your Holy Mother
am preparing you to meet the Lord; I am
educating you in your spiritual growth; I am
covering you with graces to help you and
encourage you; realize that these are special
days you are living in your times; these
are the days preceding the Lord's Coming,
they are the opening of the path where
the Lord will come; these days are a
preparation for the descent of your King;
pray so that everybody will be ready, pray

58

My little children, fervently, for those souls
who refuse to hear and refuse to see, pray
to your Father who is in Heaven in this way:
   Father all Merciful,
   let those who hear and hear again
   yet never understand,
      hear Your Voice this time and
      understand that it is You,
         the Holy of Holies;
      open the eyes of those who see and
      see, yet never perceive, to
         see with their eyes this time

59

      Your Holy Face and Your Glory,
   place Your Finger on their heart
   so that their heart may open
      and understand Your Faithfulness,
   I pray and ask you all these
         things Righteous Father,
      so that all the nations be
   converted and be healed through
      the Wounds of Your Beloved Son,
         Jesus Christ; Amen;
ask the Father to forgive the stubborn souls
who refuse to hear and see; the Father is

60

all Merciful and He will look on all His
children; yes little ones, you are the incense
to God when you pray for the salvation of
your brothers; the harder you pray all the
more powerful your prayers become ♡ thank
the Lord who called you and with His grace
made you hear His call, so pray for those
who refuse to hear; the time is pressing
and many are still unaware and in deep
sleep; the days are fleeing and My Heart
plunges in deep sorrow when I look from
above at the youth of today; love is

61

missing ... but they never met with love either ; many of them never even received their mother's warmth or love since she had none to give ♡ the world has grown cold, icy cold, and the parents turn against each other, the child turns against his parents for lack of love ; the mother refuses the child's pleadings for love ; the world is dead to love , it lies in deep obscurity because hatred, greed and selfishness dominate the entire earth all the way to its core ; I am shaken

62

by terrible sights, with the iniquities of this dark world and the apostasy that penetrated in the sanctuary itself, the disasters, famine, afflictions, war and plague, all these are drawn by you ; all that comes from the earth returns to earth ; the earth is autodestructing itself and it is not God who gives you all these disasters as many of you tend to believe ; God is Just and all Merciful, but evil draws evil ; pray hard, pray with your heart for the conversion and the salva-

63

tion of your era ; children of Mine pray with Me ; I need your prayers, pray and I shall offer them to God ♡ I assure you that I am with you wherever you go ; I never leave you, you who are My children ; I bless you all ♡

16. 5. 90

peace be with you ; I the Lord come to open hearts and deliver you all from evil ; you are living in a period of grace ; I said that My Spirit will be poured on all mankind ; blessed are those

64

who receive My Spirit of Grace without doubting, blessed are the poor in spirit for theirs is the kingdom of heaven, blessed are the simple in heart for Wisdom shall reveal Herself to them, blessed are those who do the Will of My Father in Heaven for the doors to My Kingdom shall open to receive them, blessed are My vessels of light who carry My Word and diffuse My Messages given to you by My Holy Spirit, for many of your sins shall be forgiven ♡ come, ΙΧΘΥΣ ⤳

1

22.5.90

peace be with you flower; delight Me
and meditate more, pray more be pliant
so that I form you to My Image; fear
only when you do not speak My language;
can you recognize now the Voice of Your
Master? Yes my Lord, I can. Why? Because

You are teaching me good things and Your
Language is Love.

share then all these teachings with the
others; all that you learn from Me share
it together with your friends, glorify Me;
delight Me and share My Passion on Fridays

2

enter into My Wounds, sacrifice more of your
time for Me; live holy, sacrifice by giving
all that you have received from Me; do
not count the hours you spend with Me,
I want you generous, I want you to offer
Me your will daily, offer Me your pains,
offer Me your sufferings, offer Me even the
slightest scratch so that I may use what
you offer Me to efface your sins and to
deliver souls from their purifying fires; do
not let these things go by in vain, offer
them to Me and I will use them;

3

come, before you rest, pray the Salve Regina,
I am listening, rejoice My Heart and your
Mother's Heart too ♡ ... (I prayed it.)
good; come daughter go and rest, I bless
you and your child ♡ rest in My Heart
like I will rest in yours; feel confident in
all you receive, Love loves you.

23.5.90
peace be with you, it is I, Jesus,
never cease calling Me, never cease praying,
I give you My Peace and My Love;
daughter? have you nothing to say?

4

I give You my poor love and my nothingness
Lord.

ah, I desire your love even if its poor
and as for your nothingness little one, always
remain nothing; efface yourself entirely,
annihilate all that is you by absorbing all
that is Me; fill your spirit with My Spirit
so that your soul becomes a living torch
of light; be transparent, yes, limpid, so
that your light shines through you without
any blemishes but in purity only; if you
ask Me daily to forgive you your sins and
if you allow Me to purify you, even if

5
---

this requires sufferings and trials, I will do it without hesitation; I know your needs; I do not allow you to sin, I never commanded you to sin, and I have no pleasure hearing your tongue slip, have I not asked you to be My incense appeasing Me with your fragrance? I adorned you with impressive vestments and I gave you a tongue to praise Me and remind My people of the Love I have for them; be attentive then pupil, and listen to Wisdom's instructions; keep My Name Holy and keep

---
6
---

scrupulously My Law and My Teachings and I shall never desert you ♡ I am your God and with Me at your side, who can be against you? be certain that after such a charism given to you without you meriting it, not to refuse Me anything, and I mean anything, so live for Me, do penitence and fast; fast on bread and water; do not reject with disdain the trials I am giving you, rejoice when persecuted! rejoice when threatened for My sake! rejoice when attacked by My enemies! these My child

---
7
---

are the trials with which I shall perfect you ♡ pray without cease, pray, pray, pray without counting the minutes; I shall not spare you Vassula from suffering, as the Father did not spare Me from suffering; I want you to be a living crucifix, a memory of Myself; did you not know that the gift of suffering comes out of My Infinite generosity and out of My Infinite Love? do not hesitate then to embrace My Cross, let your arms grasp My Cross with fervour and It will lead you

---
8
---

into the Path of Life; if your feet wander from the rightful Path, be certain that My Love and Faithfulness will preserve you, I will come quickly to your rescue; let your soul be in constant thirst for Me, let Me hear and feel your sighs of love; your forehead, soul, I have deeply marked with the Sighs of My Love, those Sighs I have been giving you incessantly, I have branded your forehead with My Holy Name and made you Mine for Eternity; lift then your eyes to Me and find True Peace in My

9

Presence ♡ tell Me then My daughter, you whom My Heart loves, will you return to Me this Love I have for you?

My love is poor, how will I ever replace Your Crown of thorns by a garland of roses? My spirit ponders this continually and sinks within me; explain then to me without tiring of me, and I shall learn, teach me to love You as You desire us to love You, teach me to observe Your Law scrupulously for ever and ever, so that I walk in the Path of Right-eousness, direct my steps in the Path of Love as You promised.

ah daughter... I have strained My Eyes waiting for your lips to utter your vows of faithfulness...

10

Sweet Jesus ever so tender, Beloved one, draw me then in Your Footprints of Faithfulness, let me be sick with love for You, let me taste Your Sufferings, they shall be in my mouth as the rarest fruit of Your Garden.

open to Me then so that I may breathe on you, My Breath is of the subtlest odours, My fragrance is a blend of incense and myrrh; open to Me soul so that My Spirit of Love breathes on you; My Breath is Life; open to Me My beloved, My daughter, I have been panting for this moment to show you My Divine Heart; I came all the way from Heaven to your doorstep to meet you,

11

and now that I have found you I shall not let you go; speak soul! respond to Me ♡ Come, come to us Lord and multiply

Your Seal of Your Holy Spirit's Love on our fore-head, the seal of the Promise; God, create a clean heart in us, I know that You are at the doorstep of every soul, waiting for their response, Your Eyes languishing for their door to open; Your Vineyards are flowering now my Lord and soon they will give enough fruit to feed every desert; the dead will not come to life unless You breathe on them arousing them with Your sweet fragrance; for the sake of Your Love let this land of ghosts come to life again.

I shall then smile to them and My Light shall penetrate through the hinges of their door and through every key-hole, even

12

below their door My Light shall penetrate! Alleluiah, glory be to God!

yes! shout little heart for joy, your barren lands will bear fruits! break into tears of joy, all you who hear Me, with everlasting love I have taken pity on you ♡ vineyards will grow instead of thorns and briars, I mean to show My Holiness and My Wisdom to efface this era's hostility on My Divinity and their so-called wisdom ♡

8.6.90

Lord, the vow I have made, help me fulfil.

13

peace be with you, I shall help you dearest soul, receive My Holy Spirit of Grace; remember My Teachings; remember that My Ways are not your ways, pray for discernment;

I pray You Lord to offer me the gift of discernment to protect Your Word and be able to know the right from wrong, evil from good, the Truth from the Lie.

I shall feed you with discernment, I shall not leave you unaided, remain in My Love; hear Me: cry out to the nations that My Return is near you, all those who have ears let them hear and

14

those who have eyes let them see, I the Lord descend out of My Boundless Mercy to warn you and call you back to Me ♡ listen, just before My Return I shall give mankind still greater Signs than what I am giving you today, be vigilant, for the greater My Signs become the greater Satan's fury will come upon you; I have risen prophets to announce the End of Times and I am sending My Mother as a Teacher to teach you all around the earth, I am sending Her to prepare in this wilderness

15

a path for My Return, a leveled highway for Me your God, across your wilderness, stay alert because the more I multiply My mouthpieces, all the more Satan shall multiply false-prophets to confuse you all; pray My beloved ones to discern one from the other; pray that you may not be deceived; I have warned you not to run after these false prophets; remember, he who sows good seeds for My Glory shall be later on recompensed; I want also to remind you that among the good seeds

16

that have been sown and are growing to produce a good harvest, My enemy never loses his time, he too sends his false-prophets to sow his seeds among My good seeds; let them be, until the time of My Harvest; as I have said in My parable of the darnel,* do not try to weed out one from the other, lest you weed out My crop too, let them both grow till the harvest; and at harvest time I shall say to the reapers: First collect the darnel and tie it in bundles to be burnt, then gather

* Matth. 13: 24-30

17

My crop into My barn ♡ stay vigilant though and you will always be able to tell and know the difference ♡ be prudent and ask Me to guide you, may everyone listen to My advice ♡ be alert, My enemy is like a wild beast which has been injured, thus becoming wilder and more dangerous, for the Hour of My Return is soon with you and since I shall be giving you greater Signs than these of today; Satan already spreads, in My Holy places, before the eve of these

18

Great Signs: confusion among you to lead you to dissension; be in peace all of you, trust Me and lean on Me; do all you can, and the rest it is I who shall accomplish by My Works; remember, I have all the keys to all the doors and I shall open each door on the hour I choose; Love loves you, I bless you; bless Me and love Me ♡ IXΘΥΣ

13. 6. 90

My Jesus?

I am, it is I your Jesus; ecclesia shall revive by Me! not by you mankind!

19

I am Me who shall lift My Bride; do you want to continue being My bearer in spite of the persecutions? yes. I am willing my Lord. feel how I rejoice every time you say: 'yes!' I do not need you, as you know, I suffice by Myself, but you infatuate Me with your 'yes' in your weakness! your incapacity provokes My Strength and delights My Soul; your weakness and your wretchedness overwhelms My Pardon and from My Heart you release Forgiveness in its fullness; stay near Me My child, you delight My Soul,

20

I am your Fortress; be on your guard My little one because among those who approach you are diviners and false prophets, what shall I do Lord? keep My Principles … Will You guard me from these Lord? you will live secure and I am guarding you safely; I shall continue My lamb to carry you on My Shoulders; be in peace ♡

14. 6. 90

I am the Rock ♡

19. 6. 90

My Jesus?

I am; peace be with you, honour Me by

21

imitating Me, glorify Me by loving Me, sanctify your body since I live in you by eating Me and by drinking Me, adore Me, thirst for Me, repair for those who do not love Me and are blinded by their intellect and who cannot tell their right hand from their left, pray that they may realize that they need perception so as to not deviate like many of them do now, from My Words, pray that they may understand that what I want from these wise men is adoration, I want them to come and do Me homage

22

like the first shepherds and like the Magi; I know that I have in My Hands a mere child, do not fear, do I not know where I am sending you? I have brought you up to be My bearer, to witness for the Truth, pupil, you are My Own and from My Mouth you have learned; take your Master's Hand and allow Me to guide you where I wish you to be; lean on Me when you are weary and discouraged My child and I shall comfort you, ah Vassula, every time you feel wretched My Heart becomes a

23

Burning Furnace of Love ready to consume you; listen: rejoice! for what greater than receiving the gift of My Love? ♡ understand My child that I am He who loves you most and forever will ♡

                                                                      19.6.90

Lord all Merciful, we have deviated from Your Path, yet You never stopped acting towards us with mercy and with great love; today I call on You Lord: do not desert us in the days of ordeal, save us from destruction, deliver us from evil, unite us in Your Love and Peace!

I give you My Peace and My Love My child; ecclesia shall revive in spite of all the tribulations she is undergoing; My Church

24

will be one and holy and My People shall speak one language; all these things shall soon take place; Vassula I shall rise again My Church out of My Everlasting Love and Mercy, I am going to give you all back your vineyards and make out of this valley of death a gateway of Hope, and you shall all respond to Me as once before as you did when you were young and pure ♡ you rejected Knowledge for quite some time now, offering Me sacrifices that never reached Me, but in My Mercy I shall say to each valley of death:

25

rise! let every dark valley be filled with
My Word, every mountain and hill be laid
low to pasture and let everyone who has
been branded on the forehead with the Sign
of My Love, come foreward and eat from the
Tree of Life; today I am giving everyone a
chance to hear plainly My Voice from My Holy
dwelling place, My Voice sounds like an echo
from Jerusalem and reaches all the inhabitants of the earth, no one can say later
on that I have not been warning you; from
nation to nation I let My Spirit blow,

26

I am sending you all My servants the prophets
so persistently to remind you who is your
Father and to turn you away from your
evil doings and amend your actions; I come
to stop you from idolizing theories that are
godless; I am sending My messengers to you
to remind you of My precepts and to remind
you to live holy as I am Holy so that you
will all be worthy to face Me on the Day
of My Return ♡ My daughter be My incense,
I shall always feed you, Lord I have so
many things to tell You!

27

things? - Yes! to start with I'm not
worthy of anything You have given me.
I know, but I give Wisdom to the poor
and simple; let My Love envelope you,
come, never forget My Presence; May Your
Good Spirit guide us on to level ground,
Yahweh, for the sake of Your Name keep
Your Promise to save us, amen. (Ps. 143:10-11)

27.6.90
peace be with you; daughter, pray,
giving Me glory for having lifted you from
the world of the dead and having allowed
you to enter and live in My World of Peace

28

and love and having taught you through
My gentle mastery the Knowledge of the
ancients ♡ so do not condemn anyone who
still cannot tell their right hand from their
left; be compassionate as I am compassionate;
do not judge and you will not be judged
yourself ♡ do not condemn, and you will
not be condemned yourself; resist evil and
conquer it with good ♡ do not give the
Tempter a foothold; do not say that I
your Lord have abandoned you; out of
My Five Wounds I nourish your soul!

29

pray for discernment ♡ look My daughter, I am Hope, I am Life and I am near you I am the Crucified and your Redeemer who tells you : My love for you is eternal ♡ bless Me and love Me

IΧΘΥΣ 🐟 Later on, to a priest-visitor : tell My servant this, write :
My peace I give you; take this token as a gift of My Love, take My Word and prophesy to the nations, tell them that " once more there will be poured on you My Spirit from above; then shall your

30

wilderness be fertile land; integrity will bring peace, "* a peace the world had never known before, " My people will live in a peaceful Home, " yes, they shall live in My Sacred Heart, for I shall "keep them safe", but before this desert turns into a fertile land and into fine vineyards, My Breath shall come and blow in this dark world, like a stream of brimstone which will set fire everywhere, to purify this era and renovate her entirely, uniting her into One Holy People; your renegates I shall turn

* Is. 32: 15-16

31

into holy people and their apathy into fervour for Me your God ; I shall make you holy as I am Holy ; remember that My City shall be rebuilt on its ruins ; (...) be blessed IΧΘΥΣ 🐟

30. 6. 90
Lord, they have failed to appreciate Your Great Love, this Love no flood can quench and no torrents can drown; and now I am telling You, my strength is gone and my soul is shut out from consolation. I think You have given me my fill of bitterness, is there yet more to come? I have offered my cheek to the striker to be overwhelmed with injustice; Your Lambs You have gathered lie now scattered.
— "I have trodden the winepress alone; of the men of my people not one was with me."

32

look, who is coming from Heaven all the way to your room ? it is I, Jesus ... your Spouse, so do not be afraid, I will rescue you again ♡ your flesh is weak and your spirit these days has been taken by a hurricane; I am near you by your side, do not be afraid My daughter, My bride, My Pity is stifling Me to see you taken in this hurricane, but I shall take you out of it; My enemies* are nursing My Father's Justice again, to become even greater now, how can He relent ? how can He

* here Jesus changed tone, from being tender to severe.

33

relent when wickedness is the only bread they eat! My God do not desert me! hold on to all that I have given you My child, cling on Me; these people cannot sleep unless they have first wronged you, I watch them and My Father's Justice flares up to here them coming to Me with lifeless words ... have they not read in Scriptures : "Some I have blessed and made more important, some I have hallowed and set near Me." (Eccl. 33:12) but when My Day comes, I shall spare

34

not one of them !   and as for you My child, you are My property because you are poor, but they have not understood ... daughter ... daughter ... weep not ... come ... they have been the trade of rich merchants, like expensive material they have been bought ... hope My Vassula, hope ... faith My child, have faith in Me, I shall never abandon you ... never ... never ... blessed one, My Pardon has already been given to them, yes, to these very ones who do not sleep unless they do evil, so

35

let Me hear your pardon too for them ...
I forgive them Lord, for they know not what
    they are doing.
My Eyes watch over you; I am your powerful protection and your true support, nothing therefore can come between you and Me, even if you are persecuted, threatened or even attached; was there any prophet who was not persecuted, threatened or attached? they are ranging second in the rank of My Church, after the apostles, yet they have always been mistreated and

36

abused for out of their mouth they hear the truth and the truth disturbs them ♡
    What am I to do now? (I asked Jesus very
                                sadly)
                bring My people to
            the obedience of faith* ... broadcast My Message; come I will give you the means of diffusing My Message ♡ I will supply every want in due time; flower spread My fragrance of incense abroad ♡

May Your Will be done, use me as You please, make out of me Your instrument of Peace and Love.

* He answered me this in a majestic tone and without the slightest hesitation.

37

4.7.90

Smile to us Lord and every face on earth shall grow brighter, Hope shall creep back in our hearts, and the whole earth, from end to end, will remember and come back to You.

My Heart is pining with love even for the deserter, have you not noticed? have you not heard My Sighs of Love? have you not read My theme of Love I have written for all My creation? come to Me and let Me see you stretch out your hands towards My Sanctuary, adore Me and bless Me day and night, night and day. ♡
blessed one, I will ask you a question,

38

only one, tell Me: do you love Me with all your heart, with all your soul and with all your mind?

I love You my Lord and my God with all my heart, with all my soul and with all my mind, but I know that my love is poor, miserable and insufficient for Your Bounty.

I will light a fire inside you then ...

Come then and invade me! How am I to find the Way unless You fill my spirit with Your Light to guide my soul to the Truth and the Life?

acknowledge your faults always and I shall help you surmount them; come you who are Mine and My property, you are My property

39

because you are poor and wretched, misery attracts Me; I shall revive your strength and I shall encourage you by lavishing My scents on you of blended incense, never give up My child; never refuse Me a place in your heart, I am attracted by poverty, I seek poverty and misery; I have brought you to Me so that My Fire consumes you before the very eyes of all who see you; I am showing My Infinite Love through you to all mankind so that every man may see and learn that I am a God of Love, a

40

consuming Fire ♡

My God, You rained a downpour of blessings on me, knowing that what You own and is Your "property", is wicked and imperfect, and that I was unable to give You anything in return.

I blessed My property ... - your candour delights Me ... - listen: I raise the poor from the dust, I lift the wretched and place them in My Sacred Heart, then I show them to My angels, I teach them My precepts and I become their Master and they My pupils; and their sins are forgiven by Me, like frost in sunshine their sins melt away; then I

41

ask the saints to watch and pray over them and I fill them with My Spirit of Understanding to enable them to perceive the Truth and reach a deeper understanding of My Knowledge;

Lord You who fostered me father-like, after resurrecting me from the valley of death and You who guided me in Your Light ever since and You who delivered me from evil, tell me, are we not all Your children?

Yes, you are;

Since we are all Your children I implore You then to let those who hear and hear again but do not seem to understand, to allow them to understand.

42

have they repented?

Lord, I do not know if they repented but if You open their eyes and let them see, they will see Your Glory and then they will perceive Your Faithfulness and Your Beauty; they might then come to You and repent!

child, even if I open their eyes they will not see Me! they will not see Me because they are surrounded by darkness, so how do you want them to see Me even though I am near them all the time? their obscurity blinds them; so daughter, speak out and do not be afraid of them, do not be afraid to speak out the Truth, nor

43

allow yourself to be silenced; I am with you My child, My daughter; no, do not be silent, set to work with your God, I have reared you and brought you up for this mission; like a young man marrying a virgin, I have offered you My Heart and asked for yours; it is I, Jesus, who formed you and wed you; and as the bridegroom rejoices in his bride, so am I rejoicing now in your poverty and your weakness ♡ I pursued you like a lover pursues his maiden, I went in all directions seeking

44

by what means I could make you Mine, and now that you are Mine I will keep you ♡

I am frail and my persecutors are hounding me untiringly but my hope is in You. I live in this exile just for You, nothing delights me in this world any more and already my eyes are languishing for Your world of Peace. My heart and my soul are pining away with love for You; You are my Refuge and my Joy. I had asked You to accept me if it was possible and be to You less than a slave, yes, an auxiliary-slave.

the poor and simple always praised My Name and always will ♡ (Jesus here, was as if He was talking to Himself.) this is why I thank the Father for hiding Wisdom

45

from the learned and the clever and revealing them only to mere children; happy you who are poor and miserable, yours is the kingdom of God; alas for those who have their fill now: they shall go hungry; happy are you when people abuse you and persecute you and speak all kinds of calumny against you on My account; rejoice and be glad! for your reward will be great in heaven; this is how they persecuted the prophets before you; daughter, do not weary, carry out the work

46

have given you; imitate Me your Lord and follow Me with no trace of doubt; I shall humble you more; stay poor and weak, docile and obedient; be pleasing in My sight ♡ love Me and bless Me ♡

I am Yours and under Your Eyes, I have found true peace. I bless You.

6. 7. 90

peace be with you, here is My Message: peace be with you; I am your Redeemer who speaks to you; I am He who loves you most ♡ I have come to your nation to ♡ give sight to the blind and take

47

away the sight from those who claim they see ... I have come to you so that you listen to My Voice, the Voice of My Holy Spirit, the Constant Reminder of My Word and all that I have given you, listen to Me: inhabitants of the earth, how I love you! in spite of your awesome wickedness and your apathy towards Me, I your Jesus, love you ♡ today, My beloved, I come and stand before you as your Shepherd to tell you: My Kingdom is near and before this generation has passed away, all that has

48

been foretold by My prophets of today, will have taken place ♡ pray for those whom I have given mouths to praise Me but use them only to defile My Holy Name, pray for those whom I have given eyes to see My Beauty, My Holiness and My Marvels but turned blind, with scales on their eyes from their sins, pray for those whom I have given ears to hear My Word and My Hymns of Love, but allowed their hearing to dull for fear of hearing and be converted, pray for those who out of their mouths come out false evidence

49

and are unconscious of it, their leaders will
fall and they will have to face Justice, pray
for those who never cease to throw venemous
arrows at each other, they have to realize how
they are harming My Body, pray the prayer
your Holy Mother has given you in Her precious
Message to relent and to draw back My
Father's Justice; ask the Father to give your
generation a hearing.; amend for those
stubborn souls who never cease to do evil;
pray for all these souls My little hearts,
because you are the salt of the earth;

50

and I Jesus tell you: take courage little
hearts for I am with you.; I shall see that
My Name is kept Holy even though My
enemies brought this great apostasy in
My Church and a disastrous abomination in
the heart of My Sanctuary and still hold
fast because of their pride; I tell
you truly that My dwelling place shall
be rebuilt on its early bricks, the
Day is near when I shall come upon
these wise men and destroy all their so-
called wisdom and their hostility towards

51

My Divinity; I shall pull them out by
the roots so that they will not thrive anymore.; they have apostatised from Me, yes,
they have accustomed their steps to walk
with Apostasy and have as their guide and
travelling companion Rationalism, the weapon
to combat My Divinity.; if any man is
thirsty for Knowledge let him come to Me
and drink and I shall give him living
water, do not go and drink from a man's
doctrine which is coming from his own nationality; that man is putting honour

52

from men before the honour that comes
from God; so for these I say: alas for
you when the world speaks well of you!!
the day will come when they will have to
speak from the ground, but before their
voice reaches Me they will be muffled by
the dust and the thick layer of their
sins; Justice will prevail ♡
I tell you solemnly that in these coming
days, Satan and all the foul spirits shall
not work subtly as they did before; no, the
time has come now when he and those

53

foul spirits shall show themselves openly to every inhabitant of the earth; Satan shall send false-prophets and he shall multiply them like sand, creating confusion among you, and deceive even the elect, so take care that no one deceives you; this sign is the sign of the eve of My Great Signs that are to come; the demon today is like a wild beast that is wounded, thus becoming more dangerous, but do not fear you who love Me, I will grant you the safety you sigh for; but alas for those who defiled

54

My Sanctuary bringing great apostasy in My Church, brimstone and fire shall rain upon them! I tell you truly, in the lairs where the jackals* live, shall soon run a highway, undefiled which shall be called: Sacred Way; the impure shall not travel by it, but the living will walk there, for they know how to worship Me and they will bend their knee and say to Me: Amen... Amen... ♡ little children, never have grudges against each other, be united, be united, be one; it is I Jesus who asks this from

* Here Jesus is alluding to the freemasons in His Sanctuary

55

you; I bless you all leaving My Sign of Love on your forehead, this Sign that brands you as Mine ♡ ΙΧΘΥΣ ⤳ ><>

Our Holy Mother's Message:

peace be with you; children of Mine, I would like you today to read and meditate on Luke 15: 4-7; yes, Jesus does not want to lose any of you, this is why He is in constant search of your heart; pray My little children as never before, keep God's Name Holy and remember that anyone who seeks the Lord, will find Him; anyone

56

who knocks, will always have the door opened to him ♡ work for your salvation, pray for every thing you need ♡ I want you happy and peaceful in the Lord because the Lord has given you the Gift of His Love, so what greater Gift than His Love? find Peace in the Lord, this peace that is missing from many of you; penetrate into God's Love and He will purify your soul, praise the Lord for He is good and patient; do not come to Him just for your interests, do not come

57

to Him unconsciously just out of duty,
come to the Lord to praise Him and Love
Him; consider the blessings God is giving
you daily, contemplate on the blessings He
is giving you daily and offer Him your
hearts, thanking Him beloved ones, show
Him your gratitude too ♡ Jesus is Love,
Jesus is Hope and Jesus means He-Who-
Saves, so do not doubt of the Greatness
of His Love; have Faith in Him, He
comes to rescue even the least among you,
testify to the nations of this Great Love

58

and spread His Messages to the four corners
of the earth ♡ I your Holy Mother, am
always near you My children, I bless you;
may the Peace of My Son reign in your
hearts
-Lens- ♡ Message for the prayer groups. 8. 7. 90
peace be with you all; I Jesus bless you
all... feel My Presence at this very minute
among you, feel Me in your hearts...
do not harden your heart doubting, open
your heart so that you may understand
fully My Message of Love; I descend I who

59

am King and Sovereign, all the way to you
to remind you of the Love I have for you
and of My Sacrifice; I come to remind
you to whom you belong; I have redeemed
you all with My Sacrifice and you belong
to Me; if today My Spirit of Grace is
being poured out on you so lavishly it is
because the fig-tree is almost ripe and very
soon you shall be eating from it ♡
you cannot say anymore: " where is my
God?" the pastures of the heath I shall
turn green again so that you find your

60

rest in them, My Vineyards I shall keep
multiplying and My fruit-trees will yield
abundantly, you will eat to your heart's
content from My Heavenly Stores, hear Me,
your Heavenly Father, has He not opened His
Celestial Stores in Heaven to feed a starving nation with manna? your Heavenly
Father rained down bread upon His people,
and from the rock at Horeb He let water
flow from it so that they may drink;
and I, have I not multiplied the loaves
and fish to feed thousands? O men of

61

little faith how is it then that you cannot tell the times? why do you now doubt
that My Holy Spirit of Grace* is being
poured out so manifestedly upon you? have you
not understood that My Holy Spirit is filling
you in your wilderness? I said, ' I am
going to water My orchard, I intend to
irrigate My flower beds;²; I shall pour out
teaching like prophecy, as a legacy to all
future generations, ³* do not be afraid,

1) Jesus in this whole passage, mentions the Father,
Himself as the Son and the Holy Spirit showing the
action and the presence of the Holy Trinity in times of wilderness
2) Ecc. 24:31   3) Ecc. 24:33

62

it is I, your Lord, your Saviour; had you
penetrated into the mystery of the manna
and the mystery of the multiplication of the
loaves and fishes, you would have understood today fully the outpouring of My Spirit,
you would have understood My Miraculous
Feedings from your ancestors' times, flower,
(here Jesus interrupts me, it is 16.23 hrs)
pray now for Russia with Me;
' O God make her follow You,
  O Lord save her soul and raise
her as You have risen Lazarus,

63

embellish Your daughter so beloved
in Your Eyes and place her in
Your Divine Heart so that
her image reflects Your Divinity,
raise her so that she walks
by Your side,
parade her near You and free her
from her captivity,
wed her and make her
entirely Yours; Amen,
say it to Me ♡ (I did.)
write My Vassula* to this day's feedings;

* continuation of His message.

64

realize and understand My transcendence and
fidelity to My Promise of salvation; I will
hide none of the secrets from you generation,
because I will trace out soon an open highway, undefiled and I shall call it:
Sacred Way, leading you to an open Tabernacle; no more lairs for jackals! no more
hidden works by night! no more prowl-
ings in the dark! I the Lord, shall
bring everything to light, it will never be
night again, because My Light shall shine
on you forever, yes, I will set out My

1

Knowledge in this open highway and I shall raise landmarks to lead you to it; I shall mark the road well; I shall then give you a spirit of fervour to worship Me your God and those who are My prodigal sons and daughters I shall take back with great love in My Arms, and they will live in My Light; then all Heaven shall celebrate their return; no man will say: "where is our Lord?" for I shall engrave My Law deeply on your heart, this Promise is inscribed in front of Me, I will set up Jerusalem on its

2

early bricks; I had hoped on My Return to find holiness, but I find a fallacious people gnawing on My Body, love, but I hear only a cry of hatred coming out from their desolation; where is the glory and the beauty I had once given them? where is the Spirit with which I endowed them? these Cains have substituted darkness for light and light for darkness, they have turned unspiritual and My Law that commands and is Sacred, they ignore all of it and trample it under their feet; this era is opposing

3

My Law, contradicting every iota of it; have I not said explicitly that anybody who receives My Commandments and keeps them will be one who loves Me? in your era many claim to be doctors of the Law but they understood neither the arguments they are using nor the opinions they are upholding; oh how they weary Me with their talk! they weary Me because they do not safeguard My Knowledge nor My Law; I do not come through these Messages to condemn, I come to warn you out of love and

4

wake you up from your lethargy, I also come to encourage the remnant, from priests to laity, who love Me and remain faithful to Me and reflect My Image: you, who show your love, for your sake I will lay an open highway, blessed; and on its sides I shall plant fruitful trees*; your soil will nourish many, and no one will be able to destroy the fruits of your soil nor make you barren; you will be all called: Faithful: and you will be all that is not pride, fallaciousness and rationalism;

* the priests of the new era.

5

your fruit will feed starved nations, nations
that have collapsed into atheism ♡ I intend
to clothe you all in My garments of old*, and
rebuild My Church on its old foundation;
I shall adorn My Bride in her early jewels;
and from your mouths you will exult Me
and praise Me without cease; beloved ones,
I am the Light of the world and before
you I am walking, still I am telling you
this: there are other sheep I have that are
not of your fold, I will lead all these as
well under My Renovated Church so that there

* The Early Church.

6

will be one flock and one Shepherd; go out
to the nations and teach them to pray to the
Father this prayer:

Father all Merciful,
let those who hear and hear again
yet never understand,
hear Your Voice this time and
understand that it is You
the Holy of Holies;
open the eyes of those who see and see,
yet never perceive,
to see with their eyes this time

7

Your Holy Face and Your Glory,
place Your Finger on their heart
so that their heart may open
and understand Your Faithfulness,
I pray and ask you all these
things Righteous Father
so that all the nations be
converted and be healed through
the Wounds of Your Beloved Son
Jesus Christ; Amen ♡
understand then that with this prayer
you are asking: the salvation of the world;

8

courage brothers, My pupils, courage; I am
with you every day; preach and defend My
Word without any fear, proclaim My Name
with zeal, remind the world that I am
Holy, teach them to live holy; be gentle
like I am gentle, have My patience and My
Love; only a little while now, a very
little while and the One you are waiting for
will have come; I will come as Love, yes,
Love shall return as Love in this wilderness;
I shall fulfill the Promise soon; but remember My dear friends, what My

9

prophets told you to expect at the end of Times; they told you that there are going to be great tribulations before this Coming and that the foundations of the earth will shake and a great tremour is to come; the sky will appear to you as though it is of an eternal darkness, never fear though for I will be by your side, I have marked your forehead with My Seal of Love; I bless you all leaving My Sign of love on your forehead ♡ Jesus Christ is My Name and I tell you:

10

I love you eternally ♡ be one; ΙΧΘΥΣ ⊱✠

19. 7. 90

My God! my God! come and light up my darkness! come quickly and help me! — Visit me. — My soul thirsts for You my God. When will I see Your Holy Face? My soul melts within me ... why do my persecutors persist in condemning me? O God, where have I wronged them? Lord, where are You? At least let those who persecute me say what crime they found me guilty of. O God, how I miss You ...

beloved, I have not spoken in secret, I am confirming My Word and they know it ♡ you have not seen Me face to face but I am near you; I may be absent in body,* but in Spirit I am always with you; *²

* flesh and bone   *² Jesus very sweetly tried to console me.

11

I am with you to bind you all together in love and to stir your minds, so that your understanding may come to full develop- ment, until you really know My secrets in which all the jewels of Wisdom and Know- ledge are hidden*; blessed one, I want you to have a visible image of My Divinity, meaning, by loving Me fervently, by obeying scrupulously My Law, and little by little, therefore, I shall correct those who offend Me and persecute you; I shall remind them of how they have apostatised; I shall give

Col: 2, 2

12

them the chance to repent; courage! I am telling you this daughter: whoever will listen let him listen; whoever will not, let him not ... ΙΧΘΥΣ ⊱✠

20. 7. 90

O Lord, let Your Spirit rest upon me and invade me.

let Me bless you ♡ I give you My Peace; let My Spirit rest on you; I the Lord will grant you the safety you sigh for; keep firm in your faith because I am faithful to My Promise; I will put My Love Law into the hearts of your nations and I

13

shall never call their sins to mind; I shall remind them of My Sacrifice, I shall remind them of My Cross, I shall remind them that I am God; and you, you whom I sought and found, offer Me your heart and I shall receive it as blended incense; stay loyal to Me and yearn all that is Me to efface all that is you; annihilate all that is you by absorbing all that is Me ♡ pray for the conversion of souls, pray for peace, love and unity, remember, My Love is Infinite,

14

a love no man can understand fully on earth ♡ I bless you, turn to Me and bless Me ♡

21. 7. 90

I saw in a vision that I was looking from outside a window. It was day light; suddenly the earth started to shake violently under my feet, the ground was going up and down, the earthquake was of points eight, it was not stopping. I looked from the window at the sky because it was loosing its luminosity, I was staring up at the heavens while they were becoming darker by the second until they reached to become full night. Then I saw the stars falling, or rather as though they were speeding away from the eastern horizon to the western horizon; it seemed they were leaving the heavens. Then the tremor stopped and there was a menacing darkness. I saw that I had a faint light in my room. I looked out of

15

the window, but there were about 3 or 4 houses which had light in the whole town.

Message from our Holy Mother   22. 7. 90

peace be with you beloved children, I am your Holy Mother speaking and I already thank you for coming here to hear Us; open your hearts and understand every Word We are telling you ♡ Jesus gives you His Love and His Peace; He guides you to Salvation and I am sent by Him to prepare the road for His Return; I come to open the way again for Him ♡ do not be

16

surprised little ones; I know it is hard to live in wilderness but I come to you in many nations to prepare you, I am schooling you in rules of righteousness to set you free ♡ ask the Lord to guide your steps in the path of His Commandments; let your love comfort Him, let your love console Him, be His Balm; feel loved by Me; feel loved by My Son; today I am calling the sick telling them : My child, do not be depressed, I, your Holy Mother love you, but pray to the Lord

17

and He will heal you ♡ cleanse your heart
from all impurities by repenting, then open
your hearts to God and He will shower you
with His Love ; pray without cease ; do not
slumber, pray with your heart and be like
roses in the days of spring, like a bouquet
offered to the "Most High", let your prayers
be like blended incense reaching His
Throne ; let Me remind you what the Most
High is longing for :   your heart   ♡
offer Him your heart and allow Him to
be your Guide on the road   I am

18

preparing for you ; My children, Love is at
your doors ; praise the Lord and love Him
♡ God is love ; I bless you all ; I also
bless all those who are confined in a
prison, towards them I send flowing peace
like a river in their heart ♡
Vassula, be patient ; My Son Jesus loves you
to tears of affection ; never doubt ; feel His
love, end your day always by praising
Him, have My Peace ♡ we, us ? Yes
Holy Mother, we, us .

19

Rhodos 27. 07. 90

Explain to me my Jesus how to respect and
follow Your Law and how to observe Your
Commandments. Guide me in the path
of Your Commandments, I mean to meditate
on Your precepts. Forgive my faults and
sins.
  peace be with you ♡ before you uttered
a word I have already forgiven you* ♡
if it was not for My Infinite Mercy beloved,
you would have already felt My Justice
upon you, since all that you have is
wickedness and misery ; come... do not
watch Me from a distance ... come to Me,
closer, I cherish you like the pupils of My
Eyes, praise Me My beloved, praise Me for

* Jesus understood my intentions

20

My Name is Holy ♡

Rhodos   27. 7. 90

One of the monks I met was shedding tears
when I explained to him how Jesus suffers.

come and place your ear on My Breast My
son, and hear My Heart-beats, every Heartbeat is a call for a soul, a supplication
for a smile, a thought ... shed your tears
not on Me My son but on your brothers,
your sisters, who are dead and decomposing,
not on Me My son, not on Me ... pray
for them that My Father sends them My
Spirit of Understanding, how else are

21

they to convert? Vassula, give them the prayer your Holy Mother has given you and I ask them to pray this prayer daily; come, Scriptures are being fulfilled ... I the Lord am building incense altars, on altars that were to be but have lain waste, because there was no one to handle them or light them ♡

Rhodos 28. 7. 90

Jesus, I am caught in a cloud of lethargy, and I do not seem to come out of this lethargy, I am a poor wretch ...

I know, but why do you not ask for My

22

help? and why do you look elsewhere? if you turn your eyes towards Me you will see My light and I will grant you the things you ask for ♡ you are poor but I can provide you; I suffice to say: grow! flourish! and within your desert I can make rivers flow; child, do I ever abandon you?

No my Lord, never.

then why was it that you failed to believe in My Presence*? do you not realize that I have been in constant search of your eyes? I have made you My bride

* When I had seen Him with the eyes of my soul, that afternoon.

23

have I not? yes, You have my Lord.

then look at Me now and then, this is your due! listen Vassula, I do not need you, as you know I suffice by Myself; I have told you several times that I am Omnipotent but I love weakness because My Power then is at its best; little one, I am with you every day, every hour and every second of your life; I am always among you ... remember, I am with My Mother, yes my Lord. repeat after Me again: we, us, forever and ever. ΙΧΘΥΣ ⵊⵔ

24

Rhodos. Monastry of St. Nectario 30. 7. 90

I stayed at this monastry five days. Five days of fasting and not speaking. Just praying and meditating.

Lord? I am, never doubt; My Peace I give you, enter into My Heart ♡

When the Lord said: "My Peace I give you," I saw Heaven open and I was welcomed into His Heart.

time is pressing, the hours are fleeing ... come near Me and listen to what I want to tell the church in Rhodos: look at the Palms of My Hands, My Side and My Feet; feel My Wounds ... those who will not drink from My Wounds shall waste away, they shall

25

pine away and dry; I Am your Salvation, so why does this nation fear to drink Me and eat Me? they cry for help but then no one comes to drink Me and eat Me and get healed; have I not said that through My Wounds you shall be healed? pick then your steps over this endless desert and let Me hear the sound of your step ♡ come and receive Me; this nation fails to understand the Call of My Love; I look down from Heaven anxious to save you all, I pour out My Heart to you, I am sending

26

you Wisdom all the way to your doorstep to teach you that My Theme is: LOVE, but has anybody any ears to hear? I have made a New Song of Love for you, and for the sake of My Holy Name little ones, I descend all the way to you; I your Christ come to ravish your heart with My Song of Love and delight My Heart; do not say: I sought Him, but I did not find Him; I called to Him, but He did not answer; I waited for Him, but He did not come; seek Me

27

beloved ones in simplicity of heart and you will find Me; call Me from the core of your heart and I shall answer you, open your ears and your heart and you shall hear My footsteps of My Return ♡ the fig tree has ripened and soon you shall eat its fruit; come, since many of you have wandered from the rightful path and fear to receive Me, keeping your sins secret in your breast, liberate yourselves by going to confession, repent truly and fast so that you receive Me in purity and

28

in holiness ♡ My door is always opened to all of you beloved, I am known not to be insensitive to the poor and to the sick man's needs; so do not put your God to the test and do not doubt of My Infinite Mercy; yes, the instruments I use to transmit My words to you are poor, unworthy and common, those whom the world think common and contemptible are the ones that I choose — those who are nothing at all to show up those who are everything,* Wisdom is given to mere children and not

* 1 Cor. 1:28

29

to those that call themselves wise; hear Me,
Wisdom shall remain a riddle to those who
boast and call themselves virtuous and holy,
I shall indeed destroy the wisdom of the wise
and the more severe will be the sentence they
will receive; I intend to leave in their midst
a humble and lowly people who will be able
to say to Me: 'Alleluia, alleluia; day and
night, night and day, joining the hymn
of My angels: 'Holy, Holy, Holy is the Lord
God, the Almighty; He was, He is and He
is to come*'; with no one to disturb them,

* app. 4:8

30

because I shall remove all those proud boasters
from their midst; I am telling you, therefore,
before My hour comes upon you: seek
humility, seek poverty; you who obey My
Commandments and teach others to obey them,
humble yourselves; do not judge and you
will not be judged ♡ do not condemn so
that I too will not condemn you; repent,
and I will make up to you for those years
you spent suppressing My Spirit; I intend in
these last days to lead this wicked era
with reins of kindness, with leading-strings

31

of love, stooping down to all of you to give
you My Food; I shall always be a Refuge
to the poor and needy; come, lean all of
you on My Breast, like John My disciple,
and hear My Heartbeats, these Heartbeats will
bring you all the way to My Feet below
My Cross ♡ I the Lord am among you
and I bless you all leaving the Sigh of
My Love on your forehead; remember all
that I have given to you today and show
Me your love by following Me; My Eyes
are upon you; be one, ΙΧΘΥΣ ⟨fish symbol⟩

32

31. 7. 90

(Still at the Monastry of St. Nectario.)

My Lord, revive me as Your Word guaranteed.
Take away this spirit of lethargy that lies on
me. For how long will I have this spirit?
Instil a constant spirit of fervour in me,
do not deprive me of Your Holy Spirit!

Vassula, I am only waiting to be gracious to
you, raise you and place you in My Sacred
Heart ♡ if only you were alert to My Precepts
your spirit would have been in constancy
with My Spirit; you complain, you groan,
yet My Sacred Heart overflows with Love
and Pity for your soul! put in action
all that I have given you! remember My

33

Presence, make an effort! keep your distance from all that is not Me, keep your eyes fixed on Me and Me only; a vessel of My Word you are, but do not drift away with the first current! I have called you and wed you making you Mine; should you pass through these currents, I am with you, or through hurricanes, these will not uproot you; should you walk in a nest of vipers, you will not be bitten; I have made your path easy; I will lift you every time you come upon thorns and briars;

34

I realize your weakness and your astounding incapacity, this is why My forebearance is great upon you; so do not venture to say: "where is Your Spirit?" My Spirit is always with you My child; listen, do not be impatient in prayer ... do not say: "God will consider My weakness, He is All-Merciful;" then go on sinning; open your ears instead and listen willingly to all My discourses and I shall give you My Light to understand even shrewd proverbs, for I am with you to save you ...

35

Make my heart ready dear Lord, to praise You in constancy. I am surrounded by temptations that make me forget Your Presence.

see now? now you are coming back to your senses ... you are beginning to realize in what a wretched state your soul is in ♡ a light has shone in you; rejoice soul ♡! rejoice! for if I was not standing by you, you would not be standing at all ♡ pay attention from now on, and never let your heart sink, always come to Me for help; this My Vassula is not your last fall, I the Lord will lift you every time you fall

---

36

with greater compassion and love every time; bless Me now and love Me ♡

I bless You Lord, You who fostered me father-like; if my feet wander away from Your Rightful path again, come quickly to my rescue.

rely on My massive Strength, rely on My Love; come more than once to Me today, Love is near you, I bless you ♡

Later on, the same day. I commented about something, it sounded like bragging.

daughter, consider My Work upon you, do not claim to know; man does not know what love is unless I give it to him, not

37

even a sage can discover it, though he might claim to know; I give an order from above and My Word flashes to earth, I send My Word to bring the thaw and warmth on icy hearts; elevate your spirit and seek My Spirit of Discernment; I shall in spite of your faults stand by you to enable you to proclaim this whole message for everyone to hear ♡ ΙΧΘΥΣ ⟶

— St. Nectarios monastry - August 90

My Lord, Holy Spirit of Truth, I know it is not by coincidence I am here. Holy Spirit of Truth, You who guided me and guide me, what am I to say to these two nuns

38

who live here, what am I to do for them? Please speak to me from Scriptures first. I know You shall not fail me.
(I open then the bible at random and my eyes fall on Romans 16. 1-2).

I commend to you our sister, a deaconess of My church; give her and her companion, in union with Me, <u>a welcome</u> worthy of saints, and help her with anything she needs: she has looked, (with her companion, by their prayers, their praises to Me, their penitences, mortifications and sacrifices) <u>after a great many souls</u> *

* Then Jesus turned His Head away looking in

39

space and as though talking alone, as if He was talking in place of the two nuns, He said: I have worked and laboured, often without sleep; I have been hungry and thirsty and often starving for lack of love; I have been in the cold for lack of love, so you who read Me, will you look after Me? after My lambs? do not say: do not bother me, I cannot go out there and give it to You! (Then Jesus again continued like in the beginning of this message.)
today I am telling <u>you</u> who read Me, that

40

My blessings are given to anyone that meets with the needs of this House; for all that you do, even the least, you are doing it to Me; be blessed then you who will hear Me and do My Father's Will; anyone, therefore that will meet with the needs of this house shall be greatly rewarded by My Father in Heaven; be on your guard though from these that will encourage any difficulties and trouble; avoid them; do everything in constancy with the Peace I am giving you ♡ do everything in love for the

4

sake of Love ♡ all I ask is Love remember always this; IXθΥΣ 🐟

Lord ?

August 90

I am ♡ My Vassula, are you happy to be with Me in this way? O yes Lord, praised be Your Name. pray more; this is My advice ♡ I am in constant wait for your prayers; I am blessing you incessantly;

(Jesus then asked me to open the Holy Bible at random and write what He will show me)

you should be awake and praying not to be put to the test (This was from Matth. 26:41)

I need Your massive Strength. hear Me: pray;

42

do not sleep ♡ Can I look in meditation on You? pray! (I prayed.) pray once again to Me; Synchronise my spirit with Your Spirit. Amen

(Jesus quickly gave me the start of my prayer the prayer He wanted; I think He dictated it to me.) My child, My beloved, what will I not do for you ... I have reared you and realize to whom you belong to now; be happy! I am more than happy. then show it! I shall open your mouth and you will speak ♡*

Catch the foxes for us, those that make havoc of Your Vineyards that are flowering

* I suddenly blurted out these words:

43

now. a Glorious Throne is descending now very soon; I will lay their* hiding places bare and their race shall be annihilated, extinguished; the time of reckoning is soon over, just wait and see ... I intend to refresh the earth with rich food and have My remnant full of My good things; I love you with an everlasting love and I am constant in My affection for you; allow Me you who read Me to discipline you, and if you accept My discipline I will bring you

* the foxes: free-masons

44

back to Me, I shall adopt you and teach you My Law; like a child comforted by his mother will I comfort you; Love desires love ♡ Vassula, please Me and pray the Credo looking at Me; yes my Lord. I am listening; (I prayed) good!

come, we, us? Yes Lord, we, us.

Rhodos — 4.8.90 (Prophecy)

flower, peace be with you;

— fire, justice, is soon to descend — ecclesia shall revive ♡ the earth shall be set aflame; IXθΥΣ 🐟

45

_ The Ten Commandments - Rhodes. - 5 to 29 August 90
Lord ?

I am ♡ lean on Me, think of My love; I have walked on the Way to the Cross alone, of the men of My people not one was with Me, they hated Me for no reason at all, by force and by law I was taken; suffering and humiliation was the prize of My victory; I have taken your faults on Myself and I allowed those very hands that I created to strike Me and disfigure Me, but through these Wounds you are healed ... so bless those who persecute

46

you, do not judge them, bless them and pray for them ♡   today I am telling you this with tears in My Eyes : there are many who are behaving as enemies to Me and to My Cross; of all those who preach My Gospel, very few actually are working with Me and for My Kingdom ♡ My whole Law is summarized in ♡ a single command :   LOVE ♡ had they followed My Law and examined ♡ their conduct daily they would have discovered that they are not living according to My Commandments ; and

47

if they tell Me : " how is it that we are not following Your Commandments ? how are we then to follow Your Commandments ? can we teach Your Commandments if You say we do not follow them ? " yet you are not following them because love is missing within you : the Crown of My Commandments is Love ; to love is to live according to My Commandments; do not be like Cain who had no love for Me and simply out of spiritual jealousy cut his brother's throat ...

(When I understood what God's intention was : to

48

comment on His Ten Commandments, I feared to be unable to take every thing down.)
 - O God, I will never be able to do it alone !

who told you that you are going to do this work alone ? you shall write down every word I am going to tell you; do not hurry; I can dictate you in sessions if you wish,   Lord, go according to my capacity !!

you forget My Capacity that can fill your capacity ; come .... share My Work to gain souls ; do you understand My thirst ? I am thirsty for souls, thirsty

49

for your sanctity, thirsty for your reconciliation, I am thirsty, My dear children, for all that is Me and My reflection; I am thirsty to give you back your divinity; I am thirsty for a return of love; I am thirsty to renew your original source and alliance in My Holy Name; your original source that sprouts out of My Sublime Love; I am thirsty for adoration, but behold, what have you become and what have you done! O era! you have stopped adoring Me and you have, instead, multiplied your false gods,

50

you are not obeying My Commandments, no you are not observing My Law; era of wretchedness what have you become! you rarely invoke Me to adore Me; you do not call Me out of love nor honour Me anymore offering Me your services; I have been calling you all the days of your life to remind you who your Heavenly Father is and to whom you are to turn to, but your heart is not set for Me nor is your mind willing, because you preferred to cut off the navel-string that unites us and

51

makes us one, to make out your own law and call yourself: godless; taken by Vanity you want to consider yourself equal to Me; you are now saying: "I am equal to God and I am sitting on His Throne, because my wisdom has amassed great luxury and great authority over the world," your skill in trading is such that a multitude of nations follow your example; yes, you followed indeed the primeval serpent's advice who so cunningly made your ancestors eat the forbidden fruit, assuring them that they

52

will be like gods*; you thought then you would open your eyes but in reality you turned blind and to this day you are struggling to cut off this Cord that gives you Life and Sanctity thinking you will find your freedom, but what you find is Death ♡ O era of wretchedness! you are serving Folly instead of Wisdom, you are serving the dragon instead of your Holy One; you are not obeying My Commandments, no you are not observing My Law I laid down to you; you are incessantly

* Gen. 3:5

53

putting Me to the test ♡ your era; My child is guilty of grave ♡ blasphemies because it is not keeping My Law; they are unmindful of My Commandments in which they can find life if they observe them ♡ nation after nation has deviated in all ten of My Commandments adding blasphemy to rebellion; with the empire of the dragon, the black beast* set up together with the second beast, alias the false prophet, blasphemous poles for themselves, on every high hill and under every spreading tree, to

App. 13

54

conquer the world and blow out the little light that is left in it; on each one of its seven heads the beast made idols representing its own gods; these idols are placed, with the power of the dragon, into high places; then they appointed priests out of their own number for the high places who officiate today in the heart of My Sanctuary; and they are not worshipping Me; they pretend to do so; they go out masqueraded as high priests*, worshipping and serving the beast itself and its production

* read message of 30.1.88

55

which is conformed to the world; they are worshipping alien and lifeless gods; just as their fathers once behaved in the past; they flout piety and repudiate My Commandments My child, they go out to teach all nations to worship the image of mortal man,*¹ a worthless imitation, instead of My Eternal Glory... ah! how they*² lie heavily on Me! with the power*³ given to them by the dragon, they summit their implacable hatred and spirit of revenge by making war against the saints and all those

*¹ A false Christ
*² God gave me their name   *³ Black-masses

56

who are not in their clan, and who refuse to worship the statue* of the beast; so I tell you: blessed are those who beleive in Me and worship Me; blessed are those who follow Me; blessed are those who beleive that My Promise is on its way to be fulfilled, for on these, My Sign of Love will be branded on their foreheads; I tell you truly: if a man serves Me, he must follow Me; O era, do not be afraid to come back to Me; come back to Me while there is still time, for My Day is near and how

* A false Christ

57

will you face it?

it is said: you shall have no gods
except Me ♡ do not follow other gods, gods
of peoples 'round you, but men have trans-
gressed My Father's first Commandment de-
claring <u>their freedom openly</u> by means and
encouragements of the black beasts, upon
whose heads will lie the blood of many;
<u>do not call My Name in vain</u>, is the
following Commandment; now, arrogant
nations are attacking My Holy Name,
people whom I mean nothing to them;

58

with mouths full of blasphemous talk and
ready with flattery for others when they
see some hideous advantage in it; they
curse My Holy Name when engaged in
arguments; they blaspheme against My
Deity and My Holiness, and those who
officiate today in My Church, but are revol-
ving around the beast's power, boasting
about their knowledge of My Law, are
<u>those very ones</u> who are calling My Name
in vain; they are those who shut up
the kingdom of heaven in men's faces,

59

neither going in themselves nor allowing others
to go in who want to; they 'preach'
against stealing, yet they steal souls from
Me; they 'forbid' adultery, yet they
commit adultery themselves since they follow
the black beast and are faithful to him;
they pretend to despise idols, yet they
rob My Sanctuary; so if this
generation blasphemes My Holy Name and
uses It idly, it is because of <u>the permis-</u>
<u>siveness</u>, satiated in vice, given to them freely
by these very ones garbed in black cloaks;*

* Sect of Freemasonry

60

to destroy the roots of holiness and justice,
is their aim, and bring lawlessness at its
zenith ♡ generation ... in My Return,
would ♡ I have to say: there is not a
good man left, there is not one who under-
stands, not one – who looks for Me? – I
<u>have asked you to remember to keep holy</u>
<u>the Sabbath Day</u>, yet you have reversed
It with impurity and sullied It with filthy
enjoyments and the practices with which
you dishonour your own bodies and minds
since you have given up divine Truth for

61

a lie and worship and serve creatures instead of serving Me; you have made Sodom and Gomorrah appear almost faultless and pure compared to your impurities; I tell you truly, on that Day it will not go as hard with Sodom and Gomorrah as with you now, most of you do not observe the Sabbath Day, no you are not, you are not observing My Law... scriptures say : "with all your heart honour your father, never forget the birthpangs of your mother; remember that you owe your birth to them; how can

62

you repay them for what they have done for you?" (Ecc. 7:27-30) and you are to follow this Commandment : honour your father and your mother; why are so many of you surprised that so few follow this Commandment? foolish and wicked notions led these children astray into worshipping empty productions, filling their spirit from early childhood with a spirit of sluggishness; many parents have not given their children that everflowing Source of My Spirit; Wisdom was calling them day and night,

63

but this generation barred Her out, and every day that passed, your children strayed further and further from the Path leading to Me; if any one, young or old, acknowledges Me as their God, they would reflect My Image, and out of love, would obey and honour their parents as they would be obeying and honouring Me; but all things that are conformed to the world have depraved these children from coming to Me; love is missing; many parents are complaining of their children's disobedience while

64

they are doing exactly the same thing to Me; why, can they really claim to have abundant goodness, patience and toleration? had they really all these virtues their children too would have the virtue of obedience and would honour them both; but I tell you : this generation's minds are empty and so Darkness came and filled them up; for the image of becoming a philosopher is more important in their eyes than My Eternal Glory; then, their lack of holiness is consumed by passion and from

1

early youth go out and dishonour their -own bodies; your generation has flouted My Commandments and replaced Them with blasphemous imitations, and to this day out of the beast's mouth come out evil productions to darken your children's minds and draw them as victims right into the lion's mouth; conquering their young mind to worship the first beast and serve man-made gods, giving them the honour and respect that was meant for Me, and thus reflect this virtue, on their parents ♡ I am telling you truly:

2

for the unsubmissive who refused to take My Commandments for their guide and took depravity instead, <u>there will be fire in the end for them</u>; O happy the submissive in heart, they shall attain perfection ♡ so I tell you: do not be unsubmissive to the Fear of the Lord ♡ — you know I have forbidden you to ♡ kill, generation! if you call yourself Mine and call yourself part of My Church and you preach against killing, how is it you kill? do you presume to maintain that you are in the

3

right and insist of your innocence before Me in the day of Judgement when you heap up crimes of unborn children? from Heaven I watch frightful sights, ah! how I suffer to see how the womb that shapes this child, rejects him and sends him to his death without a name and without regret; the womb that shaped him recalls him no longer; for these I say:

" you may sharpen your sword, but the weapon you prepared will kill you; now you are not pregnant with child but with

4

iniquity; you are going to conceive Spite and you will give birth to Mishap, you have dug a pit, hollowed it out, only to fall into your own trap! your spite will recoil on your head and your brutality will fall back on your head "*¹; and <u>you</u> *² you who are reputed to be faithful to Me and hold firmly to My Name, I know all about you, yes, you are reputed to be alive and thriving and yet you are not, you are dead and decomposing ♡ repent! I had entrusted you with souls ♡ beyond number; but the devil

*¹ Ps 7: 12-16   *² Here, Jesus calls out to the false prophet with a lamb's mask.

5

traded with you to exchange them for
his gold and silver; yes, indeed! I know
how you live now; you live like jackals *¹
in hidden lairs *²; these lairs upon which I
shall run an open-highway; - I shall come
suddenly upon you and expose your nakedness, and when the Day comes I shall not
allow you to eat from the tree of Life;
listen carefully: you preach against killing, yet you kill My Spirit; you boast
about the Law then disobey it because
you have not understood the mystery of

*¹ The once faithful ones "sold" themselves to
Satan and follow
the Beast.   *² The Lodges of the Freemasons.

6

Thy hidden manna; no, you have not yet
understood My miraculous feedings, nor
the mystery of My Transfiguration ♡
I have promised you to keep you alive
in the end of Times with My Celestial Manna;
I said to My church in Pergammum: *
"to those who prove victorious I will give the
hidden manna and a white stone - a
stone with a New Name written on it,
known only to man who receives it" ♡ I
am today offering you this manna reserved
for your times, a Celestial food, a nourish-

* App. 2:3, 17   *¹ Us = His
                              Creation.

7

ment of My Spirit for your starved spirit,
I pour out My Spirit in its fullness to
fill up your interiour desert, and I am
offering you My celestial manna, free, for this
is the food of the poor ... but you have
not understood .... so you refuse to eat it
and forbid others from eating it; I have
already inscribed My New Name on the
"white stone" which will be known only to
the poor; you claim to be humble and
poor _ yet you are neither humble nor
poor _ your spirit is enthroned in the

8

riches of Satan ♡ - I am the Ruler of the
kings of the earth and I have asked you
not to commit any impure acts or adultery;
adultery has been refined in such a way by
Satan, that it lost its meaning both in
ecclesiastical orders and in laity ♡ My
endurance in your sin has come now at
its end; for those* who sought Satan's
blasphemous powers and erected them as banners to efface My Divinity and My Holiness,
and My Holy Sacrifice, I tell you:
it is your fault that My Name is being

* Jesus is again referring those who worship the beast

9

blasphemed among the godless ♡ you have sullied My Sanctuary by ordaining perverted men with degrading passions; tainted all alike they do not fear Me; so if the godless today commit adultery and find it natural it is because of the great permissiveness in My Church given under the instructions of the beast whose aim is to falsify the Truth; how is it you forget so easily that your bodies are members of My Body? I would like to see you free from perversion since your bodies are

10

the temple of My Holy Spirit ♡ I, your God, would like to see you live holy since I am Holy ♡ creation! by acknowledging Me as your ♡ God you will be able to acknowledge My Law, and thus follow it, but many of you failed and now your corpses litter this desert... I have not commanded you to sin, so why use your freedom in a way that proves a pitfall for your soul? pray to Me so that I may forgive you, otherwise you would be a loser ♡ marriage is to be honoured and kept holy; I am

11

the Lord, and I have called you to a life of devotion, of peace, love and holiness: I have called you to Myself forever I called you to betroth you with My Tenderness and My Love and not until you understand that you are Mine and My betrothed, you will stop sinning and committing adultery towards Me; I will not cease, for the sake of My Holy Name, to take all means to bring you back to your senses, even if I must drag you out into the wilderness and expose to you there My

12

Sacred Heart and Its Fathomless Riches, to make you understand the nakedness and wretchedness of your soul; then like a scroll, I shall unroll to you all My Knowledge so that you renounce your sin; I have the power to cure you, so come and repent! My Holy Spirit asks you not to steal; if you call yourself Mine and if you know My Law and claim to be in the Truth, then why not teach yourself, you who ordained yourself as priest* as well as others, not to steal? but you have

* follower of the beast: the false prophet

13

allowed yourself to be bought and follow
subtly the beast, who taught you to set
banners of lawlessness; you are of the world
and I have much to condemn you for;
your tongue proudly claims that you do
great things, good things, honest things,
deceiving even the elect with your lamb's
mask; but I tell you: you do not
deceive Me, because I know that behind
your lamb's mask, you hide a hideous
catastrophy for mankind such as the
world has never seen before: your aim

14

is to <u>abolish My Sacrifice</u> *[1] and replace It
by Iniquity and with <u>a lie</u>; you profess
to be a Prophet to disown My Own prophets;
have you no fear to have your name blotted
out of the book of life, since all you do is
steal millions of souls from Me leading them
to their death? — your miracles impress
many today and even more the day you
will rid off My prophets overcoming them*[2]
by your sword ♡ now you have armoured
yourself to the ♡ teeth to make war on
them because their witnessing disturbs your

* Daniel: 12, 11
*[2] App: 11; 8

15

ears, and their obedience to My Commandments even more; they have not followed
you nor the beast, they are the ones who
have kept faithful to Me and have never
allowed a lie to pass their lips *; they are
My Abels; in the eyes of the world you
will appear to have overcome them, but
your joy will be only for a very short
time, because like thunderbolt I shall
let My Justice overpower you; I shall
descend to breathe again life in them,*[2]
raising them, before your very eyes, as

*[1] App: 14: 5   App: 11, 11

16

columns of light in My Sanctuary ... and
then heaven will open and you will see Me,
and if you will ask Me: why are your rich
garments stained with crimson? why are your
garments red, your clothes as if you had
trodden the winepress?* I shall tell you:
I have trodden the winepress alone; of the
men of My people not one was with Me,
I have trampled upon My enemies in My
wrath; they never ceased defying Me and
provoking Me; I have come to efface from
the surface of this earth all human

* Is. 63. 2

17

doctrines and regulations which were poison food to all of you and forced by the sword upon you, to defile My Divinity and My Holiness; this shall be the first battle of the end; I Am: the Majestic Rider, *' I Am: the Word ♡ if this earth mourns, pining away, and its trees have no produce and their leaves are withering, it is because you are not obeying My Law; — have I not said: you shall not give false witness or testimony? yet from the core of My Sanctuary where lies the lance's blade, *² where

*² the false prophet   *' App: 19:11

18

among My Abels are the Cains too, this Commandment is not obeyed too; Cain's appointed priests are sent out now to the four corners of the earth, not to bear witness on Me as the Resurrected, nor on My Sacrifice, but to condemn My Word by aping Scriptures, and to teach all nations a False Christ, under a false ecumenism, giving the world a portion of Rationalism and Naturism, a defiled food: a Lie; I tell you, they shall not prove victorious nor will they rule forever: Justice will prevail! I shall not

19

leave you prosper forever since I know all about you and how by the power of the dragon you are appointing your own priests placing them into high seats to crush and overcome My own priests; I tell you: the time is almost over; I will drag you from your high seat to fall at the feet of My own priests, My saints and My angels, and make you admit that you are the slave of the beast ... soon, very soon, I shall come to you like a thief, unexpected, and overthrow: the Lie, your False Christ; and

20

place back The Truth; I shall soon come to shatter this false image you are making out of Me, compelling every nation to honour it; * no, victorious you shall not be! daughters and sons of Mine, you who err aimlessly in this desert, return to Me, repent! sin no more; I know you have many a times testified wrongly for lack of love, but you were not under your shepherd's protection to be taught My precepts because of your hostility towards Me; yet, in spite of your arrogance and your hostility

* App:13; 16

21

towards Me, I cry out to you: I love you! and My forgiveness has been granted to you already; come back to Me as you are and I shall dress you with My Divinity, I shall give you back your divinity for the sake of My Holy Name; — you want to testify? testify on My great Love and Mercy, you want to bear witness? bear witness in My Name: Jesus Christ, Beloved Son of God and Saviour ♡ love one another as I love you; rejoice you who have been given My hidden manna and have already received

22

the Seal of My Love on your forehead; ♡ — from Heaven I have commanded you not to covet your neighbour's goods nor your neighbour's wife, from laity to priests this Commandment has not been kept either; I have revealed My Love, for every creature on earth, with My Sacrifice and through this Sacrifice gave you eternal life and My Message of Love; many of you preach love, forgiveness humility, tolerance, holiness, over and over again, yet to this day many of you are ready to kill because you do not get what

23

you want; you keep on throwing venomous arrows on each other, because you do not have what I have given your neighbour ♡ from the time of My Abel to this day this sin is constantly repeated; the first man to covet his brother's goods was Cain, but how many more Cains are there today? and how many more Esaus? motivated by convenience and nothing else he gave up his birthright, falling into apostasy; why not follow Abel's example and be holy? to love is to live holy and according to My

24

Commandments; if you who praise Me night and day yet covet your neighbour's goods, I ask you to repent! if you ask Me: "how am I coveting My neighbour's goods, I, who consecrated My goods to You, my life and everything, how am I coveting his goods?" I will tell you: your spirit is coveting your neighbour's spirit, those very gifts that I have given his spirit; the devil has set a trap for your soul, do not fall! where do these wars and battles between yourselves first start in My House, if they are not

25

mainly from spiritual jealousy? Cain wanted something and he did not get it, so he killed Abel; Esau wanted something and he gave up his birthright to get it ♡ you have an ambition you cannot satisfy, so either you ignore your neighbour's happiness to dissatisfy him, or you go out and are ready to kill; I tell you truly: if at heart you have the bitterness of jealousy, or a self-seeking ambition, never make any claims for yourself or cover up the Truth with lies for wherever you find jealousy

26

and ambition, you find disharmony, hypocrisy and tepidness; do not go on sinning, repent! and do not get influenced by those appointed by the false prophet and are members of Satan's dwelling; do not listen to them; I shall soon descend with My Throne among you, so come and repent while there is still time; come you who waver and hesitate between good and evil, and who insinuate yourself into your neighbour's house in order to get influence over silly women who are obsessed with their sins

27

and follow one craze after another in the attempt to educate themselves, but can never come to knowledge of the Truth; * realize how pitiable you are to look at and do not misunderstand My reproofs; realize how I love you ♡ work for My Glory and do not look to your left nor to your right; for if you look to your left you will behold ravenous wolves ready to pounce on you and tear you to pieces, and if you look to your right you will see a pit, dug up for you to fall into;

* 2 Tim. 3 : 6 - 8

28

be happy then, generation, with what I have given you and share as I share with you; My Fire is imminent and, ah ... so many of you will be unprepared, because your era does not believe, they do not adore Me, they do not hope or love Me, your generation has replaced The Truth and My Commandments by blasphemies, love is missing among you; you do not live a life of love, nor have you understood what 'the Fear of the Lord is the Beginning of Wisdom', means; if you fear Me, you

29

are blessed; if you fear Me, you can attain perfection; if you fear Me, I will intoxicate you with My sweet Wine and fill you with My produce; if you fear Me, you will live in Peace; if you fear Me, Wisdom will come all the way to your doorstep; if you fear Me, you will obey fervently My Commandments not changing one stroke from Them; so I recommend you all not to live with a double heart; infuse your soul with My Divine Grace now that there is still time, repent while there

30

is still time, come back to Me while there is still time; do not heap your sin on sin; alas! for those stubborn souls who shut their ears on these last warnings, what will you do on My Return? I am known to be Faithful and True* and I tell you: Justice shall prevail ♡ do not be bewildered, My child, do not stand mystified with what I have given you to write, for it has been foretold, that in your days, My Church would be betrayed, by one who was My very own, just like Juda,

* App 19:12

31

and Her apostasy would come from within Her; I would be betrayed by those who shared My Meals, who had bonds with Me, who drank and ate with Me; but very soon now, everything that is covered will be uncovered and what I have said in parables and in metaphors will be made clear; I shall unveil My proverbs and parables to the poor; before this generation has passed away, with My Power and My Glory I shall overthrow the False Prophet; all that Scriptures say must be fulfilled

32

to the iota; this is why I have written everything down so that after the examination of these Messages, you will understand the mark of genuineness in every letter and that these are My Own Words given by My Grace to you all; I have come to revive this flickering flame of love, before the false Prophet blows it away altogether... (Jesus wept.)... I weep, I do; he is lodging in My House and instead of offering Me fragrant offerings and sacrifices, he is replacing these by all sorts of evil forms offered to him

33

by the evil one : impurity, promiscuity, injustice, disobedience to My Law, debauchery and drunkeness with the blood of My prophets, My very Own...without cease his mouth sends his boasts and blasphemies to the four corners of the earth; false blessings and true curses come out of this same mouth ♡ I know all about him, I know him inside out, and I tell you; he shall never reach the place of rest; I the Lord, shall give you, My child, visions of he who carries on himself the blood of many, and of those

34

who worship him *; stay awake, praying at all times for strength to stand with confidence by Me; hear Me: this Rebel's sins have reached up all the way to Heaven and aroused My entire justice, followed by an Infinite Grief in My Soul, to have to condemn him and his entire stock; – My Father created them with delight and great Love, and I have loved them and sacrificed Myself to redeem not only the just but the unjust too, I laid down My Life for them, but he and his clan, instead,

* look at message 3.9.90

35

turned against Me with full conscience to wreck his faith ... (Jesus wept again) ... and break My Covenant forever and ever ... his aim is to distort the Scriptures from beginning to end and make out of My Word, Truths, Wisdom and the language of My Cross a cymbal clashing, a rational theory, a philosopher's theory; aping Wisdom, and with these empty teachings nourish a multitude and lead them to their death; – out of his boastful mouth he apes the Good News, he apes My Resurrection and My

36

entire Divinity; ah! the time of your trading is soon over; the merchants that traded with you and supplied you with the best quality of merchandise will be sunk and all people will be horrified at your fate; daughter, read Ezekiel 28 ♡ :
" being swollen with pride, you have said: I am god; I am sitting on the throne of God, surrounded by the seas; though you are a man and not a god, you consider yourself the equal of God; you are wiser now than Daniel; there is

37

no sage as wise as you; by your wisdom and your intelligence you have amassed great wealth; you have piles of gold and silver inside your treasure-houses; such is your skill in trading, your wealth has continued to increase, and with this your heart has grown more arrogant; since you consider yourself the equal of God, very well, I am going to bring foreigners against you, the most barbarous of the nations; they will draw sword against your fine wisdom, they will defile your glory; they will throw you down

38

into the pit and you will die a violent death surrounded by the seas; are you still going to parade as the High Priest clad in silver and gold? are you still going to say: I am a god, a Prophet, when your murderers confront you? no, you are a man and not a god in the clutches of your murderers! and you will die like the godless at the hand of the foreigners; you were once an exemplar of perfection full of wisdom, perfect in beauty; you were in Eden, in the garden of God, in the Core

39

of My Sanctuary, but your busy trading has filled you with violence and sin; you have corrupted your wisdom owing to your splendour; by the immense number of your sins, by the dishonesty of your trading, you have defiled My Sanctuary; then read Apocalypse 18 ♡; – now sentence is being passed on this world; now the prince of this world is soon to be overthrown; the second beast alias the False Prophet, the "high priest", the Lance, the jackals, are all one and the same; he is the one who armoured

40

himself to the teeth to make war on My Law* and on My prophets*²; he and his clan are the jackals I have mentioned to you in My previous Messages; – I have grown weary of him and his whole clan, and I take no pleasure in punishing; I wanted to redeem them adopting them as sons of Mine but they allowed themselves to be bought by rich merchants who will fall with them; feel My sorrow, feel My grief, feel My pain; they are idolaters of money ... My God, come and rest in the hearts

*alias Moses   *² alias Elijah

41

of Your Abels, those who really love You; maybe they are few and not many, but they are Your saints who endure trials', they are the people who love You, they are those who have constancy and faith, they are Your companions, they are Your first-fruits who never allowed a lie to pass their lips; I offer You these so that You may rest in them.

♡ I will rest My Head in the hearts of My devout children, (the saints of your era,) come, love Me, console My Heart; and repair for those who are depriving entire nations from My Love by building a wall between Me and My children, - I have never deprived a soul from My Love, - pray My Vassula

42

without cease, many will be cleansed by prayers; many will be purged by sacrifices and fasting; do not linger, time is pressing ♡ bless Me more, efface the world's iniquity by giving Me and showing Me more love, ah Vassula, My daughter, please Me and tell Me these words:

Jesus teach me to love you tenderly,
give this grace to those who do
not love You and do not
know the Consuming Fire of
Your Sacred Heart; amen

43

17. 8. 90

I come to You my Yahweh to ask You to forgive my sins; Lord listen to my pleading, I know You do forgive us and overlook all our sins.

I forgive you, I forgive you rather than let My wrath strike you ... desolate and uninhabited you were, you were famous for your desert; you were like a garden without water and I, like a watercourse running into a garden came to you to irrigate your soil; I saved you from the clutches of My enemy; the lion has left you and your land is a garden now,

44

thanks to My Infinite Love and Mercy; - I am your Saviour and Jesus is My Name; allow Me to write the following message for ♡:... I the Lord am before him, and ♡ I am setting fire and water in front of him; I have given him the liberty to choose; he can put out his hand to whichever he prefers; I note every one of his actions; I note down his conscious and direct sincerity towards Me and his conscious and direct insincerity towards Me ♡ hurry up and come to Me, and I will revive your flame:

* a Rhodian

45

what little flame is left in you is dying fast!
I love you with an eternal Love and My
Mercy is Fathomless; you enjoy My favour ♡ "
– many of you today say : let us drink
let us eat today, tomorrow we shall be
dead ; do not lie to yourselves ... come back
to your senses and face Me your God; to
obey My Law is to love Me and anyone
who lives in love lives in Me; I do not
need philosophers and sages of your age,
neither masters, I need weakness ... poverty...
simplicity ... see? the days are coming

46

where I will put My Law on your hearts;
I come in these days of Mercy to prepare
the nations and remind them that I can
purify your inner self from vile and dead
actions which can lead you into eternal
fires; – but this generation's heart has
grown coarse and although I am talking
openly to the nations they will still not
listen to Me; come, take your cross and
follow Me, I shall bless each step you
take ♡ ΙΧΘΥΣ ⊂▷

47

Later on, to the little prayer group:
I have invited many to My banquet but
very few are willing to come *, so I tell you:
      go to the poor now! go to the blind !
some you will find dead but do not
worry, I shall raise them; I have lifted
you all and I shall lift many more; so
go out to the poor and the sick and make
sure to fill My House ! let those who were
first invited to My banquet yet refused to

* The little prayer group attempted many times to invite
well known priests and archimandrites, even well-known
monks, but each one had an excuse and showed no
interest at all for the Lord's messages. They were polite.

48

come be astonished to see the blind with
their sight and the poor, rich with My
Knowledge ! and the dead, raised back to
life ! ♡ thrive in My Riches and do not
fade away ! be constant and work for My
Glory ... children, efface your egoism; My
Kingdom is very near you, be zealous and
follow My Word, keep yourselves pure and
learn to efface yourselves so that My Spirit
breathes in you ♡ – I have chosen you
My angels not because you are worthy
but because you are poor and wretched ;

49

glorify My Name again by meeting to serve
Me; be active in all good works — I
am with you all the time ΙΧΘΥΣ 〜◗

3.9.90

I went to meet a priest. He is of a certain
order and I recognize what the garments of
that order of priests should look like. When
the door opened and I saw him I was taken
by surprise to look straight at someone who seemed
to wear some fancy-masquarade garment! He
had on him a light-color purple long garment
like satin, I could see the interiour of his
long and large sleeves were light olive colour
and around his waist he wore a fancy belt
of gold and silver. Around his neck he wore
a thick gold chain. There was no sign of
cross on him. He looked like an ancient
king. At first I thought that maybe because
he is so special they dressed him up this way.
Then when he greeted me I looked at his face

50

forgetting what he was wearing. I was together
with 'x' another priest of the same order and
he did not react. I thought everything was
normal and so I left this as it was without
thinking of it much until I remembered the
message of the Lord when a week before this
incident He said :— I the Lord shall give you
visions of they who who follow the beast; — and
He had said that these who follow the beast
in His Church are dressed up, like High-Priests,
masquaraded in gold-and silver. They will
deceive many, even the elect. — That afternoon
I had not seen a regular priest, I saw someone
dressed as a 'king', in fancy clothes.
Vassula, I have told you that I shall point
out to you with My Finger all the thorns of
My Body, * — a man who does a thing
like that ought to have been expelled from

* I open at random the Holy Bible for a prophecy.

51

the community — (1 Cor. 5:2).

10.9.90

Yahweh Sabaoth, bring us back, let Your Face
smile on us and we shall be safe.   Ps. 80:3

peace be with you; lean on Me ... I have not
formed you for nothing; I have not commen-
ced this Work with you to leave it unfinished,
I have blessed My Work so that it glorifies
Me, and you, you who are nothing, and
with no gifts at all to offer Me, I have
given your shoulders My Yoke to confuse the
wise and disperse them, and show them
that as long as they maintain their stand,

52

I, the Lord, will not reveal Myself to them;
— and you, daughter, yes ... stagger with
bewilderment at My choice, for what man
can say: 'I have cleansed my heart, I am
purified of my sin?' yet, your persecutors,
deaf to My Teachings, hope for something
to use against you; I tell you solemnly,
of all the children born of women, a lesser
than you has never been seen; the wound
on you daughter, wounds Me too; yes, all
of this generation is adulteress... but I mean
to save your generation like I saved you;

53

even if I have to drag her out to the desert,
 and do unto her as I have done to
you* I shall expose her nakedness in her
eyes, and at the first sound of repentance,
I shall come flying to her as I came flying
to you, then in the presence of My angels
I shall sing to her My Song of Love; I
shall turn her away from the path of
delusion and grant her the grace of My Law;
then I shall take her hand into My Hand
to guide her back into My House, where

* A purification like in purgatory. When I saw my
sins with God's eyes.

54

I shall show to her all the Riches of My
Sacred Heart; these Treasures My Heart
kept for the end of Times: to enliven this
flickering flame about to extinguish into a
Consuming Fire, to give light to those who
live in darkness and the shadow of death;
— Vassula My daughter, your persecutors
will try to strip off you the garments I
have given you and rob you of My Jewels!
but I promise you to take away each
hand that will approach you; I mean
to end their debauchery and their mis-

55

guidings; I mean to display a notice that
will stand firm and forever: King of kings,
the Lamb of God, the First and the Last,
the Word of God, the Resurrected, the
Christ, the Redeemer; to abolish and end
their conspiracy against My Church, and
their false teachings of My Word and of My
Image; I am not speaking in metaphors
now, I am telling you in plain words that
they are conferring a title that does not
belong to Me and is not Me; a false Christ,
a lifeless image, a false god: subtly hidden

56

under a false ecumenism … but I promise
you My child, that I shall prevail in the
end; I will overpower these false teachers of
your era and I will give you the hidden
treasures of My Sacred Heart putting on
your tongue the language of My Cross which
is Love, with all Its Mysteries and Miracles
and Wonders! then I shall remind My
shepherds the words "leadership and service,
I will command them that they should
not be like great men making their
authority felt among the poor; no,

57

anyone who would want to be great among the poor must be their servant, and any- one who would want to be first among them must be least, just as I came on earth not to be served but to serve, and to give My Life as a ransom for many; — and you little child, do not fear Me *, I shall keep My Light inside you forever and ever! pray for the sal- vation and the conversion of your era; I bless you; bless Me and love Me ΙΧΘΥΣ ♡⚬><

* I was afraid Jesus was upset with me.

58

12.9.90

Jesus? I am, peace be with you flower ♡ write down My Message for all parts of the world ♡ : — peace be with you; children of My Heart, realize how Heaven is opening every day to you with My Grace to give you calls, for conversions .... reminders of My Word ... instructions to teach you to follow My Commandments; Heaven is opening Its Doors daily in several places of the world to bring you Peace and Love, and Wisdom with all Her Glory descends on a Throne right in the

59

middle of you all, to open the eyes of the blind, to open the ears of the deaf and to resurrect the dead who litter this desert; no, Wisdom will not show Herself to a crafty soul, She will come to instruct only the poor and the simple and pour out all Her Works on them, for these very souls know how to fear Me, the Lord, and cherish My Word; what greater gift then than bringing Her all the way to your door- step? what greater joy than Her smile on you? what greater delight than hear

60

Her sing to you Her New Song of Love? rejoice then creation ! for I Am at your very doors ... this Joy had been reserved for your times generation, when Satan and all his empire together with his worldwide authority are escalading at the peak of their power in My Church and in all nations, together with the false prophet of whose footsteps you hear clearer and clearer every day and everywhere; they are armed to the teeth to make war against My Church and all those who obey My

61

Commandments; I have reserved, beloved children, for your times, this Celestial Manna given by My Spirit; it is this hidden manna * I had reserved for times of wilderness and iniquity; it is the food of the poor and those who are starved, and I promise you, they will receive as much as they want to eat and to them I shall confer My New Name; it is this Heavenly Food I am pouring from Heaven, it is : the outpouring of My Holy Spirit, filling your interior desert; it is Love speaking to a

* See App. 2 : Pergamum, v. 17

62

hostile world; it is Love knocking on every locked door; it is Love calling from the other side of the Wall separating us, built up by My enemies; it is Love pleading as a beggar for : a return of love ... a smile ... a regret ... a sigh ... it is I :

the Sacred Heart;

I come once more to revive this dying flame in your heart into a Consuming Fire of Tenderness and Love; I descend to outpour lavishly all the Treasures of My Heart on you, humanity ... and give light to

63

those who live in darkness and the shadow of death; I come to break in splinters the doors of your dungeons and with My Flame melt your chains of sin; I come to free you from your captivity and your iniquity and end up your debaucheries; I mean to save you generation, even if I must drag you all the way to the desert and speak to you, showing you your aridity and how your whole body is filled up with darkness, I shall do it to save you; ah, creation! what will I not do for you ...

64

My Spirit is upon you and It will rest on you forever and ever; so open up your hearts and let Me fill you with My Grace; come and draw your strength from Me, strengthen your roots in Me, for what will you do then on the day of tribulation if your roots are frail? you will sway in the wind and be torn away with the violence of the storm, and your branches will snap off like thin glass; no, you will be unable to survive ♡ come to Me then and thrive in My Riches so

1

you do not fade away; come to Me as you are; do not wait to be saints to come to Me; come to Me as you are and I shall forgive your sins and purify your soul; I shall then dress you with My Divinity for the sake of My Holy Name to prepare you for our spiritual Wedding; I the Lord intend to wed you in My Glory and make you, generation, entirely Mine; I mean to make you find the Way and guide your feet away from tortuous paths; I will prepare you to be Mine forever and for all

2

eternity; today I am bending from Heaven all the way to you out of Love and Mercy, but at the same time, My Soul is sorrowful and in sheer grief, to find My lambs and My sheep, some of them scattered, others lost and others devoured by wolves hiding under lamb skins; so do not be surprised of My visit to you because every day that passes you will see Me more and more until you will meet Me face to face; I will come in flaming fire to sweep away all who do not acknowledge Me as

3

their God and I am telling you: time is pressing, the hours are fleeing and the Day of My Glory is soon with you; do not be one of those who say: "well, where is this Coming?" "where is this Promise?" — My Coming is soon and My Promise is on its way to be fulfilled and your waiting will be shortened for the sake of My Mother's prayers together with all My saints; so then My beloved, while you are waiting, reconcile and live holy so that I will find you at peace ♡ I shall be

4

coming very soon now as Love, everything soon comes to an end, and one day you will all have to answer Me and give Me your accounts; so what will happen to the wicked and to the sinner? and what will happen to those who continue to offend Me? I am Faithful and True and My Promise will come true, I shall not delay; for as much as you hear the footsteps of the false prophet and his clan on the surface of this earth, all the more will I make you hear My Own Footsteps to wipe

5

off with My Blood the traces of venom they leave on their path for you as bait; this Rebel and his clan are thriving now; concealed in robes of High Priest, concealed as lamb, concealed as the Truth, to deceive many and lead them all to their death; I am not speaking in parables now but in direct words; the Times are here, those Times foretold in Scripture, when My enemies will be conferring a title that does not belong to Me and is not Me: a false Christ, a lifeless image, a false god; an idol,

6

subtly hidden under a false ecumenism: the Lance's Blade which lies deep in My Sacred Heart and causes so much bleeding... by sword they will force you to eat their defiled food: a portion of Rationalism one day and a portion of Naturism the other day and so on; aping the Truth, My Word, Wisdom and the language of My Cross; but fire will come on them from Heaven and consume him and his clan; this is sure and will come true; I am telling you all these things,

7

beloved ones so as to warn you from these false teachers and human doctrines, and to tell you that in these coming days of tribulations, My Sacred Heart which is on Fire will continue to pursue you; as the beggar hoping for alms, I too will be hoping to win your heart before the coming of darkness befalls you ♡ I bless each one of you leaving My Sigh of Love sealed on your forehead; I, Jesus Christ, Beloved Son of God and Saviour leave you with My Peace wholeheartedly;

8

I love you Infinitely ♡ be one;

ΙΧΘΥΣ 🐟

18. 9. 90

My Lord You who guard me from evil and surround my soul with Your love Songs, let Your Holy Face smile on all who love You. Teach the youth of today to follow You and imitate You. Show them the Treasures of Your Sacred Heart and teach those who still do not understand and waver undecidedly before this Holy Name You have chosen: Sacred Heart, to learn that it is You, the Christ. Let those who keep on differentiating themselves because of theological terminology, yet are under Your Holy Name, come back to their senses and realize how they encourage this Division in Christianity, and how they are not doing Your Will, but are granting Satan one more foothold to keep us apart, thus weakening Your Church; You are Jesus Christ, the Beloved Son of God and Saviour, The Sacred Heart, The Word, The Alpha and the Omega, The Light, The Redeemer, The Pantocrator: You are ONE Christ. You are not

9

parcelled out! so I pray to You, who want us to be united to unite us again in love, in heart, in our belief and practice.

this My child is what you are to teach them to believe and persuade them to do, but, My child, there will be those who will not listen, because of their self-conceit; these people lie heavily on My Heart, they lack humility and true Wisdom, they are only full of antagonistic beliefs of the 'knowledge' which is not Knowledge at all... when it comes to judge, condemn, and argue about words, raising without cease questions;

10

yet never realizing that they are a prey to the Tempter; oh My child bear those hardships for My Sake, all these are not in vain: one day you will see the Light face to face... come and feast now in My Love and My Tenderness, repose your head on My Heart and listen to the calls of Love, rejoice in Me, rejoice in My Splendour and My Riches, I have stored this Wealth for you, generation, to lead you to Me with chains of Love, and if you ask: " how long until this Wonder takes place?" I will tell you.

11

it is already taking place, My Footsteps have been heard by some of you, the Lord whom you are seeking, will suddenly come upon you, the One whom you are longing for, is coming; so I tell you, do not resist My Holy Spirit who will come now in full force to unwrap the death shroud, which covers your nations, prohibiting you to see the Light; I will descend in full force with My Spirit, to unmask the deceivers and drive out the traders who infiltrated into My Sanctuary ♡ turn your eyes to Me, generation, and see the

12

Joy that is coming to you soon; My Holy Spirit will descend in its fullness not only to save the wretches but I will descend also for judgement, to give sight to the blind and take away the sight of those who say they see, and from those who call themselves wise and instructed I will confuse to the point that they would not know who they are and where they come from; I tell you solemnly, I will instruct the unworthy, and those whom you call foolish and contemptible, I will raise and instruct them

13

with My Knowledge turning them to devout pupils of the Truth, to shame those who hold back My Kingdom from them♥ I tell you: "the dead will be making their way into My Kingdom before you*; My Spirit of Grace came to you at your doors but you did not want to believe in My Marvels nor in My Miracles and yet the ones you call contemptible and who are the rejects of your society, believed with humility, with fervour and with love; this is why I will bring back the sinners and raise the dead as columns of light,

* the "wise".

14

but to My sheer grief even after you will see these great marvels, you will still refuse to think better of it and believe in My present Divine Works; so I am telling you:

My Kingdom will be taken away
from you to be given to a poor
people., a people who could not tell
their right hand from their left
and it will be to these wretches
I shall confer My New Name ♥ "

Ι Χ Θ Υ Σ 〈fish symbol〉 ☧

15

18. 9. 90

Vassula of My Sacred Heart,* do not allow anyone to take away from you the gift I have given you ♥ Lord! forbid them to do this to me, by myself I cannot do anything and I am limited as You know!

do not fear, Vassula My daughter; My enemies who are also your enemies, I shall overpower, and My Teachings shall convert many more; see? how many times have I rescued you from the lion's mouth? and how many times have I enlightened you My child? and how

* Here, I was just thinking that probably I am the first Orthodox called: 'Vassula of the Sacred Heart.'

16

many times have I shown you the Way? ah My sweet pupil!* have confidence in Me, rely on Me; ask and it shall be given to you ♥ come, evangelize with love for Love; earn souls for Me; desire Me, love Me, and trust Me ♥ Ι Χ Θ Υ Σ 〈fish symbol〉 ☧
ecclesia shall revive!

17. 9. 90

Lord, take my soul and my heart and place them in the middle of Your Sacred Heart.

Ah My child, how I longed to hear you say again these words to Me! how I

* Jesus was so full of joy as He cried out loud these words!

17

long to hear these words from everyone's
heart ! ♡

Lord ?

I am; come and console Me, come and
comfort Me, rest Me; I have created you so
that I may be the One and only in your
heart; I have created you to remove My thorns
that penetrated My Body; I have created you
to be the victim of My Heart; I love you to
passion; accept My Love, accept My Knowledge, accept the trials with patience and
do not look on them with disdain; I have

18

accepted My Cross with great Love, with
obedience and I drank My Cup to its last
drop, out of Love and to please the Father
in Heaven ♡ I am only disciplining you in
moderation My daughter; if you listen to
Me you will learn; My Eyes are constantly
watching you, guarding you and blessing you;
I am He who loves you most so do not
fear My daughter Vassula, do not dread
My discipline which will orient you in My
direction, showing you the magnificence of
My Works, their Splendour and the

19

Riches of My Heart and the Consuming Fire
of My Love ♡ have I ever failed you?
have I ever resisted your calls when you
needed Me? - blessed nations, blessed people,
blessed creation! then how is it you resist My
Love and have gone astray to become an
easy prey for Satan allowing yourselves to
call My Name in vain? the spirit who is in
you, generation, is a rebellious spirit, ruling
you all to live a sensual life, an aimless
life, a godless life, thus interchanging
holiness with perversion ♡ oh generation !

20

where is the Sign between Me and you?
what have you done with It? where is
your faith in Me? how have you allowed
to bring yourselves to give Me up? have
you not heard before that the nearer you
come to Me, the nearer I will come to you?
keep your eyes fastened on Me without
looking to your left nor to your right;
let Me one day say: My child, welcome
into your Father's House, you have been an
appeasing fragrance to Me, you have kept
My Law and lived holy; you have

21

been fruitful and you have nourished the
poor; come then, My child, thrust yourself into your Father's Arms and live forever and ever in My Heart ♡ ΙΧΘΥΣ ⤳
21.9.90
My beloved Yahweh, make us once more
divine, renew us; fashion us into Your Divine
Image; this Holy Image we lost.
My Vassula I shall hear your pleas and
like I have rained down on you My Blessings, I shall cover this earth with splendid
vestments, clothing her in glorious perfection,
and make her people fall on their faces to
the ground, in adoration to Me; but first

22

I must descend My Purifying Fire upon this
generation, I must descend to pull out
the foxes from their lairs that make
havoc of every new vineyard; I have told
you this now before it happens, so that
when it happens you may believe; like
rousing a corpse from death, I shall resurrect
this earth's decaying body into a glorious
body, transfiguring you from priest to lay-
man into a divine people; today your
generation lacks faith and refuses to believe in
Me, and every day that passes, more and

23

more of My shepherds are being taken by
the world and the lure of riches; they are
aping Wisdom and when Grace comes to them
at their feet they refuse this Grace; they
do not want to receive Grace in return
for grace; there is a division in My Church;
like Cain and Abel, brothers, yet divided;
one blood, yet different; Abel was competant
but Cain, incompetant, one was sincere, the
other not; one was well disposed and
pleasing, the other one was ill-disposed
and displeasing Me; and today My Abels

24

who officiate in My Church, suffer... they
suffer because they see that their own
brothers are betraying Me; this is the
plague that weighs heavily on My shepherds
and makes this brotherhood: broken, and
divided ♡ happy the man who keeps My
Commandments, for he shall feel My
appeasing Love, happy the peacemakers
when they work for peace, they shall be
called sons of Mine; soon Love shall be with
you, this is why there must be constancy in
My Abels who keep My Commandments and

25

keep their faith in Me ♡ My Nassula, I
shall give you the rest ✱♥ later on, be perse-
vering in your prayers and be thankful,
delight your Father who is in Heaven ; do
not fear... I am with you ; Love's Eyes
are on you ; Jesus is My Name ♡ ΙΧΘΥΣ
⟨fish⟩ Alleluia !

24. 9. 90

peace be with you ♡ Nassula, I shall
never fail you ; prolong your prayers to
Me, this pleases My Heart ; say : "Jesus, You
who saved Me, be blessed ; Jesus, You who

* the rest of a certain passage of the Bible He wanted to
teach me.

26

feed Me be blessed ; Jesus, I love You, teach
Me how to love you more ; amen ♡"
caress Me with simple words, yet coming from
your heart ; ah My beloved ! bless Me without cease ; rest in My Heart and console Me
as I console you ; this My Nassula is what
I need now ♡ ✱

25. 9. 90

Our Holy Mother's Message to us all.

peace be with you, beloved children ; allow Me
to remind you that the Lord knows each
heart ; the Lord is in search of your heart ;
come to Him with a pure heart and He

27

shall teach you ; the Lord shall comfort
your soul, He shall lead you in His Path
and in the Truth ; I beg you, you who
still waver, do not shut your hearts to
reason ; return to the Lord and He will
return to you ; a Joy from Heaven will
now descend among you, a Light will
shine in the midst of you ; be prepared
to receive this Light, be prepared to meet
the Lord ♡ — today, whose hands are
clean ? and who can say truly, his heart
is pure ? whose soul is in perfect harmony

28

with the Lord ? beloved ones ! My own !
My children ... the road to the Lord is
in the midst of you, it is found in the
land of the living ; stretch out then your
hands towards His Sanctuary and the Lord,
from Heaven, will reach to pull you to
Him ; stretch out your hands towards
Him and Me, full of Compassion will
lean down to you ; come to the Lord
without delay ; lift your eyes to Heaven
and look to no one else but Him,
the Lord your God, delight in no one else

29

but Him, your Saviour; seek, seek no one else but the Lord your Redeemer; sing, sing to no one, but to the Holy One;

am I to remind you that the Lord is Tenderness and Compassion, slow to anger and rich in Graciousness? _ Jesus was the Stone rejected by the builders that became the Keystone; I tell you truly, that the Kingdom of God is among you and His Holy Spirit of Grace is blowing sweetly now on your nations, to revive you, so come and see the Wedding of the Holy Spirit

30

who will wed your lands; do not reject the Holy Spirit that so manifestly is poured upon you; do not be like the "builders" who rejected the stone that turned to be the cornerstone ♡ God wants everyone to be saved, and now this is My solemn warning to all who hear the prophecies of this book:

do not suppress the Spirit, the Spirit that now blows on you in the middle and in the peak of your apostasy; do not say later on, on Judgement Day:

31

" I had never heard, I had not known; " Jesus and I are revealing things beforehand, before they happen, so that you cannot say when you meet God face to face: " I was unaware .... _ ... the citadel of the proud shall fall ... and the devils shall be cast out from within her womb ♡ _ may you be blessed; may you all ♡ be blessed for hearing Me; I am your beloved Mother, the Théotokos who loves you all ♡

32 _

Jesus? I Am ♡ lean on Me, lean on My Shoulder, as ♡ I came to you and lifted you from the pit and carried you to My House where I healed you, so will I continue to help your feet to be in the Righteous Path; let your hands clutch on Me; I know you to be faint-hearted * but I shall make you strong to oppose evil; _ ah creation! Mercy now descends before Judgement; welcome My Mercy now and My Spirit shall rest on you ♡ approach Me you who desire Me, and take your fill from My Inexhaustible

28.9.90

* Jesus was smiling

33

Wells of Life, for they who eat Me will hunger for more and they who drink Me will thirst for more;* and I, like Manna, will replenish your soul, and like a potter, shall form you into what you have lost: My Divinity; – then I shall show you My Kingdom and I will send you Wisdom to teach you My Knowledge of My Holy things, and I shall make you Mine forever and ever; you will be My sons and daughters glorifying Me together with My Assembly in Heaven; then I shall send you out like

* Eccl. 24; 21

34

mist, to display like one displays a banner: My Knowledge you received from Wisdom Herself, to teach others to grow upright in purpose and learning, so that generation after generation My Holy Name may be kept Holy; your descendants would have a rich inheritance born of you, and thanks to My Infinite Mercy, so will your children's children; and in the future the nations will know the meaning of, the Fear of the Lord ♡ My favours are not all past, My favours are inexhaustible, filling every valley, and My Tender-

35

ness is renewed every day upon you; I am pouring out continuously from My Heart My Love like flowing rivers to water your desert and revive you; — it is not I who forced you to dwell in darkness; it is not My wish to watch from above how you wall yourselves in and imprison your souls in the darkest dungeons; My desire is to bring you Home in peace; My desire is to make out of your deserts and parched lands, green pastures, to fill you ♡ Vassula, all My Messages are prayers, read and

36

write down Romans 8 : 26-27 :

The Spirit too comes to help us in our weakness. For when we cannot choose words in order to pray properly, the Spirit himself expresses our plea in a way that could never be put to words, and God who knows everything in our hearts knows perfectly well what he means, and that the pleas of the saints expressed by the Spirit are according to the mind of God.

meditate upon this ... I love you, repeat after Me this: Jesus, neither death, nor life, no angel, no prince, nothing that exists, nothing still to come, not any power, or height or depth, nor any created thing, will ever come to separate me from You,*

* Romans 8 : 38-39

37

vow to remain faithful to You; this is my solemn vow; help me keep this vow forever and
ever; Amen; (I repeated what Jesus gave me)
———— 28. 9. 90

soul, pray, this means, speak to Me! do
not ignore My Omnipresence just because the
tempter keeps tempting you, hear Me, resist,
resist him; come now, I shall manifest
Myself again through you, if you submit
to Me humbly and allow My Spirit to rest
on you in My hours of My Passion ΙΧΘΥΣ
⳥ your Jesus; I Am ♡

35

My Vassula, it is I, the Lord, feel
Me, I am near you, discern Me;* I am
sharing My Cross with you, My Crown of Thorns
and My Nails; I have chosen you out of
the land of the dead and revived you in
My Heart to make you the victim of My
Insatiable Love, and make you an atonement
for many souls who prefer to remain divided
and differenciate themselves under My Sacred
Name; I am sharing My sufferings and My
grief with you, daughter, console Me and
I will console you; Vassula My child,
* thee, Jesus touched my arm.

39

I have raised you to appease My Justice,
I have raised you to delight My Soul; do
not fear then My child, My Father has
found favour in you for all that you are
not; you have no merits, none at all, but
I favoured you in spite of your wretchedness,
for My Loyalty and My Gentleness are
without measure; sacrifice more My child;
— incense and myrrh of Mine! how I love
you! I shall make you zealous for Me,
your God, and loyal to My Commandments;
I shall anoint you with My oil; O property

40

of Mine, live in Me and allow Me to live
in you! I am He whom you should never
resist, never fail, never deny! I am He who
breathes in you Life! allow Me to invade
you entirely, show no resistance to Me; am
I not overwhelming you with favours? am
I not consuming you entirely with My
Flaming Fire of My Heart? have I not
shown you to My angels and to the Holy
ones living in My Assembly? have I ever
deprived you from suffering, soul? hence,
it is your due to Me now to love Me,

41

it is your due, soul, to prostrate yourself to Me and adore Me; it is your due now to delight My Soul and receive Me in My Holy Sacrifice ♡ Come ... come ... approach Me, allow Me to whisper now and then in your ear My Love for you; allow Me to caress you with My Tenderness; allow Me to caress you with My Blessings, come and lean your head on My Heart; you are not just My tablet, soul, you are also My beloved bride whom My Heart loves and desires to sing to you; My Voice is sweet

42

and My Heart a Blazing Furnace of Love, and My Fragrance attractive and delicate; see how I come flying to you before you even open your lips and have the word in your mouth for Me? as a flower among the thistles I have you now, as a net cast into the sea I have thrown you to catch souls for Me your King; if you do not know this, Vassula My daughter, I tell you now: follow the marks of My Blood and take the Cross I have entrusted you with, follow the marks of My Blood, these marks you

43

sought from your youth*; they will lead you to Me, into My Arms and into My Heart; O Vassula! I shall guard you like the Pupil of My Eye; I have lifted you from the pit to give you a place together with My predilected souls of My Heart; I have wed you to share My Cross as our matrimonial bed and henceforth made you Mine for eternity; lower now your eyes before your King and Spouse, lower your eyes and allow My Hand to rest on your head to bless you and breathe on you

* When I was a child, I had visions of following Jesus on the way to Golgotha and being near Him under the Cross.

44

My sweet Sigh of Love on your forehead, the Breath of My Tenderness ♡ My child, I would like to see you free from all worry, I am only waiting to be gracious to you, I am only waiting to hide you in My Sacred Heart forever, where you will find <u>True Peace</u> ☩

10.10.90

peace be with you child, allow Me to use your hand, it is I, your Jesus, it is Love who speaks to you, and asks you ...

O come and invade me!

45

Ah My Vassula I shall then fill you ... hear Me and write My Message for the entire world ♡ peace be with you; Love is speaking; Love is offering; Love is healing, even injuries that appeared to be beyond healing; Love is consoling those who are not cared for; My Love for you is eternal and I am known to be constant in My affection; approach ... come close to Me, by praying with your heart; I am offering you a place in My school, I am offering you Wisdom to teach you My

46

Knowledge; blessed are they who humbly accept My Instructions and lay My Words to heart; hear Me, My beloved; Scripture says: "the language of My Cross may be illogical to those who are not on the way to salvation, but those of you who are on the way see it as God's power to save" * and it is this language I am coming to teach you, it is this language of Love you will hear in My school, and you, you who are willing to learn, be blessed, be strong and happy; though

* 1 Cor. 1:18

47

obstacles are bound to come, do not fear, rely on Me; but alas for the one who provides them, he shall have to answer Me on the Day of Judgement! My Return is imminent, and I am giving you constant signs to prepare you; Love is on the Path of return, I am on My way back to you; tell Me, when a king enters into a city, will there be no preparations to receive him? the whole city will be in turmoil and the king will send before him his elect and his imperial court to prepare a way for him

48

and make his paths straight; he will send his messengers to announce his coming; he will ask them to shout with a loud voice: "here is your King, your King is coming with His Heart in His Hand to offer It to you! Mercy now leans down from heaven and from His Throne; He has taken pity on you;" this is why, before My Return, I am sending you before Me, the Ark of Alliance, I am sending you the Woman of the Apocalypse, the second Eve, who will crush the serpent's head with her heel;

49

I am sending you before Me : My Mother, to open a broad highway and level it in this desert; I am sending you the Queen of Heaven, the Door to Heaven to prepare you, and to school all you who still lie in the dust, to come forward and make your peace with Me, your King, before My Great Return; I am sending you the Queen of Peace to thresh from one corner of the earth to the other and gather you one by one; I am sending you before My Great Return, My servants the prophets, to remind

50

you of My Law and to turn you back from your evil ways and live holy; and announce to you events before they take place; I am sending you My angels to remind you of My Holiness, My Magnificence and My Splendour, I am sending you My mouthpieces to shout and proclaim on the rooftops of your houses the Wedding of My Holy Spirit, I will not grow weary of calling you to wed Me, I will not get discouraged by your hostility nor by your aridity; I will be in pursuit of your heart and like

51

a young man marrying a virgin, the One whom you wounded all along will wed you; and I, in My Love, shall make you replace the Thorns encircling My Heart, by a flowered Wreath; and like a bridegroom wearing his wedding wreath I too shall wear it, because this wreath will be My Wreath of Victory, this will be the Prize of My Mercy .... generation, I shall make you Mine; I shall lift you up and carry you as a bridegroom carries his bride into his rooms, and in My everlasting Love I

52

shall carry you into My Sacred Heart and make you Mine for eternity; soon, very soon now I shall tear the heavens open and come down in full force ! if you were to understand fully what I mean, you would not spend your time being lethargic, you would be in constant prayer to Me, for suddenly and as quick as thunderbolt I shall descend in flame of devouring fire and unveil all that has been hidden from you; I shall with My Finger point out to you all those that honoured Me with lip—

53

service, never serving Me with the Language I had taught them : the Language of My Cross, the Language of Love, the Language that teaches you things beyond human understanding; I shall reveal to you the Cains whose language is not My Language but this one of rich merchants and trade; pray for these Cains, do not judge them, spend your time with prayers for them, do not allow your tongue to slip ♡ - do not be one of these who say   to My seers : 'see no visions' and to My prophets : 'do not

54

prophecy'; let My Imperial Court prepare for Me My Way; no prophecy ever came from man's initiative; when My seers and prophets speak for Me, it is by Grace that they do and by My Holy Spirit that fills them, moves them and opens their mouths to repeat My Words; and I shall continue recalling you the Truth, by My mouthpieces, even if you know the Truth; I shall keep revealing My plans to My servants the prophets and show My Magnificence in visions to My seers; leave My elect and

55

My predilected souls free to prepare the Way for Me your King; let them complete their witnessing; I am sending you My Celestial Court to prophesy for these end of Times, in the wilderness of your era to convert you before My Great Day comes; realize that I do not descend only for Mercy but also for Judgement; I do not tell My messengers to call only the just, I tell them to call also the unjust, the poor, the lame, the rejects of your society, and everyone they meet in the streets, to come and fill up My school; I want

56

to call all those who never sought Me nor ever knew Me, to come and prosper in My House, for these are the Times of Mercy and of Grace ♡ then let all those who see you, gaze and stare at your transfiguration, let it show on your faces and by the glow of your heart that you have been attending My School and that you are My pupils and I, your Master; let them see in your eyes the reflection of everything you have witnessed, let them see on your body the marks of My Wounds; and if anyone

57

asks you how you received them, tell them
that you received them in the House of your
Master's friends where He at first received
them ... then lift up your cross and follow
Me; I, Jesus Christ, Beloved Son of God
and Saviour blow My Breath on you and
bless you all leaving the Sigh of My Love
on your foreheads; go in peace and be
one in My Name ♡ ΙΧΘΥΣ ⤳🐟

Message of our Blessed Mother.

peace be with you; incense of God, take
courage for I am with you, I am with

58

you and with My innumerable angels I surround you, to protect you; I come down
with the saints to guide you; I am the
Queen of Heaven, I am the Queen of Peace;
I am the Mother of your Saviour; I am
the One who precedes the Lord's coming,
I am the One who opened a broad highway
for your Redeemer to descend on earth, and
today again, the Most High is sending Me
to make smooth and level a Path for His
Return; although Satan uses men to delay
My Work and put obstacles in its midst,

59

do not fear, the Lord is Almighty and in
the end Our Hearts will prevail; rely on
His massive Strength for He can uproot
mountains and melt the rocks, nothing
can stop His Powerful Hand; – what do
you see above you? look above your heads
what the Lord is raising. the Lord
is raising over you the Banner of His
Great Love and Mercy; He is coming to
restore you with His caresses and feed you
with delights; He is coming to fragrance
you with His delicate perfume of Myrrh,

60

He is coming to soothe your wounds with
His balm of Tenderness; He is coming
down to pour out His oil on you generation
and anoint you; the King will bring you
into His Rooms to console you and wipe
away your tears; like the pupil of His
Eye He is watching over you; and you,
would you in your turn return His Love?
offer Him your heart and your will;
– many of you have forgotten God's ways,
you have been drifted away, – like taken
by a current in a lake, into a pool

61

of lethargy; polluted with materialism your
course changed direction and from holiness
and the rightful Path you have been led
right into the devil's nets and into the
lion's mouth! you have not followed the
marks of the Precious Blood Jesus left behind
Him as a signpost for you to follow,
no, you have followed the polluted directions
Satan put up for you, directions leading
all to the desert where there would be no
one to care for your sores, and no one to
console you; and where you would die;

62

your generation failed to appreciate God's
great Love, this is why your lands are set
aflame by egoism, by godlessness and by the fury
of Satan; and still to this day his hand is
raised to strike you and set aflame all the
nations; because of your atheism and your
perversity you have wrapped yourselves in the
shroud of death, you have wrapped your beloved ones in a cloud of flint; I call in agony
from above, to you all to make peace with
God, to reconcile with your families; when you
come and pray in pilgrimages do you come with

63

a clean heart? have you ceased to do evil? are
you in peace with your neighbour? have you
confessed and repented truly of your sins? have
you blessed your enemies and forgiven them?
have you repaid evil with love? are you indeed ready to meet the Lord with your hands
full of good works? — bless those who persecute
you, and pray for them, do not judge them,
keep on praying, for what use are your offerings
when your heart is unforgiving, holding grudges?
where is your holiness then? purify yourselves
and live in the Light of God and in the

64

Love of God; be a true witness of the Gospel
by the warmth and glow of light in your
heart; be a witness for Jesus by bearing His
Cross with Him; be a witness for the Church
by being constant in your faith and by
being united with Christ's Vicar; never allow
your tongues to slip; be perfect as the Lord
is perfect; let it show that you are indeed
the first-fruits of God's great Love; let
every eye witness your good behaviour and
know that it is because you are children of
the Most High; let the marks of His

1

Five Wounds be noticed on your body too, let these be the Sign to show you are His pupils and Me your Divine Master; live Our Messages and be like grains to spread them; let your cry of love go out through all the earth and to the ends of the world; I bless each one of you, and I thank you for giving Me your time; ♡ go in peace ♡

17. 10. 90.

Jesus, you have told us in these books many things before they happen, so that when they do happen we may believe. You have told us how you will re- surrect my sister Russia, and how You

2

will make an end of her atheism. And look! On the 14th St. Basil's Church on the Red Square opened her doors for You! and I, her sister rushed to her that day; to rejoice her feast! But what I got from her was a slap on my face... Your servant and brother of mine whom I love, struck me. — Your servant refused to bless me, because he said : I was going to our brothers the Catholics and receiving from their hand Holy Communion. Am I to feel ashamed, before You my Lord? This would have been an affliction I could bear had it not been for worse to come. He said: 'This means excommunication!' You had given me a sign before this happened, making me feel Your sorrow by turning my mouth, just before, dryer than wood, and my lips dryer than parchment. How long will the Christians be divided? Come, and set our hearts right,

3

give us back our innocence, come and make a dawn of darkness; I thank You my Lord for giving me an occasion to be struck and humilia- ted, and giving me the courage to line up with the others inspite of my injury to go back to him again and kiss the cross he held and the hand that just struck me.

Vassula, your pain is nothing compared to Mine ... even though he drew a sword on you My daughter, do not despair; there is hope for reconciliation; soon, I shall overwhelm you with a great Miracle,*

* I saw suddenly in an interiour vision, some- one dressed up like a bride, in dazzling white silvery clothes and all glittery.

4

very soon now, I the Lord, shall adorn My Bride with Her glorious perfection of Her youth; hence a covenant of peace will be sealed between brothers; like the Morning Star My Church shall rise; the ban will be lifted ... like an olive tree loaded with fruit She shall stand solidly before Me ... like a vine putting out graceful shoots, Her blossoms will bear fruit of glory and splendour ... and there will be only one flock and one Shepherd ... I am the Resurrection ... daughter?* let not your hope be void,

* Jesus turned and looked at me His Eyes full of compassion.

5

you need not fear; the terrors of the night will soon be over*; remember, by your side I Am; I do not leave My Eyes too long on their misconduct lest My wrath flare up My Justice, so I let My Mercy take over ♡ I am curing all your diseases and wiping away with My Blood all the traces of venom, to redeem you all from the Pit; I am Love, and Love in all His Tenderness is forgiving the strikers, the mockers, the unjust and in My Holy Compassion I shall lift you all in My

* Jesus was consoling me, His Words were like a balm of caresses healing my wounds.

6

Heart; do not despair Vassula My daughter, there is still hope for reconciliation and a revival ... there is still hope ...*' do not be afraid of those who kill the body but cannot kill the soul; fear him rather who can destroy both body and soul in hell; Matth. 10:28 I will come to bring peacefulness to the brothers and remind them of My Tenderness of My Love and Mercy so that they too in their turn may imitate Me; — do not hurry away*² ... come, ecclesia shall

* Jesus was once more trying to console me. It looked like the one who was wounded more was trying to console the other one whose wounds were less grave.
*² I thought it was over and I was getting ready to leave.

7

revive, ecclesia shall revive, wait and you shall see ...　ΙΧΘΥΣ　⊰-◦>　⳨

Jesus? I Am; all I ask from you is love; this is My Theme, I need every drop of love in your heart; I want all the love you have to redeem those who are heading for the eternal fires; when I say: ' revive My Church', or ' embellish My Church', or ' unite My Church', I mean you to pray, pray, pray without cease, pray from your heart, love Me fervently and with your expiations which will join

20.10.90

8

these of My martyr saints, you will glorify Me, yes daughter with your expiations and your fervent prayers offered to Me with love you can alter coming disasters, you can alter natural disasters, you can extinguish the flaring wrath of My Father, God can relent, with your prayers He can relent; you can embellish My Church; you can bring together My People under My Name to celebrate mass around one altar; you can repair their shepherd's staff, this staff they broke first in half then into splinters; for men

9

this unity appears impossible, but for Me, everything is possible; so pray and expiate for your brothers; I need victim souls, I need generous souls to repay evil with love, to repay evil with self-sacrifice; so offer Me your will and I shall make you My instruments of Peace and Love; I shall make you My instruments of Reconciliation and Unity ♡

Lord, our own apostasies are rebuking us. Forgive us and help us to make reparations. Bring us back in the love of our bridal days, the early days, and remind us the affection we once had in our youth for You; Do not allow anymore any evil to overcome us.

10

yes, offer Me your prayers and I shall restore My House which is your House too; be loyal and this special favour will be granted to you; like in the transfiguration, I shall transfigure My Church to have all the radiant glory of Her youth, in Her bridal days; I will do all these things for the sake of My Holy Name, I shall unite you to demonstrate My Power; Lord, there are other things too, I asked You this before but I would like to ask You again and I do not know how to say it !

I shall open your mouth and you shall

11

speak ! * Lord have You not said that the Advocate, the Holy Spirit, will teach us everything and remind us of all You have said to us? Then doesn't Scripture say: "...in the Church God has given the first place to apostles, the second to prophets..."*² and doesn't Scripture say: ... 'there is a remnant, chosen by grace. By grace, you notice, nothing therefore to do with good deeds, or grace would not be grace at all !"*³ and last doesn't Scripture say: ... 'at all your meetings let everyone be ready with a psalm or a sermon, or a revelation ...' *⁴ So why Lord nowadays most of the prophetic or private revelations are looked upon by some priests with contempt? with one eye instead of the two? and why are some priests and bishops even, attacking with contempt Your messages?

in reality, My child, they are wrestling against Me; because they are suppressing the Advocate,

* Suddenly a flow of words came out of me. *² I Cor. 12:28
*³ Rom. 11: 5-6
*⁴ I Cor. 14:26

12

daughter, these people are not objecting to you, no My angel, they are not, they are objecting to Me, not to you; if they ignore you My flower it is because you have grown in the middle of their desert; they will not water you so that you wither and fade away; they keep forgetting though that I Am your Devout Keeper; Vassula, I shall remind you of the parable of the wedding feast * ♡ daughter, many are called, but few are chosen; to believe is a grace given by Me, to have faith is also

* Matth: 22: 1-14

13

a grace given by Me; these are the Times of Grace and Mercy; these are the Times in which My Holy Spirit is poured out upon you; these are the Times when My Holy Spirit shall lift you out of your great apostasy, to wed you; your era's wretchedness shall peel off you, because with My Own Hand I shall unwrap your death shroud to clothe you in the garments of your wedding; feel My delight My Vassula! feel how I already rejoice at this coming event! My Holy Spirit will come to bring Fire

14

to the earth, and how I wish it were blazing already! these are the Times of the Wedding of My Holy Spirit: these are the Times your King of Peace is sending His servants, His angels, His prophets and His Celestial Court to go out to the four corners of the earth and invite His friends to His Banquet and into His Kingdom and offer them His Celestial Manna ♡ I have been sending My messengers in true ✓righteousness all the way to their doorstep to announce My Return, but many of them did not believe them,

15

and treated them as imposters, others would not come because they put honour from men before the honour that comes from Me; since I have invited you and you have refused Me, since I have beckoned and you do not want to take notice, since you have ignored all My supplications and rejected Love's offer, I shall fill up My House and give My Kingdom to the rejects of your society to confuse you all, I shall give them back their sight and heal them, I shall open the Doors of My

16

House wide open to let them in; My messengers will call aloud in the streets, and in the public squares, they will be sent by Me to invite the corpses they meet at each street corner, and those who have never been told about Me will see Me, and those who have never heard about Me will listen and understand; I shall be found by those who did not seek Me; like I have revealed My Holy Face to you, daughter, I shall reveal Myself likewise to those who did not consult Me; of My Spirit you do not

17

want! neither of My Heart offered to you in
My Hand! I tell you this now, before it
happens, so that when it _does_ happen you may
believe that I Am who I Am:

My Kingdom will be taken away from
you and it will be given to a people you call
contemptible and foolish, the rejects of your
society and My House will be rebuilt and
risen by those you call simple minds, they,
with their love shall restore the ruins of My
House and all that has lain waste, and
it is My Holy Spirit who shall shepherd them

18

and console them ... the citadel of the proud
shall soon fall into a heap of dust ... Justice
shall prevail; pray for these shepherds, pray
for their conversion; be blessed, My child,
I shall not be long, soon you shall see Me
face to face; I Am ☧

22.10.90

Vassula, beloved, I am the Holy One in your
room; it is I, Jesus; are you happy of
My visit? Very! I bless You ... very much Lord!
hold fast to all the teachings I am giving
you; let no one deceive you; reap progressively

19

My harvest of kindness and tenderness; I will
increase your visions so you may testify in My
Name; I shall provide you with words to be
able to testify; My daughter remind the
world of My Great Love; this will be the
message for all times: peace be with you,
I am Jesus your Redeemer, I am the Holy of
Holies who speaks to you; I tell you truly:
I shall pour special graces on those who accepted
this testimony, because by having accepted this
testimony of Love they are attesting the truth-
fulness and the Infinite Love of the Most High,

20

since all that is written comes from Me; beloved ones, I give My Spirit without reserve;
I give My Spirit to remind the world over
and over again of My affection and the great love
I have for you; I give My Spirit without
reserve to remind you all of My
Five Wounds and of My Passion; My child,
you who read or hear Me, look around
you, Dawn is soon with you... and you will
not have to consult the shadows of the
night that whisper and mutter, nor will
you have to walk in distress and darkness,

21

for your wizards who blasphemed My Holy
Name and substituted darkness for light
will be wiped away; beloved ones, Dawn is
soon with you and as soon as it is light
your seedlings shall blossom; the traders
who infiltrated My Church will be dismayed
and all the buyers dejected, every merchant
grown rich shall swoon, dazzled by My
Glory and by My Light they will remain
baffled and stunned before Me; the signal
is being hoisted on the roofs of your houses,
My ambassadors are sent to their post now

22

to wait for My signal, My Return is imminent, so you, who are My messengers, swiften
your step, go on every hill and announce that
judgement shall soon fall on those traders,
for they have become an _abomination_ in My
Sight! have you not read before to stay
awake and watch so that when you
see the _disastrous abomination_, of which the
prophet Daniel spoke, erected in My Sanctuary,
you would know that this is the sign spoken
of by the prophet for the end of Times? how is it
that you cannot read the Times? the

23

bricks of My Sanctuary have fallen down, and
you are living in the middle of this great
apostasy of your era; My oppressors think now
they have the upper hand, and the traders
believe they will continue trading in My Sanctuary, but I tell them: "you who have corrupted your wisdom by trading My Image
for a lifeless statue, a false god, an
idol, you who struggle to erect this disastrous abomination and abolish My Perpetual
Sacrifice, you will drink the full winecup of
My Justice;" the figure daubed with assorted

24

colours, this figure these traders are trying to
make you revere to and follow, is _not Me_; it
is an invention of perverted human skill to
degrade the concept of My Holiness and My
Divinity, it is a false ecumenism, _it is a_
defiance of all that is holy; I suffer because
of the sins of these traders; pray for these
priests who became traders, their sin is grave;
pray that I may put My Spirit of Truth in
them, and make them keep My Laws and
sincerely respect My Divinity ♡ beloved ones
you whom I marked as Mine on your

25

foreheads do not allow these traders to compel
you to follow this false image; be on your
guard; I am telling you all this before because I want you to feel confident in Me your
God when the times of great distress are upon
you; I mean to visit you, already the hour is
coming of My Great Return, and woe to these
merchants who are struggling to erect their
disastrous abomination in My Sanctuary and
abolish My Perpetual Sacrifice, by forcing you
to eat their defiled food! woe to these traders,
who conspire to ruin My Word by rationalizing

26

it! woe to the blasphemers who blasphemed
ten times My Holy Name! woe to the followers
of the Beast who carved images* blaspheming
against My seven Spirits! their citadel will
become a heap of dust by the Breath of My
Mouth! and you My child, who read Me or
hear Me, you whom I visited your grave and
made My Breath enter you, I tell you: follow
the marks of My Blood I leave behind for
you as a sign and if you are stopped and
interrogated on your way by a passer-by,
tell him that you are My pupil and I your

* False Christ. False teachings. Rational and Naturalism teachings.

27

Master and that you are on your way to
witness a crucified Christ, a resurrected Christ;
and if you will be stopped by a trader beware of his dishonesty, beware that he does not
exchange the Cross I have given you for a corrupt so-called wisdom; without a sound,
without a word embrace more fervently than
ever the bar across your shoulders, and follow
the marks of My Blood and they will lead
you to Me; and if anyone of these start proceeding against you, do not cover your face against
insult or strike, offer your backs too, so that

28

they know you from your wounds, let them be
a perfect imitation of My Wounds for they will
be given to you by the very same ones who
struck Me, your Master; and then the Sign
of the Son of Man will appear in the skies,
a great light shall be seen in your darkness,
for I, the Holy One mean to save you for
the sake of My Name; come, My child, you
who hear Me or read Me, I have shown My
Love for you again in this testimony, do not
say, that I am too far away to love for
at this very instant My Eyes are upon you

29

with a special tenderness and an affection you can never understand fully; had I to return just for your sake alone to redeem you, without the slightest hesitation I would come and repeat My Passion, for your sake alone! Now do you believe Me when I tell you that a man can have no greater love than to lay down his life for his friends? I am telling you all this so that you may find your peace in My Sacred Heart, so that you may find true life in Me, so that you may find true love and rest in Me your God;

30

I know that you are weak, My child, but your weakness attracts My Omnipotence; can you take in what I say? I say: peace be with you! I am the Victim of Love who speaks to you, I am He who gave you this testimony of Love as a reminder of My Love; absorb Me and allow Me to invade you ♡ feel how My Heart yearns for a return of love! do not resist Me, come to Me as you are, come and drink the flow of My Heart and you shall thirst for more; oh so many of you wandered away from the Truth and went

31

this way and that; the Truth is LOVE; I am the Truth; be witnesses for the Truth; receive the Holy Spirit of Truth, receive the Holy Spirit of Grace ♡ I bless you all leaving My Sigh of Love on your foreheads; be one under My Holy Name ♡ ΙΧΘΥΣ 🐟

23.10.90
Lord, I am daily facing marvels beyond me and my poor knowledge, to meet You every day in this way is quite beyond my mind!

peace be with you, realize what joy you give Me little one, how I wish to be now up with You, do You know that? My child,

32

yes I know that, but you have to wait, you must accomplish first your mission, it is your due now ♡ fertilize these arid lands with all that I have given you; nourish the lands, I love you to folly, never doubt of the greatness of My Love; alone you are not, never, I am wherever you go, I am your Holy Companion; Fountain! that turns arid lands into fertile gardens! Well of Living Water! give us flowing streams so that we may live ♦ allow me to share with You Your Cup. Then take My Cup and drink from it, and if you feel faint from its bitterness come and

33

lean on Me, come and rest in Me; Vassula, My property, I your King, hold you captive of My Love; and I shall be guarding you like a sentinel is guarding a gate; I have given you the gift of My Love espousing you to Me, so I shall make sure that no intruder trespasses upon My property; My property now I have turned into a garden, where I can go to, and rest ♡ allow Me to breathe in you, allow Me ♡ to accomplish My Works in you; be docile and accept Me your Master and King; Love is My

34

Name ♡ come to Me to eat from My Hand *
I shall feed you till the end ΙΧΘΥΣ ⤳ 〉⟨

                                      24. 10. 90

My heart wants to serve Your Greatness but I am needy and in misery and unable to lift my finger without You,

true, for if I was not standing by your side you would not be standing at all; soul! enwrapped in My Light, are you willing to obey My precepts? I am willing to obey Your precepts. come and share My cloak then, let Me be your Guide and I shall continue to reveal to you the secrets

* Jesus means in this manner with writing which feeds my soul.

35

of My Sacred Heart, I shall continue to unfold to you the depths of Heaven, I shall not fail you soul... remain poor, needy and fervent for My food, yes, hunger for My Food and desire it; do not be like the rich who do not hunger nor seek My Food; seek the Riches of My Heart; through your nothingness I have revealed My Greatness, through your misery I showed My Mercy, and through your frailty My Strength; I have shown the world now the ardent Flame of the Burning Desires of My Heart,

36

all I want from you now is a return of love; daughter? I tell you truly, you who wish to serve Me your God, every time you will open your mouth to witness for the Truth, I shall bless you; each time you speak of Me I shall light a fire in you, pray and ask and I shall give more than you have asked; I shall remind you always My Instructions so that you may repeat My Words, I shall not leave you, I am known to be the All-Faithful, so My Vassula, allow Me to use you until

37

I come and fetch you; blessed one! * remnant of Mine! flower come to Me in the right spirit and trust Me; will you kiss My Feet? come, take your Master's Hand and follow Me ♡

30.10.90

Vassula, puny little creature, do you know how many thorns you plucked out of My Heart? No Lord. sufficient to rest Me, sufficient to rest Me My child; the purpose of your creation was also to rest Me; I have

---

* A thought passed my mind; to what will the Lord do with me after He fetches me; it was not an intelligent thought. That's why Jesus surprised said: blessed one!

38

created you and even though you are dust and ashes I find in you a profound rest, accept Me, accept My Cross on you, be grateful to Me now; child look at My Lips and listen to Me carefully: faith, have faith in Me and trust Me; I know your ineffable weakness and that without Me you cannot raise your little finger; this is why I have chosen you, I have chosen weakness to show the world My Power, I have a reason why I have chosen you in your state; trust Me and draw your strength

39

from Me; I shall remind you how the devil hates you and today you felt his claws on you; yes, if I had left him he would have torn you to pieces, but you are under My Divine protection; every single minute of his is aimed on you and all My other chosen souls; I tell you: because of your nothingness and because of your poverty, puny creature of Mine, you are undoing Satan's patterns, you are undoing stitch after stitch of his embroideries; he called you worm when he knew that you are My chosen one, yes, be

40

like a worm and eat up and ravage his designs, see? I can use for My Works even worms ... yes, eat up like a worm his patterns, I have allowed you to feel his hatred, he hates you because the Father himself loves you for loving Me, this infuriates him beyond one's imagination; happy is the man who does not lose faith in Me; delight My Soul and fill Me with joy by remaining nothing ♡

41

3. 11. 90

Our Holy Mother's Message.

peace be with you, little children; like a mother feeding and consoling her little children so am I too feeding your souls, by giving you the Word of God, like a mother consoling her children in times of distress so am I too leaning towards you to console you; I am looking after your soul with My prayers; the Lord is not slow to carry out His promises, but is waiting patiently that everyone will have the grace to see the light and be converted; the New Heavens

42

and the New Earth promised are ever so near you now; in the meantime while you are waiting sanctify, I beg you, your lives and live holy; I want to see in you dear children, a real conversion! anyone who has escaped the vices of the world but then allows himself to be led by principles not coming from Wisdom but from Folly are certain to fall; God is Love, He is forgiving and slow to anger; God is a most Tender Father; examine your soul now and then to know whether you are

43

standing in His Light or not; be like a garden for the Lord where He could enjoy His rest in you, where He can delight His Soul in its delightful essences, and where He could rest His Head on its green grass, let Me transform your heart into a beautiful garden for the Lord, so that when the King of kings comes to visit you, He would not turn away His Eyes from you, but would offer you to become a victim of His Soul, a captive of His Heart; lose no time therefore, for His Eyes keep watch on

44

each one of your steps; the Prince of Peace exhorts you to pray for peace and I, the Queen of Peace begs you to pray for peace; Satan is now like a mad bull and My Heart is sick at what I see coming, though out of Mercy, the Father, has not shown Me everything; I roam all around the earth to look for generous souls but I cannot find enough generosity to offer Jesus and appease the Father's Justice; tremendous amendments are to be done still; Jesus needs generous souls who are willing to expiate for others; this

45

is why I weep; My Eyes dissolve in tears of
Blood at these terrible sights I see coming;
today if I tell you all this, it is not just
to impress you or frighten you, but to
ask you to pray for Peace; it is God for
His Own loving purpose who sends Me all
around the world and in every house to
gather you one by one and convert you before
His Day; beloved children, do not come
to these gatherings to look only for signs,
if I come all the way from Heaven to your
doorstep it is to bring you the Peace of

46

the Lord and My Peace ♥ allow Me, therefore,
to transform your hearts ♥ into a beautiful
garden for the Holy One, so that He may
find within your depths a spirit of holiness,
love, peace, purity, obedience, humility and
faithfulness; then your King will use all
these virtues and combat the powers of evil;
rise up from your sleep children and change
your hearts; I am happy to see so many of
you fast on bread and water and today
I ask these generous souls to add something
more to their days of fasting, I ask you

47

to repent and confess, dear children, watch your
lips from judging one another, do not, with
all your fasting, allow your lips to be the cause
of your condemnation, love one another, live
our Messages; your King is addressing to you
His Peace; I will keep patrolling the world
to bring to the Lord those who are far
away from Him; I need your generous prayers,
children of Mine; I bless you all, I bless
your families, your friends and even those
you carry heavily in your hearts, yes, all
are children of God; ♥

48

7.11.90

Lord, let everything founded in the Truth
remain, and everything founded in Falsehood
be extirpated and thrown into the fire.
Lord, I feel you far, yet I know You are not,
have I been insensible to Your Presence?

My child, do your best and I shall do the
rest, even though I may seem far from you,
do not fear, I am not far, I, the Lord
keep a vigilant eye on you; pray soul!
pray that justice relents and does not come
suddenly upon your nations like a thunderclap; Vassula*¹ I have prayed for you to
the Father and asked Him to hasten His
Step*²; read Jer. 44. 7-9 ♥

*¹ Jesus changed tone here.
*² diffusing the messages.

49

allow Me to use your little hand; use it Lord, and use all of me as an atonement for Your Sacred Intentions.

I am happy*, and I like it when you repose entirely your confidence in Me, for you are speaking to Me your God, not a man, you are reposing your confidence in Me and you must trust Me fully; so when you come to Me to offer Me your will, look at Me full in the Face; I delight to hear you abandoning yourselves, reposing thus your confidence in Me; I rejoice to hear this

* Jesus was smiling.

50

adoration, for adoration it is if you offer Me your whole being, heart, soul and mind; Vassula, little soul how could I resist your pleadings? to know that these come from such a vulnerable soul, a soul that I resurrected only yesterday! how could My Heart, little soul, resist your calls? draw from My Heart, little soul, and cling to Me! and pray for your brothers, for those who still lie as corpses under a thick layer of dust, pray that My Breath sweeps away this dust and My Finger touches

51

their heart so that they too turn to Me, for they have deserted Me in favour of leisures and not to say more than that ♡ be blessed My child ♡ bless Me IXΘΥΣ 🐟 ♡

11.11.90.

Lord? I Am, rest in Me, all Heaven is full of joy, this is what you call the beatitude in its plenitude; daughter, if souls only knew how wonderful it is to live in God, no one would be lost so easily; unless they chose to be lost like Judas; he chose the way to perdition, not that My Heart did not

52

melt with sorrow every time I saw him take one further step away from Me; not that I had not prayed for him; not that I had not cried My Eyes out for him; I had opened so many ways for him to take, all leading to Me, but no sooner had he started one than he came out of it when he would realize I had laid it for him, for to sin he added rebellion, heaping abuses in his heart, for Me his God, when he realized that My Kingdom was not an earthly kingdom in earthly glory; he shut his heart and cut

53

out our bonds and estranged himself immediately from Me; his senses of what is righteous or not was darkened and obeyed the
ruler who governs the air; today I am asking
the sick like I asked the sick man at the
pool of Bethzatha* : 'do you want to be well
again?' I can heal you instantly, and all
Heaven shall rejoice and celebrate! My gift is
free, so come to Me as you are, I shall
heal you, soul, so that you can share My
Kingdom and live in Me your God ♡

IXΘΥΣ ⟝⟨∘⟩

* John 5 : 1-9

54

15.11.90

'I will celebrate Your Love for ever, Yahweh, age
after age my words shall proclaim Your Faithfulness;
for I claim that love is built to last for ever
and Your Faithfulness founded firmly in the Heavens.'*
But now a Greek orthodox theologian is attacking me
and hounding Your messages, O Lord show them
that You are my help and consolation and that
only through Your great Love You have saved me
and others.

Vassula of My Sacred Heart,*² My Holy Spirit
has been your guide, so do not pay attention
to the theologian's conclusions; pray that
she too may receive the Spirit to understand
that human reckonings and human doctrines
made a devastating desert out of My Church,
Lord, she is shocked to have read in Your

* Ps. 89 : 1-2   *² Jesus made it a point to call me in this way
because the Name, Sacred Heart, is not Greek orthodox.

55

messages that You are like a beggar begging for
our love. _____ has she not read : 'happy those
servants whom the Master finds awake when
He comes; I tell you solemnly, He will put
on an apron, sit them down at table and
wait on them.'* ♡ I am known not only
as Omnipotent, Majestic and a God of
Justice but as a most Tender Father and
only those moved by My Spirit will call
Me : Abba ♡ I am a God full of pity
and My Mercy is Boundless; Lord, she is
profoundly disturbed about this intimacy I have

* Luke 12 : 37

56

with You, she calls it sweet and sentimental!
she has not penetrated My Wounds to understand; had she penetrated My Wounds she
would have understood that these Wounds were
given to Me out of Love for her, a man can have
no greater love than to lay down his life
for his friends, and you are, all of you
My friends, I have lain down My life out
of love; but daughter, this is the Cross I
have charged you with, remember, I am
bearing It together with you; to unite you*
Justice will have to intervene; My Vassula,

* The Churches

57

I am with you always till the end, do not be afraid then and disconsolate; I knew, My angel, all along that these people would hound you, like hunters each one would pull out his weapon and pursue you, because I am sending you <u>to a people not your own,</u> the leaders of your nation shall persecute you and deject you and treat you as they please because what I have given you to carry in your hand is not a man's teachings but Mine, and since My Language and My Teachings do not penetrate them, they would disagree

58

and they will treat you as an imposter; I have told you already that the world will condemn you, but even when they are condemning you, declare to the world what you have learnt from Me; daughter, if My Language cannot be understood by the world it is because their doctrine is not grounded in the Truth which is Love; I have deported you from Egypt to a people not your own, to unite My Church, but no one yet knows the whole way to unity and no one yet has grasped the outsitting of My Plan; they

59

have not yet recognized the paths I am preparing for them to tread; the theologians and the philosophers have not yet found the key to Unity that Wisdom holds; I speak but they do not take in what I say, only My Own take in what I say; I know them and they know Me; so My Vassula do your work before the appointed time; I have entrusted you with My Cross, bear It with love, soon there is going to be a time of great distress unlikened to any other, but soon after that a fountain will spring from My

60

House to water this desert; so courage daughter, bear this bar across your shoulders with love and nothing will go in vain, if clay* washes away with the first drops of rain, your soul remains forever; so death is swallowed up in victory ♥ Love is near you to guide you, so beware of these philosophers and theologians, the more severe will be the sentence they receive! bless Me and love Me as I taught you to love Me intimately but never forgetting that I am Holy ♥

* In other words: "If you, who are but dust and ashes die, your soul is immortal."

61

23.11.90

peace be with you; daughter do you wish to progress? Yes Lord, I do. then My child I shall help you progress; this is My wish too; do not fall asleep, be awake of the dangers surrounding you; flower even though My enemies tear upon you and pluck out your petals, I shall always replace them, should they leave you crumpled up, do not fear, I shall pour from the heavens My Dew and revive you; beautiful you should look and beautiful I shall make you and keep you; you are My envoy and you have

62

nothing to fear of men; if they accuse you because you call Me Father it is because they have not understood that the Spirit of Love you received and speaks through you, brings you peace and love to cry out: Abba! My Spirit is united to you My child; I have given you Spirit anointed Messages for your era to revive you; every word I have given you are Spirit and they are Life; the sheep that belong to Me recognize My Voice from far; soon I shall send My Light far and wide, from one horizon to

63

the other, yes, I shall make discipline shine out; have My Peace, this is My Blessing; love Me as I love you and remember, I am your King, so give your King the love He deserves! be blessed; I Am ♡

27.11.90

dearest soul, peace be with you, are you happy to be with Me? Yes Lord, very. Praised be the Lord. daughter, when you strain working for Me I use your efforts and your fatigue to heal other souls; yes, learn that everything you do with a spirit of sacrifice

64

I make good use of it ... I am the Teacher of mankind; remain near Me so that I whisper in your ear My intentions, stay My beloved near your God, it is He who loves you most; stay near Me My child and allow Me to feed you My Bread, come near Me My daughter and with Me you will find no brutality, I will only watch over you and be your adviser; I shall sing to you My Song of Love, a Song that will save you and all mankind; clay you are, but does it matter? I have given you an immortal soul;

a soul that shall shortly return to Me; you are without majesty and without beauty, unless you reflect My Divine Majesty and Beauty through the purity of your soul and this, My child, can manifest itself only if you imitate Me; to imitate Me is within your power; so approach Me, My child, and offer Me your will and I shall not delay, I shall come flying to you with chains of love, to bind you to Me and teach you how to praise Me and how to worship Me day and night; I shall teach you the

hymns of My angels, I shall show you My Glory and My Strength, I shall teach you how to cling to Life, I shall teach you how to prostrate before Me and worship Me, so come near Me and I shall watch over your soul; but Lord, what do You like in me, the sinner? your nothingness and your misery... when the coldness of the world becomes unbearable for you, come quickly into the Furnace of My Heart; I am your Refuge and I shall shelter you; your Father in Heaven knows that you do not belong to the world

yet He is sending you into the world, to show the world the Heart of your God and that I Am who I Am, sent you, come now and rest in Me and allow Me to rest in you ♥ — ΙΧΘΥΣ ⊰•)))

4. XII 90

Lord, You are All, and I am nothing. You are stupendously Great, so what are my praises for You the Holy of holies? No man can glorify You enough, yet my heart calls incessantly Your Name because You have set my heart on You.

your praises and your calls are not in vain; love Me and praise Me without cease, for as long as they come from your

heart, they are acceptable to Me ♥

Lord, You have opened the doors of heaven for me, and from the Stores of heaven You fed me the Manna You reserved for my soul, You gave me the Bread of heaven!

all the words I have spoken to you are Spirit and they are Life; grow in My Spirit so that you become a perfect witness to My Holy Name; and now I ask you not to give way to distress;* see My Vassula, My Cross is heavy and, ah! I need to rest now and then; I said: "who is generous enough to bear My Cross for Me?" and you answered:

* I was sad because of more persecutions.

5

"take me, purify me and use me as You please;" the Cross of Peace and Love to unite you all is at your charge now ... but pupil! since all eternity I had predestinated you this Cross; you belong to Me and for this reason you must reflect My Divine Image; I am He who provides your soul from My Infinite Resources, I shall not abandon you, soul, I shall fill you like an incense bowl so that your love reaches up in heaven like a column of perfumed smoke ♡ therefore, do not weary of writing, do not weary of blessing your

6

persecutors, do not weary of giving your back to the strikers; you may be sorrowful to the point of death, but the Queen is always nursing you back to joy and life; the Queen provides you with courage and comes and dresses your wounds with Her Maternal Love and Affection; your Mother is caring for you My child, like She has cared for Me; in your misery and distress She comes flying to you and takes you into Her Room,* that same Room of Her who conceived Me ♡ so do not hold back your tears, because while you

* Her Heart.

7

are shedding them in this exile because of the walls My people built in all directions in My House, dividing themselves, I too shed Tears of Blood to blend them in yours, so that when the Father sees your tears blended in Mine, He would not refuse your pleadings to lift the ban, for they will be no longer your tears but Mine ♡ shout pupil, that the whole earth, from end to end, will repent and come back to Me under My Holy Name as one ♡ Vassula, bear My Cross with love and not with consternation, be happy; ☓ ♡

8

6. XII 90

Message for a consecrated soul.

My Lips have uttered :

Come; come to Me

and I shall shepherd you

I shall never fail you

nor will I ever forget to pasture you,

with Me you will never

hunger or thirst ♡

ΙΧΘΥΣ ⋊≻

9

10.12.90

God! How You make me suffer from Your Love! how You make me suffer for thirst of You!

daughter, how would you like to live in My Wounds?

I would like anything You like me to have.

then I shall robe you in holiness; I shall make you strong in your love for Me to last forever; although you are still far from being perfect I can make you perfect; I have formed you in this particular way to witness for the Truth and glorify Me; I have sent you to a people not your own to proclaim

10

My Love, those who want to hear let them hear and those who do not want to hear let them not hear; tire not of meditating and writing; bereft you must not feel, I am with you, by your side, in this exile; love Me, adore Me and live for Me, your Lord; allow Me and leave Me free to en- velope you into My Infinite Love; ah ... how I delight when you desire Me and thirst for Me! Born-Again*! worship Me! surely you will not make the Bridegroom

Jesus called me by that name.

11

wait too long? come quickly to your Holy One and He will place your head on His Sacred Heart, and when you will listen to His Heart-Beats you will no longer resist Him ♡ you would only desire to glorify Him; and He will pour out His Spirit on you to invade your spirit and annihilate all that is you; never again shall you be "you", your "you" shall be no more; I shall invade you little one completely so that your motives will be My Motives, your desires shall be My Desires, your words shall

12

be My Words, your thoughts My Thoughts, and I shall hide you in the deepest place of My Sacred Heart; I shall efface your "you" altogether, if you allow Me; from now on after your consecration* to My Sacred Heart, you will worship Me from the depths of your heart and serve Me with a Fire inside you, you will serve Me in fidelity and more fervently than ever before; weak, you are, but My Strength shall sustain you; I will not allow you to lose sight of Me nor will I

* I had an act of consecration to the Sacred Heart that I intend to do this evening.

13

allow your heart to flutter elsewhere; your heart will look for Me alone and desire Me alone without cease, I shall make you dislike all that is contrary to My Holiness and to My Will; I shall sift you through to make sure that not one rival remains within you; from today, the bonds I have enlaced you with shall be tightened even more now by Me, I shall make your soul thirst for Me and your heart sick with love for Me your God; I am only writing now to consume your whole being with the Flames of My Heart and

14

My Love; whatever you do from now on will be done merely for My Interests and My Glory, and nothing for you; you shall from now on, in other words, be the slave of My Love, the victim of My Heart and the benefit of My pleasures, the toy of My Soul; I shall make your traits resemble Mine, from the sorrows when you see the deafness of souls, and the agony to see them fall; My Vassula, I shall give your soul its fill; no, I shall not spare you from My Cross, like the Father had not spared Me; how can I?

15

My Affection for you is unmeasurable, besides, everything comes out of My Generosity and My Infinite Love; I shall arrest your eyes, your thoughts your desires to become captives of My Heart, Love is seeking love; unworthy you are, and you deserve nothing, but your frailty, your misery, your total incapacity and your nothingness besieged My Affection and retracted My Wrath; look at Me in the Eyes...

(I looked into my Saviour's Eyes) see? you have seen Fidelity and Truth face to face; henceforth, your consecration must be loyal

16

invoking My Name day and night, night and day; I shall make your spirit repulse all that is not Me, like a thirsty traveller you will thirst for all that is Holy, but I shall be always ready to offer you water from the Springs of Life and Blood from My Divine Heart; your soul shall bear more than ever before, the Marks of My Body, for the conversion of many souls; this is why you shall voluntarily take the road to Calvary; I shall develop your zeal to please Me furthermore and observe My Law,

17

so that you build up and plant all that
I have given you ♡ ... rise now and
restore My House; do not stop loving
Me, otherwise you will wither as quick as
grass and fade away; and remember one
major thing: ♡ Love loves you ♡

ΙΧΘΥΣ ⊱⊱

Praised be the Lord! Glory be to God!
like clay in the hands of a potter I shall
mould you as I please since you have
given Me the liberty to do so, and your will;
  Praised be the Lord! You have asked me

18

to be the slave of Your Love; since I am not
worthy to be Your slave, the slave of God,
lead me into Your purifying Fire and refine
me, my King, as gold is refined so that I
am able to glorify You, for I am only committing sin after sin. Out of pity Lord, allow
Your Light to shine in my darkness.
Teach me to be the victim of Your Heart,
and embrace Your Cross ardently and not
with consternation, while on the road to
Calvary, this road that leads to happiness
since its The Path of Holiness and in which
You, as the Perfect Victim, first tread on It.
I am constantly sinning, yet You do not punish
me as my sin deserves, You are sparing me
without cease, and You allow Your Light to
be in me; this is why I know that: God is
on my side. Now I must fulfill the vows
I made You in the consecration to Your
Sacred Heart; allow me to stay in Your Tent
forever, allow me to cling on You and gaze
on Your Holy Face and I will bless You
all my life, and my soul will feast in Your

19

Love and in Your Presence.

pupil! rejoice then in My Tent, and worship
Me; remember, I have given you something
very precious, guard it and embrace it with
love; My Cross will guide you into holiness
little soul ♡ I give you My Peace; I bless You
Jesus. the ♡ One who loves you most, blesses
you; ΙΧΘΥΣ ⊱⊱

                                    18.12.90
(I feel in me that I am entering another
phase of my life in God, like a student,
going to a higher class which will require
harder work ...)

20

Lord?

I Am ♡ take My Hand and say with Me
this prayer: " Father, take all I have;
amen;" offer the Father everything, and you
shall be saved; do not fear Him; abandon
yourself to Him ♡ Vassula, allow Me to
breathe in you; be confident for I am with
you ♡ ΙΧΘΥΣ ⊱⊱ read Isaiah 55 ♡
♡ Vassula, add these lines to My Message
given for the meeting ♡
      I am coming to you today to tell you
how complete My joy is; since I am

21

the One you are looking for and you have come from far to hear Me, I tell you, My very beloved ones : I, your God, am smiling on you ; remain in My Love ; pray for Peace and be witnesses of the Truth ; I, God, am with you and bless you ♡

19. XII. 90

My Lord !
I am ; if only my people* would listen ... the ban would be lifted and they will listen, so courage little one ... I am with you ... Love is near you .... oh Vassula, beloved, I am so close to you*²! I Am ; and I watch

* The Orthodoxy. *² Jesus meant by my little writing table.

22

every step you take ; rise and kiss Me, I am near you ; kiss the Sacred Heart in front of you ... (I Kissed His Sacred Heart)
yes ... please Me now and write ♡ (I looked in His Holy Face and my heart leaped with joy)
peace be with you ; it is I, beloved children, the Sacred Heart ; it is I, your Saviour who pursues you to gain your heart and make it entirely Mine ; today I have assembled you as in a school, to be together and learn directly from Wisdom ♡ I intend to give sight to the blind so that they may see

23

My Splendour, and instruct the unlearned to grow in My Spirit and know how to tell sin from virtue ; I intend to gain every heart, even those who turned into granite and are unyielding as millstones ; like a man who invites his friends to share his property, I too invite you to share My Property ; My assemblies are similar to a school ; they are to progress you into your spiritual life and remind each one of you the contents of My Word ; in My School I prepare your spirit for My Great Return and by My Grace I discourse to you

24

now and then of future things to let you know their outcome ♡ if you do not learn from Wisdom how ♡ then will you be able to live according to My Law ? besides, many of you did not know Me, no more than the one I have sent you ; but I am the Resurrection, see how former predictions have come true ? I raised her from her grave and have taken her by the hand and formed her to court her ♡ yes, I am the Resurrection and the Light ; have I not done the same to you too ? have I not taken pity upon you ? and

25

those who were far away from My Heart, have I not sought and found? and have I not with everlasting Love taken you back to Me? and have I, your Lord, not been courting you all these years to win your heart?

I have roused up My Mercy to suppress My Fury, and I poured out My Love instead of My Justice; and My Peace was offered to you followed by Grace, and My Compassion leaned down from heaven granting you the requests of your prayers; I have never ceased blessing you; like a watercourse running into a

26

garden, I said, I am going to water My orchard, I intend to irrigate My flower beds, and see, My watercourse has grown into a river and My river will grow into a sea*; today I tell you: your Shepherd shall soon live among you and shall pasture His flock in the gardens of His City; no-o, you are not yet one flock, but I shall fetch you one by one out of the desert; therefore, My little flock, when from far you see your Shepherd coming up from the desert, know that I shall have with Me the rest of My lambs, and all the things I have

* Ecc. 24:30-3

27

done to you, daughter, I shall do to your brothers too; I shall save you; I shall unite you to your other brothers and Wisdom shall be your Holy Companion to instruct you without cease; I shall soon lift the ban and your great apostasy will come to its end; and the prayer I have given you shall be accomplished; My Will shall be done on earth as it is in Heaven, and under My Hallowed Name, many nations shall come from far away, from all the ends of the earth, to dwell close to My Holy Name, extolling My greatness by the divinity I would give you

28

back; and My Kingdom shall come; because, My Throne shall descend from above into My Holy City; and I shall reign among the remnant left, who will see Me face to face; - Love shall return as love - ♡ and My Will shall be done on earth as it is in Heaven because you will be one, worshipping Me around one Tabernacle with love in your heart and a Fire burning inside you; I shall accomplish My priestly prayer on earth as in Heaven, your souls shall be rooted in Me, in Love, in Unity and filled up with the utter fullness of My Spirit; yes, My

29

beloved ones, I shall not only give you your daily bread, but also a hidden Treasure out of My Heart : The Celestial Manna, that trans-figures, uplifts your spirit into a copy of My Spirit ; you shall be transfigured with the out-pouring of My Spirit ♡ to know how to forgive fully those who tresspassed against you, I shall put inside you a Spirit of Understanding and Mercy to make you understand what 'the fear of the Lord means'; yes beloved ones, and once you do, I shall give you Wisdom to be your travelling Companion and guide, to

30

lead you into sanctity, this sanctity which will paralize Satan for a thousand years, obstructing him from coming between us and between you and My Love; so when you will see the sky dis-solve into flames and the elements melt in the heat, know that this is the sign of the beginning of My Promise; and of the New Heavens and the New Earth : the Renewal of My Church, the Revival of My Church,

the Revival of your hearts ♡

and you, you who are consecrated souls to Me, you who represent Me, I tell you this : do

31

you remember how I heard Elijah's complaint to Me about Israel's behaviour ? and how he believed that they had killed all My prophets and broken down all My altars ? do you remem-ber what My answer was to that ? I said: I have kept for Myself seven thousand men who have not bent the knee to Baal ♡ and today I am telling you beloved brothers : I have kept for Myself a remnant; chosen and transformed by My Grace to remain faithful to Me; this remnant I am raising up to rebuild the altars that once were, and reconstruct My

32

Sanctuary; they are the builders of My New Church; so while the wicked are continuing their evil deeds, persecuting you, My prophets and My saints of the end of Times, and while the proud are struggling for worldwide authority, I, your Redeemer, am raising up and training these builders in My Sacred Heart, to be the pillars of My Church; brothers, I shall never abandon you, never ... come ... lift up your cross and follow Me and when you feel weary on the way, lean on Me, lean on My Heart and My Heartbeats will give you the

33

courage you need and the strength to proceed on your way to Calvary; be blessed ♡ I have told you all this today so that you ♡ may find peace and hope in Me; I have spoken to you today in plain words ♡ beloved ones, stay vigilant and awake and ♡ you will hear My Footsteps; the Word now is very near you and on His way of Return; I bless you all, leaving the Sigh of My Love on your foreheads, this Sigh that marks you as Mine; be one under My Holy Name ΙΧΘΥΣ 🐟

34

22.12.90

My Jesus ? I Am; I treat you very gently so that you, as My flower, grow; I want you strong and believe Me I shall make it possible; you shall be strong, daughter, since you carry My Word; in front of you, I Am, to break all barriers that come up while you are witnessing; I am the Most High, and I tell you, daughter, that I shall see to it that no power from beneath stops you from proclaiming My Message; I have taken you out of the land of Egypt to respond to

35

Me in a foreign land and witness to a people not your own; so although your behaviour was appalling and your senses blemished unabling you to see the Light, Mercy* and Compassion was seized by your astounding misery, guilt and wretchedness and came to your rescue; no-o Vassula, you have not deserved any of My Gifts, why, I had servants in My Hand who honored Me, never uttering but My Name in holiness, who blessed Me without cease, who praised the Holy Trinity wholeheartedly, but yet My Heart, an Abyss of Love

* Mercy and Compassion = The Lord.

36

cried out for you; you had accumulated sorrow upon sorrow in My Heart, treason upon treason; you were wrestling with Me, puny little creature ... but I knew that your heart is not a divided heart and that once I conquer your heart, it would become entirely Mine; an object of your era, you were wrestling with Me, but I have thrown you down in the wrestle and dragged you in the dust and into the desert where I left you there all alone; I had provided you with a guardian angel, since the beginning of your existence, to guard you,

37

console you and guide you, but My Wisdom ordered your guardian angel to leave you and to let you face the desert on your own; I said: " you are to live in spite of your nakedness !*¹ because no man is able to survive alone*², Satan would have taken over completely and would have killed you; My order was given to him too; I forbade him to touch you ♡ then, in your terror you remembered Me ♥ and looked up in Heaven searching desperately for Me;

*¹ I became "naked" as soon as my guardian angel and all Heaven had turned their back to me.
*² Abandoned by Heaven.

38

your laments and your supplications suddenly broke the deathly stillness surrounding you and your terrified cries pierced through the heavens reaching the Holy Trinity's Ears ..." My child !" the Father's Voice, full of joy resounded through all Heaven, " Ah... I shall now make her pene- trate My Wounds* and let her eat My Body and drink My Blood, I shall espouse her to Me and she will be Mine for eternity ♡ I shall show her the Love I have for her and her lips from thereon shall thirst for Me and her heart shall be My Head-rest; she

* The Son then spoke.

39

shall eagerly submit daily to My Righteousness, I shall make her an altar of My Love. and of My Passion; I, and I only shall be her only Love and Passion; and I shall send her with My Message to the ends of the world to conquer an irreligious people, and to a people who are not even her own, and volun- tarily she will carry My Cross of Peace and Love taking the road to Calvary ♡ " And I, the Holy Spirit shall descend upon her to reveal to her the Truth and the depths of Us*; I shall remind the world, through her, that

* The Holy Trinity

40

the greatest of all the gifts is : LOVE ♡ " let Us* then celebrate ! let all heaven celebrate !" ... I have taken you by the hand and formed you to become a living sign of My Great Love; - a witness of My Sacred Heart, and of the renewal of My Church ; (The Father, then the Son, then the Holy Spirit spoke) I am the Resurrection ♡

(For this message, Look for further explanations on p. 47) ΙΧΘΥΣ ⊃〇▷

23.12.90

O Father, like thirsty Land I yearn for You. Rest me for a while on Your Knees now and console me. Let me feel enveloped by Your Consoling Heart. I need Your warmth.

* The Holy Trinity spoke.

41

repose your head on My Heart, rest and feel consoled ♡ ... your Abba is caring for you; your Abba is happy to have you near Him; repose your head on My Heart, My child, and listen to the Desires of My Heart: My Heart is still seeking, longing, pleading, for the rest of My children's love... (a few seconds pause) child?*

what would you give to console your Abba?

O Lord, anything You want. My Love, my will, my heart and my soul,

and what more?

My life, as an atonement to Your Desires.

* Suddenly the Father's Head turned and looked at me.

42

descend then from My Knees and go and bear witness in My Name; go and tell the nations of My Great Love; remind them that My Promise is very near to its accomplishment and that My Return is imminent; the New Jeru- salem* is at hand; I am going to renew My Church and My people; so My child, descend from My Knees and go out into the world... for My Sake... and make My Love known to the world, let the world realize how I love My children; as it is, you have not sought Me, it is I who found you and have

* Church.

43

chosen you to go out to the world before My Great Day; it is I who formed you and although you were aloof to Me, I have chosen you and revealed My Holy Face to you; so when you have accomplished all the work I have commis- sioned you for, My child, I shall take you up to Me and you may then rest on My Knees; I shall, in the meantime while you are in the world, protect you from your oppressors; I want you for your part to look up in Heaven constantly for Me and talk to Me; 'Yahweh is with you', have always

44

these words engraved on your mind and on your heart, for I-Am-With-You; now let your heart treasure all that I have told you and remember: offer Me prayers to reach Me like incense, for the conversion of souls and the revival of My Church ☧

Christmas Day　25.12.90

I shall announce Your Name to my brothers*² and praise You in full assembly* whether they*² like it or not.

daughter, although many of you do not know the way to Peace and the way to Unity, do not despair; hope in Me, I shall come to

* Ps. 22:22　　*² The Greek Orthodox

45

comfort you soon; and you, My child, your pleadings* have been heard in Heaven by everyone; I shall come to unite you; My Word has been given and My Will shall be carried out; in the meantime summon a nation you never knew and give them the instructions I have given you, and if a 'sage' now and then accuses you of calling Me Father, remind him that today a Child is born and His Name is: Wonder-Counsellor, Mighty-God, <u>Eternal-Father</u>, and Prince of Peace*²; pray for those who call themselves doctors of the Law, that their

*¹ for unity.   *² Is. 9:5

46

spirit becomes a humble and poor spirit; pray that all nations come to My Light and that the vengeance eating their hearts be ripped off so that I may wrap their hearts in My Peace; pray that east makes peace with the west and the north with the south; pray that this excessive pride and haughtiness that seized certain shepherds of Mine be replaced by humility; pray that they understand what I have meant by: "Anyone* who wants to be great among you must be your servant; and anyone who wants to be first among you must be your slave;

* Matth. 20 : 26-28

47

yes, just as the Son of Man came not to be served but to serve and to give His life as a ransom for many;" <u>imitate Me your Lord and you shall live</u> ... ΙΧΘΥΣ ⊃—▷

(Explanation of message p. 34, date 22.12.90)

In the beginning when I was suddenly approached by my guardian angel to open the way for the Lord, I, as a "professional" sinner, had no love for God; even when my angel was telling me things about Heaven. I was just satisfied to be together with my angel. I was not looking for more. — When God approached me, replacing my angel, I was somewhat disappointed. I felt Him as a stranger whereas having already been acquainted with my angel my surprised feelings had turned to love feelings. And then I could not understand why God wanted to take my angel's place; I even went as far as to believe that

48

God was jealous from the love I was giving to my guardian angel and I had felt sorry for my angel. — Later on, after a very painful purification given to me by my angel, God approached again for the second time to take my angel's place. He stayed with me for a few days, opening my heart slowly, and with Wisdom, so as not to frighten me away. When I've just about started to open for Him, He ran away and hid. I turned around to look for my angel and I could not find him either. I felt a few souls* approach me, begging me for prayers and blessings; I prayed for them and blessed them. Then they asked me to bless them with holy water. I ran quickly to the church to fetch holy water for them, and I blessed them sprinkling on them holy water. I took the opportunity to ask them whether they had seen where my angel was and The One whom my heart already begun to love. But I did not get an answer. — Every day that went by seemed like a year. I was looking for Peace and I could find none. I was surrounded by many people and many friends but I

* from Purgatory

49

never ever before felt more lonely and abandoned as those days. I was as though I was going through hell. — Many a times I cried out for my angel to come back to me, but no, he had turned his back and gone!" My soul failed at his flight. I sought him but I did not find him, I called to him but he did not answer." (Song of Songs 5:6) I roamed for 3 whole weeks in the desert by myself until I could not bear it anymore; then out of my distress I cried out to Yahweh, searching Heaven: " Father! O God, take me and use me as You wish; purify me so that You are able to use me!" With this cry coming from the depths of my heart suddenly Heaven opened, and like Thunder the Father's Voice full of emotion cried back to me: " I, God, love you!" Instantly I felt as though I dropped out of a tornado into a beautiful peaceful world. My angel re-appeared and with great tenderness started to dress my wounds, those wounds I received while in the desert. — This happened during Easter 1986.

50

30.12.90

Lord and Saviour?

I am; delight Me and work for Me, pray to Me and remember Me ♡ come;
                     Epiphany — 6.1.91

While in the Orthodox Church I said to Jesus: ' I wish I could have had a voice to have been able to sing to You in the church choir.'
    — Jesus answered: 'Sing to Me with your heart; I rejoice much more to hear your heart sing to Me.'
Later on my eyes were wondering all over the icons and the frescos on the walls. I was thinking: "Wow! look at all this great Holy Family, and that one day we will make part of it. Angels, saints, our Holy Mother, and the Holy Trinity. What a wonderful Holy Family! And my soul longed to be with Them already, to be part of the family, and be in constant adoration to the Holy Trinity.

51

O God! let me be part of this Celestial Family! So pray for me Holy Angels, pray for me to be with you in heaven one day and join you together with the saints, in a constant adoration to the Holy One.
Pray for me, saints of the Most High, to learn to love God to perfection.
O sweet Holy Mother intercede for me and teach me to be submissive to my Father and obedient, that I may do His Will.
O Holy Trinity, Source of Sublime Love, Fountain of Inexhaustible Tenderness, come and teach me to be intimate with You, uniting me in Your Spirit of Love. O make me ready for this Hour, because the night is almost over and the real Light is soon to come.
       Holy Father, I pray not only
       for myself, but for all mankind too;
       Since we are all Your children,
       I pray and ask You to look upon
          us with Mercy,
       Eternal Father, teach us to love
        one another, so that we may

52

           do Your Holy Will, and
           be rightfully called Your children. Amen.
beloved child, I Am who I Am, it is with full Compassion and with great Force that My Kindness and My Love are now being revealed to you all; I am revealing you My Holy Face without reserve to purify a people who cannot tell their right hand from their left, and who live in profound darkness and wickedness ♡ your Abba is calling you without cease; I am love; if only you would listen to Me today...

53

Lord Jesus Christ, Beloved Son
of God,
Sacred Heart,
Blessed be Your Name,
Sacred Heart, help us to
carry our crosses in this world
and be submissive to the Father
as You were submissive and
obedient to the Father till the end.
                                                    amen.

I the Lord Jesus bless you; I am
the Word and the Word was given to you
and made His Home in you, so sanctify yourselves   that the Word may come and live
in you ♡   O Holy Spirit of Truth
descend upon us and be our
Guide and Holy Companion,
Holy Spirit of Love,

54

come upon us and teach us
to be in the real Love of God.
Remind us the True Knowledge,
this Knowledge the
Father had given us but
that we lost because of our sins,
Holy Spirit of Peace, give
us Your Peace
a Peace the world cannot give;
make out of each one of us
vessels of Light and
"peacemakers, so that when we
work for Peace, we will be
able to sow seeds which will
bear fruit in holiness." (James 3:18)
                                                    amen.

beloved, I tell you solemnly that I, the Holy
Spirit of Truth, provide you day and night,
night and day with considerable graces to

55

help you all on your way to perfection; since
I am your Life, allow Me to direct you and
be your Guide in this exile you are living in;
I can be your Oasis in your wilderness;
O how little do you know Me, creation!
you spend your whole lifetime, creation, seeking your happiness in futile things, when I,
Omnipresent, offer you: Love, Joy, Peace and Freedom to free you from the dungeons of Evil;
My Graces are multiple, yet, you are unaware
of My Presence and of how many graces your
spirit can obtain from Me; I ask from My

56

faithful ones, prayers, for the salvation of souls;
all will vanish one day, all will wear out
like a garment, but your soul remains forever;
the Harvest is ready and soon the Reaper shall
come and reap His Harvest ♡ be prepared
for the Reaper ♡
                                                    8.1.91
Our Holy Mother's Message for the prayer group, for the 19.1.91

peace be with you, My beloved children; I
am inviting you all today to pray for Unity;
to unite you must love, to unite you must
be humble and obedient; do not let anyone
lead you astray by other doctrines; remain

57

faithful and you shall not stumble; today the
lands do not yield happiness nor virtue, because
your generation has deserted the Lord; the out-
coming of this is sin; happy the man who has
been sheltered from it; had your generation
walked in the way of God you would have lived
in peace; O children! I am calling to you; My
cries go out to all nations; the dead* cannot hear
nor praise the Lord, but you, you who are
attentive to My calls, praise the Lord, glorify
the Lord with your love, with your faith and
with your hope ♡ heaven belongs to you My

* spiritualy dead.

58

child, so I beg you, you who have a mouth,
speak to the Lord and bless Him; you who have
eyes, look at His Beauty; take more of your
time to contemplate His Wounds, the Wounds
which were given Him for your salvation; you
who have ears, hear Our supplications; you
who have a heart, love the Lord, adore Him
and offer your heart to Him; no, the dead* cannot speak nor see, they cannot hear, nor feel;
beloved, He who has created you is stooping to
you, with His Heart in His Hand, offering It
to you; as a bridegroom offers his bride a

* spiritualy dead.

59

ring as a sign of alliance, so is the Holy One
offering you His Sacred Heart as a Sign of His
Love, to wed you; like a bride adorned in
her jewels, the Lord, the King of kings shall
adorn you with His Jewels*; do not sleep but
stay awake; you have been bought and paid
for with His Precious Blood, drift not away
with the first current; let His Fire consume
you into a living torch in His Church, let
Him mould you into a Image of Himself to
be faithful and sturdy and He will use you
to be the pillars of His New Church;

* His Thorned Crown, His Nails and His Cross

60

O children! do not be afraid, for God has
always done great things, have confidence in Him;
a mission of angels is being sent to you to
spread the Heavenly grains, everywhere in the
world and bring a message of Peace and Love
in your great tribulations; these grains will be
welcomed as rain on a thirsty soil; have you
not noticed how God has opened the Doors of
Heaven to rain down His Celestial Manna? yes,
His Holy Spirit of Grace? the Almighty has
taken pity on you and said: "let My people
eat; let them eat the Bread of Heaven";

1

His order was given from above; like in the times of Moses, the Father fed His people with manna in the desert, more than they could eat; and Jesus, His Son, has He not multiplied the loaves and fishes? have the crowds not eaten as much as they wanted? and today, why are some of you surprised that the Holy Spirit descends with full force on you to feed your nations with this Celestial Manna? Oh how little do you know the Holy Trinity! distressed and starved you shall not be left, never, nor shall you be abandoned to wander, starving

2

in this desert; the blackness of your era shall not last forever, your sins shall soon be purged and the Beast will be paralized soon, together with His clan they will grovel in the dust, because a Light shall soon appear in the horizon, this shall be the Great Sign; so if your feet still waver between good and evil, pray, that they will not lead you into temptation; if your heart still refuses to sing to the Lord a Love Song, pray, that the Evil one may not deceive you; if your eyes avoid to look up in Heaven seeking heavenly things, pray, that your room in heaven

3

shall receive you one day; if your soul still belongs to the world, pray, that the vices of the world will not coil in you, for you would be nestling a Serpent within you; pray with your heart; sacrifice with joy; let your labour be worthwhile and I promise you that your lamp will not go out at night; be thirsty for God! I am watching over you all and at this very minute I stoop to you to bless you all ♡

_____ 8. 1. 91

Blessed be our Lord, who performs constant marvels of love for us. You hear our supplications and our petitions when we call to You for help. Blessed be our Holy Mother, who offers me a Church

4

for my birthday present, where we* could unite and pray. You are our protector and our hope.

flower, be with Me; ten more days to come, then it is your birthday, the day I called you and planted you, flower; Ah! look at Me, it pleases Me; My property, My own, how I the Lord love you! how I delight in you! spiritually you were dead, but now I have risen you to come and live in My world; feel happy! for look at what I have given you! look at the treasure I have given you; your meditation is worth a lot; this dialogue between us is a treasure

* the prayer group, & the monthly meetings.

5

sought by many; but I brought it to you
and offered it to you; I came down from
Heaven all the way to your room to give it
to you as a gift; My treasure is sought by
many, but few can have it; Vassula, Vassula
be in union with Me desiring Me at the same
time, for this is the perfect fruit of devotion;
how I delight to take this fruit! offer Me
your time, offer Me your hand, be My tablet;
have I not sanctified you in My Holiness? so
offer Me in your turn yourself, your will, your
energy; allow Me to use you little one, allow My

6

Love to cover you My dove; love Me; ♡

9.1.91
(I wept for all the false accusations said about me
by "..." and that damage so much.)
flower, this is My Cross too ♡ but allow Me to
treat you as I please; your love reaches Me as
incense; when a sudden deadly scourge descends
on you, My child, offer it to Me; I shall make
good use of it; nations are at the verge of
war, do you understand?! little one, offer
Me your sufferings, because there is an anger
ready to flame ... have My Peace ... have confidence
in Me, My Vassula, remember, I shall comfort

7

you; then there is your angel by your side to
console you and dress your wounds; but for
the time being allow Me to leave My Cross on you;
courage, daughter! My Cross is heavy and weighing
on you, but I know that you will be willing to
carry It till the end; I the Lord bless you, I
shall reward you in heaven ♡ (Daniel, my
angel) your Jesus loves you, it is I, Daniel,
remember, the Lord has rested you, but now,
would you not want to rest Him too? Vassula,
satisfy Him then, and allow Him to crush you
with sufferings, there is a big price to pay for

8

Peace, there are many lives at stake; how often
does the Lord crush you with such a weight?
Not often. no, not many times; so the few
times He does, accept them and do not be
vehement about it; Vassula, all these sacrifices
are not going in vain; they fortify you as well;
remain in God's Love;

        eager He is, to purify you,
        eager be, to glorify Him ♡ Daniel
your angel ♡ d

(I smiled. Somehow my angel always manages
to make me smile. I smiled at the prose
he has written. That is typical of my angel.)

9

16.1.91

O Lord! where are You again? like thirsty ground I yearn for you, reach down from above and visit me; my Lamp is running short of its oil; come as usual to fill my Lamp.

have My Peace; upon My Shoulders I am carrying you; like a shepherd carrying His weak lamb, I carry you, because I know you are weak, miserable and unable to walk by yourself; I, the Lord, am pouring on you grace after grace, for your survival; I overlook all that you do not do in My favour, daughter; have confidence; I have rescued you from Death to walk by My side, I have rescued you, flower, so that you

10

walk in My Presence, but Jesus talk little, shsh ... listen to Me *; listen: ... how many have I raised up in this particular way and educated little by little? Not many my Lord. then trust Me *² ... I shall bring you to fulfill every vow that rose to your lips in your act of consecration; listen ... who was more determined than I and My Mother for your salvation? No one. no, no one; in spite of your childish insolence I offered you My Sacred Heart to become your dwelling place; why, Vassula, I have taken you by the hand

* Jesus said these words like a soft melody, whispering them, I could have died from His Tenderness.
* Jesus again whispered softly.

11

across the desert and have shown you Heaven, and your eyes saw thousands of myriads of angels surrounding Me ♡ daughter, I granted you many favours and all this from the Love I have for you *; listen to Me *² ... I have come to educate you and millions of others through these Messages, I have not come for you alone, I have not come to raise you up alone, but to raise through these writings nation after nation to glorify Me; and as I have taken you to My Banquet Hall, I intend to take soul after soul in My Banquet

* I was trying to interrupt. *² Jesus was whispering tenderly again

12

Hall too; do not stand mystified at My Beauty ... I Am Perfect ... listen to Me ... do not let your eyes turn away from Me, praise Me, and I shall, if you allow Me, hold them captive, I shall hold your gaze on My Perfection to arouse in you a desire for your own perfection ♡ I want you beautiful, blessed and holy; so allow Me to lead you step by step into Heaven. it is true that I have lifted you to be a sign of unity and to go out and witness but am I not providing you for your mission with everything that your soul needs? you were uninhabited, a desert,

13

hear Me, then, to fulfill My purpose, I came into your wilderness to pitch My Tent in you to prosper you and make out of you My Property and My Dwelling ♡ now you belong to Me and you are My Own and My Temple; for this reason I guard you like the core of My Eyes, from the Slanderer, who without cease endeavours in various methods to invade and ravage your land and make a desolation out of you ♡ like a watchman I watch over you day and night, like a sentinel I guard you from all intruders, aha! no-o, no one will be allowed

14

to enter into My Property ♡ O beloved, blessed of My Soul, allow Me to whisper in you My Desires so that they be written and read by a multitude of souls, and that out of these lines they may hear:

<u>My Voice</u>,
<u>Love's Voice</u>,

I have not spoken to you only, <u>I am speaking to every soul</u>; so come to Me, you who are needy, I shall lift you out of your misery and press you to My Heart; come to Me you who are desolate and I shall make rivers flow out of you;

15

oh come to Me, you who are weary and place your head on Me, rest in Me, soul; your hardships, your worries, I shall bear, give them to Me, offer them to Me and I shall relieve you, rejoice! for in your nothingness I Am Everything, in your poverty, I am King, and in your abandonment to Me I can do My Will! Righteousness and Justice are observing you, so do not fail Me, soul, Salvation is at your door ♡ — Vassula, let My Love cover you; be attentive and do not neglect Me, remember, I am your Spouse; I, the Lord,

16

bless you; keep Me locked in your mind; this pleases Me so much; I love you Infinitely; come ♡

Message for my birthday — 18.1.91

peace be with you ♡ My Divine Heart shall encourage you to proceed without fear and the Father <u>is</u> generous; have confidence in Me, trust Me little child; I shall fill you with consolation;* I have tested you, allow Me to assess you now and then; Vassula, even when everything may appear to you as lost, do not get discouraged;

* For the past days I neither felt God near me nor "saw" Him; I felt as though He deserted me, and I was melancolic.

17

I shall smoothen your way, but at the same time I shall have you exposed as a <u>sign</u> of rejection; the rejection for Unity ♡ sincerity is missing among them, so how can they make up the differences between them? but Lord, do You mean that they shall reject Your Messages in the end?

no; My Messages shall follow their course without you ♡ but you shall be tossed around; I shall permit your persecutors' defiled hands to strike you and mistreat you openly; I shall allow them to contradict you ... and like crows ravaging the crop they will attack you; you will appear

18

in their eyes as the loser because the wounds they will inflict on you will be impressive; these wounds, My child, shall be given to you from within My House and by My Own; they will be given to you from Cain's clan; I will allow them to strike an innocent child, but their gladness shall turn into mourning; yes, you will appear as the loser My Vassula, but have I not appeared as the loser too? I appeared to have failed My Mission, I appeared in the world's eyes as the greatest loser ever; you are a sign given to them to arise questions that will be controversial; I do

19

not mean to discourage you, Vassula, even when some of them try to stop My Messages from spreading any farther among the people, be firm, My Vassula, be firm as a rock;

Lord, if they "brake" me as You seem to make me understand, wound my soul near to death, how would I be able to be firm and standing?

lacerated you shall be, but I, the Lord, shall be standing by your side, <u>and your strength shall be My Strength</u>; come, fear not, bear witness for Me;

20

Message for the prayer group.

19.1.91

peace be with you; I, Saint Michael ask you to consecrate your days and nights to petitions, fasting and prayer; soon, all things that have been hidden to you shall be revealed; may it be the Lord's Will that you shall find His Mercy in His Day; if only you who have hardened your heart would listen to Him today... if you would only open your heart to hear His Voice ... open your hearts, not your minds... everything goes in accordance with the Scriptures, soon many will start bending their knee to God and many tongues that have not uttered

21

a prayer shall start praying; be united, you who are God's people, in your convictions and in your love; be united in prayer; I bless you all, in the Name of Father and of the Son and of the Holy Spirit ♡ rest in the Lord's Heart, Vassula; be the sign of His Love; have My Peace : Saint Michael;

_____

21.1.90

"You, who have seen my wretchedness, and known the miseries of my soul" Ps. 31:8 take pity on me, take pity on all of us.

daughter, when this time of Grace is over, so will be My Mercy; then your era shall have to

22

face My Justice; I bless you for lending Me your ear, your time and your hand; I bless you and your companions ♡ take My Hand, I shall offer you Joy and Peace; Love is near you; have My Peace ΙΧΘΥΣ ⊃○<

24.1.91

My Lord ?

I Am; I give you My Peace; write :

(Message for prayer groups)

peace be with you; beloved, you whom My Heart seeks to attract without cease; you whom My Heart loves to folly; you whom I created out of My Sublime Love; you whom I made

23

out of your body, My Temple, live holy ... and you who sin constantly, offending Me, My Heart has forgiven you; rejoice! be joyful! for your Master is not far away, your Lord is on His way of Return; come and praise Me, come... even the pebbles and the rocks will soon cry out on My Return : " blessings on the King who comes !" whoever comes to Me, even in his or her state of sin and is repentant, I shall not turn them away; yet to this day there are some who do not believe in My Mercy, nor in My Love; not only do they not believe, but it

24

is they who betray Me; today I am telling you as I had once said : " no one could come to Me, unless the Father allows him;"* this is why I am telling you to pray, that all may receive through the Father's Mercy : Grace ♡ Grace, to be converted; yes, to "come" to Me, it is necessary that one be brought by Grace given to him from above; I shall never reject anyone who accepts this Grace; so do not waste your time seeking objections to object My Spirit's Works; if I call and you do not respond, you are not responding to Grace; beloved ones, I ask

* John 6 : 66

25

you to pray that everyone receives this Grace to believe and be converted; the Words I am giving you are Spirit; they uplift, they revive and they give Light in your inner darkness; I have, children of Mine, given you many signs to believe that the Spirit is active and alive, so do not wait for material signs; My Spirit comes with full force in these days to help you now when night is yawning its darkness all around you; how My Heart pities you to watch your little hands grope their way through this night! I am giving you many signs that

26

you may believe that these are the days when My Spirit is being poured out on all mankind as never before, so you who still waver, distrustful and doubtful asking Me to give you a sign to show you that these Messages among others, spread in the world are from Me, I tell you again most solemnly: it was not Moses who gave your ancestors bread from Heaven, but My Father, it is Me who gave them bread from Heaven; it is My Father who feeds you, for the Bread of God * is that which comes down from Heaven and gives life to the world; your

* Jesus now means the Holy Spirit.

27

ancestors ate manna in the desert; and I have given the multitudes already a forerunner of My Eucharist, I had multiplied the loaves to feed them, as I feed you My Body to give you Life, I had multiplied the fishes too, a symbol of My Name, a symbol of He-Who-Feeds-You, a symbolic sign of My Name: ΙΧΘΥΣ which means: Jesus Christ, God's Son and Saviour ♡ so I tell you most solemnly today that the ♡ Messages My Spirit is outpouring on every nation, are not merely words, they are Spirit and they are Life; have you not read

28

what Scripture says: " He gave them bread from Heaven to eat; " Ex: 16:4 are these signs not enough to convince you? today I am feeding your interior desert with a Celestial Bread, still another miraculous food ♡ a Miraculous Food that does not perish but enlivens your spirit, for as the earth makes fresh things grow, as a garden makes seeds spring up, so does My Glorious Food reactivate in you, life, ardour and devotion; like a spark that can give fire, so does My Holy Spirit come down on you to re-animate this flickering flame inside you into

29

a consuming Fire of Love; Scripture says:
" an unspiritual person is one who does not accept
anything of the Spirit of God: he sees it all
as nonsense; it is beyond his understanding
because it can only be understood by means of
the spirit (1Cor. 2:14) the New Heavens and the
New Earth are right at your doors now, yet
many of you have not understood and see
it all as nonsense; these unspiritual people
prefer to take all of My Signs in a superficial
way and scorn   My Celestial Messages; but
Scriptures are being fulfilled, for they had

30

indeed announced that during the last days there
will be people who will make fun of My Promise;
since I knew that men have an infinite capacity
for sinning and that the Enemy would be enthroned, in the end of times, into My Sanctuary
I have, for this reason, kept for Myself a remnant to be the builders of My New Sanctuary,
the First-Fruits of My Spirit; as I had once
kept for Myself seven thousand men who had
not bent the knee to Baal in those days of
Elijah, today too, I have by My Grace kept
for Myself this remnant, a hundred and

31

forty-four thousand people,*[1] all with My Name
and My Father's Name written on their foreheads *[2]
these are the ones who never allow a lie to
pass their lips*[3], these are My first-fruits of
the New Heavens and the New Earth, these
will be the trees*[4] of life which would bear
twelve*[5] crops of fruit in a year, one in each

* Symbolic number: From all around the world,
a perfect people. (Ap. 14:1)
[2] Ap. 14:1
[3] Ap. 14:5 :
*[4]   Trees of life = the new-born = the first fruits
*[5] Symbolic number: The New Church. The
People of God

32

month, and the leaves of which are the cure
for the pagans*[1]; to refresh your memories, I
shall explain to you once more through what
the book of Ezekial the prophet says : " along
the river, on either bank, will grow every
kind of fruit tree," this means: Spirit - anointed priests to lay-men, " with leaves that never
wither and fruit that never fails, they will
bear fruit every month, because this water*[3]
comes from the Sanctuary, since this water will

*[3] Water coming out of Christ's Heart

*[1] Ap: 22:2 The new disciples who by means of the Spirit
will go out to convert godless people. *[2] Ez: 47:12

33

come and rise from the throne of God and of the Lamb and flowing crystal-clear, down the middle of the city street*," and their fruit will be good to eat and the leaves medicinal", like a tree, you shall be, renewed by My Holy Spirit that never fails you, and your leaves shall be medicinal, yes, your witnessing shall cure the sick, converting nation after nation, but not on your own, it will not be you speaking, but My Holy Spirit who lives in you; and like builders, I shall send you from the ends of the world with a cane in

* Ap. 22: 1-2

34

your hand like a measuring rod*', to reconstruct My Sanctuary and the altars that lie in ruin and have become the haunt of the devils*²; pray My beloved ones, that everyone may have time to convert; pray that Grace comes upon them so that they recognize and acknowledge the Truth; pray for those who have turned to myths rather than the Truth; pray for the conversion of the world; pray that I inhabit every soul, and that I make her My Property, pray that I may flow in these

*' App. 11:1   *² App. 18:2

35

souls, "like a river down the middle of a city street"*' sacrifice for these conversions, little children; stay near Me, for a leopard *² is lurking very near by, stay near Me in constant prayer: an infinite prayer ♡ allow Me to leave My Sigh of Love on your foreheads blessing you all ♡ be one under My Holy Name IXΘΥΣ 🐟 there My Vassula, this will feed many; I love you My child ♡ Love blesses you; bless Me;

    Lord, I bless You; Maranatha!

*' App. 22: 2   *² Dn. 7:4-6 App. 13:2 Hos. 13:7

36

31. 1. 91
Our Holy Mother's Message for the 23rd Feb.
praised be the Lord and peace to you all; God is calling you to Himself, meditate upon this; God has been calling you since you were born; born for Him, born to love Him, born to please Him; born to return to Him; respond to His Call; I have been trying through My Messages here and in other parts of the world to bring you back, with love, to the true Life in God for your salvation; little ones, yes, I call you little, because the Lord has revealed His Face to you and not to the learned nor to

37

the clever; realize too that it was not flesh
and blood that revealed to you the truths, the
imminence and the grace of these Messages of
your era for your salvation and made you believe
them, but the Father Himself, by His Grace
upon you; so if your neighbour has not yet
been stamped with the seal of the Holy Spirit
of Grace, pray, that He too receives this Grace
for his conversion and enters into the Kingdom
of God ♡ God is calling everyone to Himself;
try to ♡ understand God's Call of Peace, I ex-
hort you to pray for Peace, be zealous for Peace;

38

blessed children let Me tell you once more that
I need your prayers of Peace, for I take them all
and offer them as a bouquet of spring flowers
to the Almighty ♡ your prayers do not go in
vain, they are a real glory to God, they are
a proof of your love ♡   Satan is very powerful and his fierce anger is pursuing all the
first-fruits of the Lord, those who bear witness for Jesus; Jesus, in His earlier Messages had
made you understand how Satan is trying to
extinguish the small flame that is left in this
world and leave you without light, without

39

happiness; without mercy, he is blaspheming all
God's Powers; indeed the earth, without your
fervent prayers for Peace, will feel Satan's vomit*
pour out to blow away the little light
that is left in you; I am melancholic
beyond words; I have prayed for you all,
I will always; children, please meditate on
Our Messages; live to the word Our Messages;
I, your Blessed Mother, bless you ♡
_____
                                                      4. 2. 91

daughter, have My Peace; Take pity on me Lord,
I seek and do not seem to find You, I call
* Ap. 12, 15

40

and I do not seem to hear Your Voice. I do not know
where I am walking; my persecutors are hounding me,
if Your Strength will not uphold me I shall surely
be crushed, O for the wings of a dove to fly
up to You! God, how I love You!

peace daughter! come, I want you to look for
higher things; I am constantly helping you to
reach a higher level of prayer; I remain always
near you ♡ be strong; I love you to passion
and My ♡ Love shall remain; – dearest soul,
be patient, I shall unfold everything in its own
time, yes, everything has its own time ♡ My
Spirit has come down to rest on you so let
nothing disturb you; – the prince* of this
* Satan

41

world has great power and this was given to him to accomplish the Scriptures; I have told you this so that you understand ... never doubt of My Presence ♡ I am with you to guide your feet into the way of perfection but My Vassula no one reaches perfection unless they go through My Cross; learn that self-abnegation will lead you into the path of perfection, I will be glorified and you purified ♡ I know with what reluctancy* and difficulty your spirit accepts this special way I have given you, but this is one more reason why I have chosen you;

* for fear I am wrong.

42

I desired to have in My Hands a simple and weak instrument, a nothing, to shame the wise and the learned; I wanted someone without any knowledge; I have chosen you and not you, Me; I am the Holy One who came to pitch My Tent in you; I have come upon you suddenly, like a sweet breeze, and like the wind, no one knows from where it comes from; lean on Me now, I shall guide your step, I shall never abandon you ever; you are living under My Light; you have, soul, inherited My Love; so:

43

Hope, daughter, tell Me that your hope is in Me ♡ My Lord Yahweh, my Hope is in You.
Faith, daughter, tell Me that you have put your faith in Me, in all its fulness and I will tell you that your soul shall be rewarded; have faith and exult Me by offering it to Me;

My Lord Yahweh, I believe and I have faith in You and Your Promise. I trust You.

Love, daughter, tell Me that you love Me with all your heart, your soul and with all your mind; show Me that your love is pure, beloved, show Me that you love your neighbour as

44

yourself; Teach me my Lord Yahweh how to love You and love my neighbour as myself.

I Am; pupil? Yes Lord? have faith in Me, love Me and reach perfection, you are not alone, even in your sleep*, beside you I Am; learn that Heaven is rejoicing for I have through your pains²* saved a soul ♡ I have with the love you have for Me warmed a heart ♡ do not fear, Vassula, My daughter, have My Peace and honour Me by remaining faithful to Me; despise all that is not holy, thirst for all that is Me; — I

* spiritual sleep *2 physical back pains and interior sufferings

---

45

have cultivated your soil to yield a harvest and through your perseverance, (do not take this on yourself) I have worked and toiled in you; I have lifted your soul to Me; I tell you, My Mercy is great! oh if you only knew and realized fully, what I have offered you ... I am like a mother to you, I am Protective like an over-sensitive mother who cares for her child, I Am; I have in these past years revealed My Face to you, have I not? Yes, You have my Lord. I, the Light, have come in you and have given you Light in your darkness; are you

---

46

happy to have been with Me all these years? Yes my Lord, as happy as in Paradise. wait and you shall see how happy you shall be in Paradise ♡ I have prayed to the Father for you that He may overlook your astounding weakness, My Vassula, and that He maintains your strength by giving you His Strength; I have guaranteed to you that you will glorify Me in the end; pray My child that peace may come in this world ♡ love Me, be blessed;

5.2.91

Where are You again my Lord? Why are You

47

hiding? or am I in the dark again and cannot see You? are You withholding Your favours? Yet I know You cannot be far; "if my feet have wandered from the rightful path, or if my eyes have led my heart astray, or if my hands are smirched with any stain" (Job 31:7) forgive me.

My child, be blessed! peace be with you; adjust Vassula to Me and stop listening to the Tempter; I tell you: approach Me, approach Me My child, I am He who provides you with real Knowledge; O Vassula! a light has shone in you, so how could you doubt? it is I, the Lord, who saved you; — I had said through My prophets that I shall give My Spirit even on the least and

---

48

the most wretched of all, but My child this is only the beginning of My Promise ♡ I Am the All-Faithful, O My child rejoice! rejoice! because soon I shall bestow My Spirit to all mankind; I will make crystal-clear waters* flow out of every living creature; — Vassula, I hid My Face from you for just a few days so that you look for Me; forsaken you are not; I was horrified Lord! O no, do not be dismayed, how else would I revive in you a spirit of concern? concern to finally raise your head and search Heaven looking for Me, the Holy One? you

Ap. 22:1

49

are from below and I Am from above; you are living in a place where your spirit fails to satisfy you because you are surrounded by all that is not Me, and I Am to be found where your spirit, your soul ought to be languishing and yearning to be; blessed of My Soul, until you learn to constantly seek Me and desire Me, I will continue to put you to the test now and then; it is My pleasure to drench you with My Spirit today and not yesterday, tomorrow and maybe not the day after; see? Yes, Lord, I finally think I understand now.

50

bathed in My Light, search for Heavenly things keeping My Principles ♡ without Me you are alone and you cannot do a thing, you could not even master your thoughts, so I tell you: give your eyes no sleep; I do not mean to discourage you Vassula, but from My Lips come Teachings and Wisdom; I mean to make you walk by My Side and in the way of virtue; I mean to enrich your spirit so that I display My Knowledge through you so that you may glorify Me; lift your eyes then in Heaven and look at Me, daughter, and when you see again My Holy

51

Face, you will grow, once more, radiant and your heart will throb again with delight, see? your heart will be arrayed majestically and in holiness once your eyes meet My Magnificence; lean on Me, I had only examined you My child ♡ I bless you, bless Me, Love Me; ΙΧΘΥΣ ⟨fish symbol⟩

6.2.91

My Lord, guard me from all these evil attacks, defend me, who else will? Satan is putting people to plot against Your messages and against me; will You allow things to go out of hand my God? We are with Your help constructing and they are destructing; how am I to go on? I am no one, and if You will not stand by my side I can be "massacred" interiorly.

flower have My Peace; do not be distressed, beside

52

you I Am; and I know, oh, how I know everything that goes on inside men's hearts... nevertheless, realize that in spite of everything, I, the Lord shall augment; yes, I mean that I shall make My Voice be heard through these Messages more and more; and the more men will abuse you and try to efface My Voice, the more will I be heard ♡ daughter, no one will stop Me from proceeding; I the Lord Jesus, shall help you, My Vassula; let this be Always in your mind; (I wept.) weep not... beloved, weep not... come ♡

53

trust Me ♡

Message for the world.   7. 2. 91

peace be with you ♡ I Am Jesus; I am the
Hope the world is looking for; this Hope
they are looking for is within their reach; they
have but to stretch their hands towards Heaven
and search Heavenly things, they could seek Me
and I shall respond to them; I am not hiding
My Face, nor am I turning My Eyes away from
them; My Eyes observe you all and survey all
your steps ♡ My Spirit indeed fills the whole
world to brighten this darkness and give Hope

54

to those who grope their way in this endless
night; beloved, with Heaven your homeland and
earth your pilgrimage all the more reason to
rejoice and to hope ♡ O creation, am I
to unveil your death shroud and not bring you
to life? or I, who bring to life, am I to send
you back to death? I am Mercy, I am Love;
look up in Heaven and see the Signs of the
Times; I am coming to gather nation after
nation and show My Holy Face to each one
of you and remind you of My Love;
but look, the beginning of sorrows has

55

started; the beginning of your birthpangs too.
you are witnesses, since you became believers, that
what you read in Scriptures is coming to reality:
the outpouring of My Spirit in these last
days of darkness is being poured out lavishly
upon mankind; you are witnesses to things
which were in riddles and said in parables
before; you are witnesses of Satan's cruelty,
but I promise you, little children, that soon after
your sorrows (which will aggravate) will come
Joy, and after your birthpangs, Love will
be born among you! but today I look with

56

dismay from above on this generation's crimes
which now have outdone the sins of Sodom
and Gomorrah, because your hopes are built on
a false Christ; this generation is vile, rebellious
and polluted with blood, and living under
Satan's shadow, O era! your fine and so-
called wisdom has indeed walled Me out because
your hearts pompous and filled with arrogance
consider to be the equal of Me your God;
"are you still going to say: I am a god, when
your murderers confront you?"* already blood
is   flowing in your streets; in your

Ezk. 28:9

57

wickedness you build up your hopes in all that is not Me; you have put your hopes on men, and not on Me, on riches that do not save you disregarding the Treasure I offer you in Heaven; you are building your expectations on mankind based on a lie, because you believe you can accomplish everything in your own human strength; indeed, you* have amassed great wealth in your busy trading, but tomorrow you shall die ♡ few are those who ask: "why is it that the Lord and His Mother descend suddenly upon us?" and only a

* God is referring this passage to the Freemasonery thinking.

58

remnant of My sacerdotal souls are concerned about Our regular manifestations; I have said, that I am going to send My Messenger to prepare a way for Me*; and this is exactly what My Mother who is your Mother too is doing; Scriptures are being fulfilled and I tell you solemnly, that the One whom My Abels and My Jacobs were longing for, will suddenly come, entering His Temple to extirpate the Cains and the Esaus who made havoc and ruin out of My Church ♡ you have industrialized My House, this House which should have been a House of prayer!

* Ml. 3:1

59

you have indeed, turned My House into a den of thieves! if I am as you* say: "the Holy One," then where is the honour you owe Me? if I am indeed, your Master, where is My respect? if I am your God, where is My adoration and My incense? where is My devotion? how is it that you cannot read the Signs of the Times? how is it that you cannot understand Heavenly things? how is it that you do not believe anymore in My Marvels? why are you persecuting My Abels and My Jacobs? if not openly, in secret? I appear as well as your Holy Mother, and We

* The Cains & Esaus

60

manifest Ourselves through souls, in many nations, but Our manifestations weary you, and even anger you; "how tiresome it all is" you say* for to this day you have not understood the Heavenly things like My Abels and Jacobs, no, you have neither understood My Love nor the devotion you owe My Mother; you call to faith and rely on your strength your authority and your reasoning; My Voice calling out today for repentance to the sinners disturbs your ears; when Righteousness suddenly shines out with healing in its rays, you refuse My Gift

* Ml. 1:13

61

which is offered today in your dark era; am I to accept your persecutions over and over again? am I to sacrifice year after year My Abels and My Jacobs who are the incense of My altars and the sturdy pillars of My Church? you have closed your ears to My Voice to listen only to your own; you have deprived many of eating the fruits of My New Vineyards because Satan has entered you and ambushed your spirit, and lo, others are atoning for your crimes;* others are atoning for your vanity and your

_____

* Suddenly Jesus' Voice became tender and sad

62

folly: _to save you_; everyday, these generous souls offer their cheek to you, to be struck, to be abased and afflicted, for your sake, these generous souls expiate with their own blood: _to save you_; I am waiting to hear you, but you are not saying what you ought to; _you do not repent_, but you go astray as you pursue your course dragging millions behind you; you go for seats and authority but not for conquering and saving souls, but you shall fall ... and this continuous apostasy shall cease ... and in you My Abels and My

63

Jacobs I shall rebuild My altars that once were, but that now lie in ruin; I shall make crystal-clear rivers flow out of you and your witnessing shall be fruitful because these waters will be coming out of My Source; and like trees of life growing by this Holy river, My children shall prosper from your witnessing; children, courage, I have not abandoned you, nor have I forgotten you; anyone who lives in Me will feel My Love, anyone who feeds from Me shall not be cut off to die, he who remains in Me shall live; I, the Bridegroom descend to

64

wed you in My Peace and Love and remind you that from the Beginning, you were Mine; I, the Lord bless you, leaving the Sigh of My Love on your foreheads; be one under My Holy Name ♡ ΙΧΘΥΣ ⊂≡◦

1

14.2.91

peace be with you; flower love Me; sanctity does not come in one day; abandon yourself entirely to Me, adore Me and love Me and I shall do the rest; do not sleep; soul, your sins are numerous, and so are the wounds you give Me; each time you sin it comes on Me, as a stroke, or a scourge, or a hole in My Body by a nail; why Vassula? why? I, who revealed to you My Holy Face, have I revealed to you My Face to be struck? and have I shown you the Wound of My Heart so you would pierce

2

it more? on earth there is no one to be found more wretched than you are! O what a wretch! do not go now, sit and hear what I have to say ♡ had it not been for My Infinite Mercy, the Father's Justice would have struck you and you would have withered instantly; have I taught you to sin? where are the offerings you owe Me? where are the sacrifices you promised Me, soul? why have you been neglecting Me? lent is here; lent will bring My Passion back to you, yet you are neither ready nor prepared; I

3

filled you with Celestial food to grow in My light and become a vessel of light, I made you Mine, and with everlasting Love I have risen you from the pit to become My bride in My Presence and the presence of My angels for ever, yet your eyelids heavy with sleep took the best out of you ♡ O My Vassula! if only you knew how I ♡ the Lord love you! I am thirsty for love; I know dear child that the times you are living in are evil but have I not made you discern good from evil? and now My Territory's soil is growing

4

coarse again; tell Me, was it by your efforts you saw the Light? No, I toiled *in you; to maintain you in My Light I poured on you grace after grace; I treated you not as your sins deserved, I treated you as I never ever treated a soul before; I gave Love for apathy; Tenderness for unholiness; Mercy for wretchedness; yes, I showed My Holy Face to sin; I treated you as I treat the jewels *2 of My Heart; I prayed for you to the Father, Vassula, so that He remembers My Sacrifice and thus spares you ♡ O God, I did not want to hurt

* God means, he worked in me. *2 jewels: perfect souls.

5

You nor anger You! I am constant in My
affection flower, and My Love for you is
everlasting; learn from Me; be constant;
come, I want you in My Presence, perfect!
I want your soul to be like a watered
garden filled with My Dew and exhaling a
delicate fragrance so that My Soul delights
in you; Vassula, are you willing to do My
Will?   I am willing to do Your Will, but
    I only seem to be doing the opposite, Lord...
I shall help you carry on My work; leave
everything in My Hands; O My child, subject

6

to sin, you are, but come to Me, shed those
scales from your eyes and behold who is standing in front of you ... I Am is face to face
with you! speaking and offering you in His
Hand, His Heart; do you want this Heart of
your God? take It,   I am offering It to you,
soul; stretch out your hands to receive My Heart;
I'm not worthy of Your Love Lord...
I know, but no one is worthy of My Love, and
this is how I come to you all today, I come to
you all with My Heart in My Hand; do not
say: I have sinned and refuse It; I tell you:

7

My Great Mercy has forgiven you, so come, come
and take this Heart which loves you; have
you not heard that My forbearance is long?
My Compassion is great; come, do not put
Me off day after day; from now on, daughter,
I want you to be faithful in your convictions
and sincere towards Me; concentrate on My Holy
Presence; I am never absent, it is you who
dim the light in your eyes from the accumula-
tion of your sins and the impurities your soul
absorbs every day to the point that you turn
blind; the light of your body is your eye,

8

when your eye is sound, your whole body too is
filled with light, but when it is diseased your
body too will be all darkness*, and in your
darkness, with the light of your eyes dimmed,
you cannot see Me, but I, I am never absent;
Vassula, today I have spoken to you plainly,
out of Love; since you are more apt to
rebellion and to sin, than what is holy, I
shall allow Myself to speak to you plainly
in My jealous Love; do not imagine that My
jealous Love can be easily put aside; oh no,
when I open My Mouth, it is for your

* Luke: 11:34

9

salvation that I speak, not for your condemnation; allow Me to reprove you out of My
Love, now and then ♡   ΙΧΘΥΣ ><>
                                            24. 2. 91

Before my journey to England, Scotland and Ireland.

My Vassula, take this passage as an introduction
for each of these countries (Jesus showed me John 10, 14-16)
tell them that it is I, the Lord, who sends
you to them ♡ the sheep that belong to Me
will listen to My Voice; I am coming to them
to lead many on what was an unknown
Path to them back to the Truth; I am coming
with a blazing Fire of Love to guide you, beloved ones,

10

back Home; My Sacred Heart is your resting
Place ♡ for you creation ... o what will I
not do! I am your Holy One, but your era
has recrucified Me; I am He who loves you most,
yet the One who receives unmerciful lashes
from the apathy of this era; I am the Light
of the world, who comes in this dark era to
give you the Light of Life; have My Peace,
My little children, I offer you My Peace,
I offer you the gift of My Love; come to
Me as you are, do not wait to be saints
to come to Me; come to Me as you are, do

11

not fear Me; I am the most Tender Father;
I can be your Holy Companion; I and you,
you and I, and I shall reveal to you My
Holy Face; I shall reveal to you the Holy
Face of your God; your eyes shall see Love
face to face, and when this happens, angered
demons shall take flight, and you will then
understand, beloved one, that from the beginning
you were Mine and I was yours for all eternity;
be one with Me; Love is at your door;
I, Jesus Christ, bless you ♡ ΙΧΘΥΣ ><>

12

                                            25, 2 90
Love seeks a return of Love ♡ (I suddenly
was thinking of the spelling and grammar mistakes
now and then in these texts, and what He had
said about it to another mystic who is dead now,
when she had the same problem.)

yes, you are obliging Me to reduce Myself to your
level of grammar to reach you, and your
limited knowledge of words, oh yes! you are
most imperfect as an instrument, (Jesus was
smiling) but I can use you even in your im-
perfection, little one; your Jesus has blessed
you over and over again, and one day, Vassula,
one day, I shall appear to you in My Light

13

and absorb you into My Light ... but now I
and you will continue as it is ♡ Praised
be the Lord! (Satan said: "Finally", as
it had taken me some time to write those praising
words. Immediately Jesus' Voice resounded telling
him: "Silence!" Satan wanted me to think it
was Jesus telling me "finally".
                                            26.2.91
Today I was thinking, if I could get a message
from St. Paul, or St. Peter, I wanted to penetrate
into mysteries and I asked the Lord for this response.
Lord?

I Am; listen flower, today My concern is your
redemption; why seek into My mysteries which
I am not willing to give you? sanctity is
My concern for you; repentance is what I seek

14

from you; daughter, understand what My
Interests are, understand what My concern is;
even when Lazarus had departed for four days
into My mysteries and had seen and understood
these mysteries, I had requested him on his
return to keep silent and keep those secrets for
himself; I did not want him to give away My
Riches to souls who would not make sense out
of them; wealth is to be converted, wealth is
to admit you are a sinner and come to Me
humbly, repenting, and lead a holy life following My Precepts; wealth is not to try and

15

decipher My mysteries, and if you try, this will
only lead you through winding ways leading
nowhere; so come to Me as a child and
allow My Hand to cultivate and enrich you
in this kind of Knowledge, let your wealth
be Me, let your Knowledge come through
My Word; let your interests be My Interests:
                    your perfection;
I love you, come; do not be impatient in
prayer; Love is near you; we, us Lord?
flower, yes!   ♡

16

                                            28.2.91
Lord You have been our Refuge age
after age. (Ps. 90:1) Lord?
I Am; lean on Me, beloved; rest in Me,
absorb Me; I am All you need; — come
we shall pray the Rosary ♡
                                    London 1.3.91
(Before the conference and prayer meeting with one day:)
O Yahweh, You are my God, blessed be Your
Name; You have carried out Your Plan and
brought me here, in this Land to witness and
give You Glory. Open my mouth in Your Assembly
to only glorify You.
I shall; I the Lord bless you; listen to Me:
prophesy to them ♡ rely on My massive Strength,
every achievement comes from Me and not from
you; — I set fire and water before every

17

soul and I let them choose; I shall never violate man's liberty, never ... I allow man to chose and I want them to know how I delight when they choose what is right; nevertheless, I shall always pursue the sinner to give up sinning; I shall always go in all directions to conquer him; and every time he falls I shall be there to lift him; I shall not push him away, or reprove him; his enemies might rejoice, but I, I will only have tears in My Eyes and I will ask him to thrust himself into My Arms, and if he

18

does I will then ask him if he would allow Me to inhabit him; if he accepts I shall then make out of his soul My Possession and in this Territory I shall pitch My Tent (in him) and from thereon I shall encircle My Property with My Love to make sure that no intruders will trespass into what I have just made Mine and forever ♡ happy the man who keeps house with ♡ Me, he shall gain Knowledge and enter into everlasting life ♡

Church of Holy Ghost-Balham, London 2. 3. 91
(Just before leaving for my first big meeting at
Holy Ghost Church.)   —   Lord ?

19

I Am, serve Me now My beloved; I shall be with you; victorious I shall be; do not fear little messenger, proclaim My Word in My Assembly; I am He who says to My souls: "come and eat this Celestial Food," let your interior desert bloom; I will bring back the exiles into their House: My Sacred Heart ♡

York   4. 3. 91
At All Saints Lower School. I was invited by fr. Ian Petit.
I Am; Love is near you; Love is Generous; remember My Presence and you shall not falter; daughter come and pray with Me to the Father:

20

Father,
though night still covers this earth,
I know that above me,
Yahweh,
who sees His children in darkness
will take pity on them;
with Power and Glory
He shall descend to dissipate this
menacing night into a bright day,
Peace and Love shall fill us,
and our soul will be filled with His Light,
I Am will be back,

21

I Am will return,
I Am will be with us,
Glory be to the Highest!
                                    Amen

(Later on, I came to the Lord wondering if I really had
to be sent out, like now, travelling to witness;
travelling every day by car, trains or by planes in
different places was not easy, but quite exhausting;)
— My Lord?

I Am; little one, every time you call Me, My
Heart leaps with joy; if only you understood
this My child ... you have asked Me if you
had to go out and witness like you do now;
yes, it is necessary, not that I need you,

22

but, Vassula, going out and witnessing in My
Name, glorifies Me and at the same time purifies
you; flower, I shall give you the strength
you need, the words you need; treat Me now
as a King deserves; treat Me as your Holy One
has to be treated; I Am is with you; come
My Child - Saved - by - Me, come; your step
must follow My Step, your foot where I had
My Foot, till the end of your mission ♡ we,
us? yes, forever linked ... so come to Me
as often as you can and I shall fill you everytime you come to Me; lend Me your ear My

23

child so that I may train your ear to hear
My Voice; satisfy Me My child and you will
prosper in Me; love is with you and blesses
you; (Later on again I went to the Lord.)
ah yes! you are back with Me; I shall elaborate
your talk tonight; I am He who shall clarify
many things; repeat after Me these words:
        "Jesus, touch My heart,
            You are my Delight,
                speak to me,
                    lead me,
                        and humble me," amen

24

delight Me and praise Me all the time; I love
you and because of that, I shall leave My Cross
on you; I Am He Who bore It till the end;
honour Me and glorify Me by bearing My Cross
now and then to rest Me, come ♡ IXΘΥΣ ⤳

                                    8. 3. 91

daughter, be in peace, I am Love; little one,
I am with you to help you sanctify your life,
I speak to every soul through these Messages and
through you ♡ I have fed you My Bread, I
have fostered you and made you Mine; have
I, in all this time, ever been harsh with you?

25

have I been punishing you? so, never doubt of
My Love; lean your head on Me and rest,
rest your mind on Me, think of no one else
but Me; I am He who loves you most; all I ask
from you is Love: love Me, adore Me, think
of Me; allow Me to be ever present in your
heart and mind; I awakened you from your
sleep so that you see My Beauty and that you
live with Me; every drop of My Blood made
you Mine; I payed for your soul by pouring
out My Precious Blood for your salvation;
every agony I suffered was with Love knowing

26

that My Sacrifice would save you; everything
I did was for your salvation; My daughter,
let all this be clear to you; I Am Love and
Love continues to save; I have not stopped
just there (on My Cross), I continue to call for
your salvation; I continue to pursue the sinner;
be prepared, therefore, because I shall soon come
to fetch you; I the Lord love all of you to
distraction; love Me, praise Me and be holy;
feel Me so that you may remember My Presence;
come ♡

27

— Scotland 9. 3. 91

I've been discussing with fr. McGinnity which prayer
is the most pleasing to the Lord. We were saying
that silence in contemplation was best. — Lord?

I Am; lean on Me I am your support and
strength; yes, indeed, My Vassula, Silence is
the most efficacious prayer of all; meet Me in
My Silence; let your spirit be drawn towards
Me and be absorbed in Me, in My Silence; allow
Me to invade you My child, allow Me to envelop
your soul in My Love; open up to Me and
let your God invade His Property; I Am owns
this Property; let I Am free to increase, let
I Am multiply His Virtues in you; do not fear

28

Me My child when I decrease you; I Am is
here to look after His Property and shine in you;
allow Me, soul, to encircle you with My Tenderness; you will be overwhelmed by My Beauty,
do not look at your nakedness, soul, and refuse
Me, come to Me in Silence and as you are;
abandon yourself to Me in Silence and you
shall live; be blessed, be blessed soul; let
nothing become My rival, Lord, let nothing
become or be Your rival! fast then on Fridays,
this is your due now to Me ♡ come;
(I had stopped fasting on Fridays because of my

29

schedules and travelling. I realized that in spite of my travelling I could easily fast but I had wanted it more "easy" on me, by pure laziness and weakness ...)

Belfast   10.3.91

(Just before the meeting at St. Brigid's Parish Hall

My Vassula, treat Me now as a King and glorify Me by serving Me; My Own will recognize My Voice, I will call them and they shall come;

Lord, my Strength, my Stronghold, my Refuge, my Light and Life, here I am, I'm coming to obey Your Will. Lord, I ask You to give me Your Strength to glorify Your Name again. Be PRESENT among us and open their hearts to receive Your Holy Spirit.

I shall be very PRESENT, daughter, My Holy Spirit shall be PRESENT; Justice will prevail

30

in this country, I the Lord shall place My Hand on this country and I shall make them feel My Presence*, those that have ears let them hear; go now My beloved, beside you I Am; ♡

Dublin   12.3.91

For the priests and nuns of Blackrock College.*² (p. 31)
My Lord, my Delight, my Everything, I love You to death. Lord?

I Am, lean on Me My child, I am the One who loves you most, ah Vassula! child of Mine allow Me to use your hand again to convey My Message to My children: a Message which I

* I saw in an interior vision, the Lord's Hand blessing all Ireland.

31

held in My Sacred Heart for them*² ♡ Peace be with you; I have come to your very doors; it is I, the Sacred Heart who speaks to you; I come to offer you My Heart; today I am coming to you in this special way to remind you of My Ways; I am coming to you because you are poor and although you do not have much, you still have your sight, for the Grace of your Father in Heaven is upon you ♡ —*¹ but My Soul is grieving beyond your understanding to see from above dissensions like never before in the Heart of My

*² It seemed as if Jesus was waiting for this hour for quite some-time.
* Then Jesus speaks to them of His Church.

32

Sanctuary; My Body is bleeding and My Heart is one big Wound; the shepherd's staff which I had given them whole, lies now broken in splinters; but I mean to visit you soon to put together the shepherd's staff I had left behind Me; therefore, beloved ones, you who have received this Grace, pray for those who still do not know their left hand from their right, pray as never before that they too may receive this Grace before the day of Puri-fication; I am telling you that soon, very soon, Love shall be with you as Love; pray that all may be ready and converted so that

33

no one will be drawn in darkness and the shadow of death for all eternity; mindful of My Mercy I come to warn your generation and out of love I come to call you by the Power of My Holy Spirit of Grace back to your senses; Love is seeking a return of Love; this is My Theme ♡

18.3.91

(Message of our Holy Mother.)

My Vassula, here is My Message ♡ have My Peace; children of My Heart, God is in your midst and His Kingdom is near you, if you have eyes you will see it; dearest children, listen to God's Voice

34

in these days of lent, listen to God's Voice by diminishing yourselves so that God can augment in you, efface yourselves so that His Spirit would be seen in you; die to yourselves so that God may live in you; be nothing so that He may be Everything; allow Him in this way to take full possession of you and make out of you His Property; so I am telling you children of My Heart: so long as you struggle to become something, the Spirit of Holiness that wants to live in you is choked by your rivalry; do not let your spirit become a rival to God; diminish so that He augments,

35

allow His Spirit to form you in this way into the way of Sanctity; bear in your minds that humility, docility and self-effacement are the key virtues pleasing God and with these you become poor in spirit and thus blameless; dearest children, Jesus was humble even to accept death; never be the one who says: "I have everything and I know everything and I do not need anyone's advice"; stay poor, be poor, so that in your poverty God may reign in you and be King; allow no conceit to overtake you; My prayers are that your holiness augments in Him who created you and that your

36

love for each other increases and overflows to purify this world of its wickedness and its apostasy; never stop praying your rosary; come with joy to pray the rosary; the rich man will not reply, but the poor man will come to Me with his rosary and in his poverty I shall listen to him while he prays this simple prayer; for all that is poor and simple is deadly to Satan, who is Vanity Itself; this is one of the main reasons why Satan hates the rosary; Satan is powerful and today he is sifting you all like wheat, because this is his hour; this is the reign

37

of darkness; remain faithful to the House of God and keep the Traditions that have been taught to you and listen to My beloved and blessed Vicar of My Son; every priest has been given the grace by God to act and represent My Son, and so I pray for those who are not yet submitting humbly to the Vicar of the Church, to submit and be willing; Jesus is Faithful and True; imitate your God, He who is Perfection ♡ be perfect by imitating Him in His Humility, His Submissiveness, His Obedience, His Docility, so that you too may receive the

38

greater gifts of Suffering and Mortification, all of which will lead you to sanctity and into His Sacred Heart: <u>your Abode</u> ♡ My priests, be like a field that ♡ has been well watered by frequent rains so that Jesus' lambs are attracted by its green pastures and may have something to feed upon; no lamb is attracted to graze on thistles and brambles; allow Me to rebuild your temples and make them pleasing to God; happy the ears that hear and understand what I say, for I tell you, not everyone's name has been written down in the book of

39

life of the Sacrificial Lamb ♡ so pray for those who do not seem to understand nor are willing to open, that they too may be given God's Grace, to hear with their ears, understand with their heart and thus be converted and see God's Glory ♡ I bless you My dearest children, every one of you ♡ I love you;

20.3.91

I, Yahweh, am your Father, come, you will accomplish your work by My side, daughter; I shall reinforce you every day because this will be necessary for My Work that will go over the whole world;

40

I have lit your lamp so that you see, My child; I have chosen you to teach you from My Hall; from My Own Mouth you have received My Word; keep My Teachings as the apple of your eye; yes my Lord and God. even now in your nothingness, <u>I who am Everything shall expand</u> and like mist that creeps everywhere I intend to envelope all My creation in Me, from the stranger to My best friend, for My Jealousy* has bypassed My wanting to check it; I have created you for one purpose: <u>I have created you out of Love to love Me</u>; when body and flesh are

* Jealous Love

41

going to be consumed and wear out, he who was pleasing to Me shall be drawn into My Soul for ever and ever; but alas for him who did not fear Me! alas for him who never saw wickedness as folly and foolishness as madness! alas for the heart who believed that he could reach the zenith of his strength by his own efforts and without Me! alas for him who has not obeyed My Commandments! alas for who's heart is filled with malice! alas for the jackal that plotted by night! alas for him who judged his brother and caused him to live in terror! alas for the lips that bore false-

42

witness! alas for those who shed innocent blood of unborn infants! your compensation shall be hell! alas for the impure who receive My Son's Flesh and Blood in a state of sin, how abhorrent you are to Me! alas for him who offend Me by re-fusing confession and absolution and come to receive My Son, guilty! repent! repent for your sins! what good is your offering to Me when you have a serpent coiled inside you? if you ask Me: "what must we do then to gain eternal Life?" I tell you: repent! follow My Commandments, produce the appropriate fruits, and I, in the

43

presence of My angels I shall offer you the room I have reserved for you, watch and be on your guard against all these things; allow Me in your wilderness to manifest My Spirit as I please and when I please and upon whom I please : to save you ♡

Correct us Yahweh, all loving Father, gently and with mercy but rapidly too!

love Me, adore Me and place Me as first and above all ... Teach us to love You without anymore offending You. I am desperate without You O Abba!

My Eyes are upon you, My child, constantly, and

44

My Spirit shall invade you more than ever to leave nothing of you, "I Am All and I can fill you with My Light; Oh creation! I am Loyal and Gentle, leave Me free o creation and with most loving affection I shall fill your spirit with divinity out of My Spirit; leave Me free to annihilate your lethargy which led you into this great apostasy and the ruin of your soul; allow Me to fill you with My Fire to become loyal and fervent servants of Mine; let Me transform you to become the delight of My Soul, I Am

45

whom I Am is with you ♡ be blessed and
have My Peace, you who read Me;

24.3.91

Let every creature do Your Will, my Lord.
daughter, the thing I want most out of you
is love; I want you to love Me, love Me,
love Me; praise Me and feel My Presence; this
is what I request of you My Vassula; Lord,
teach us to love You as You want, Teach us to
love one another. We need Your help because
we cannot love by ourselves unless You give us
the grace to love.
I shall teach you by Grace * I shall teach you
as I am teaching you the Knowledge of your

* Jesus smiled showing His dimples.

46

fathers; I shall supply you all with what you
need most: spiritual food; I shall infuse in
you all, love and holiness; I shall not delay
My Promise, soon all that I have been telling
you is going to happen and he * who crushed
you all these years will lose his grip ♡
I will sow love everywhere! there will be no
more stumbling in the night; come daughter,
we, us? Yes my Lord. so love Me, do not
fear Me, love Me, do not neglect Me, love Me,
do not forget Me, this is all I ask from
you soul ♡ IXΘΥΣ ⊱⧕

* Satan ♡

47

25.3.91

Lord, this week is the Holy Easter week for the
Rom. Catholics and next week is the Holy Easter
week for the Orthodox. I feel it is not right to
have different dates and to be differentiating ourselves in You to the point that one hears remarks
as: their Jesus is not our Jesus!

I love you all the same, but many of you do
not seem to understand this ♡ wretched you are
all; sinners you are all; frail you are all, but
all of you are My offspring; see Vassula? have
I made any difference? I have come to you
and showed you My Sacred Heart; * I went in all
directions seeking by what means I could make you
Mine, I showered blessing upon blessing on you

* Jesus means that He has come to a Greek orthodox and
not to a Catholic and speaks to me in Catholic terminology.

48

to raise you from death and form you since you
lacked Wisdom; I courted you and in My Tenderness
I Myself have chosen you to become a witness to
a people not your own and of whom many are
far from understanding why Wisdom has chosen
a foreigner among them ♡ I, the Sacred Heart
am determined to show them that I have taken
you, a foreigner to them, to share the Riches of
My Sacred Heart, and share its delights and
sorrows; yes, I have come to teach foreigners too
of My Sacred Heart's Riches, today I have
made a new song for them for I am one

49

and the same! so pupil, continue not to differentiate yourself under My Name, even if you are
whirled away by the breath of My enemies I
shall not leave you defenceless; I shall always
come to your rescue My child; if they challenge*
you do not respond, I shall respond in your
place ♡ Scripture says: God does not have
favourites, but that anybody of any nationality
who fears God and does what is right is acceptable to Him; (Acts : 10 : 34-35) but men have
divided themselves, they have segregated themselves

* from laity to priest and bishops (Rom. Cath.). Some
say I should change to prove myself as authentic by become
a Rom. Catholic.

50

under My Holiness, but wait and you shall see,
My Holy Spirit (to the great astonishment of
many), shall be poured on the pagans too; I
tell you solemnly, these things shall take place
before this generation shall pass away; so courage
My child, do not be afraid; I shall unite you
all in the end ... and the viper shall not
be allowed to throw his venom in your food
anymore, generation; your food shall be whole
and pure; sorrow and lament will be ended;
I love you and My people shall bear My Holy
Name* in one in this unity;

* Just christians, under Christ.

51

Oh that You would tear the Heavens open and
come down! At Your Presence not only the
mountains would melt as the prophet Isaiah
said*, but the three iron bars You made me
draw, representing the Rom. Catholics, the Orthodox
and the Protestants.

I promise you : I shall not leave My Church
divided for long; I Myself shall come upon Her
with full force and rebuild Her; have confidence
in Me, My beloved one; I shall not put up
with this faithless generation anymore, after all
the Father's wrath cannot be withheld any longer;
this is why My Graces upon you will be multiplying: to save you ♡ Vassula, the earth

* Is. 63 : 19

52

has not yet enjoyed My Peace fully, like a dry
soil it thirsts for this Peace I bequeathed to all
of you and I, like a watercourse running into a
garden, I shall come down to irrigate you, and
you My child, rejoice! for I have taken root in
you and made My Home in you; and in you
I shall grow, if you allow Me; pray now
with Me, My child, to the Father, repeat
after Me this prayer :

Father,
blessed be Your Name,
since Your Beloved Son Jesus Christ

53

came to the world,
not to condemn it,
but to save the world,
have Mercy upon us,
look at Your Son's Holy Wounds,
that are wide open now and
remember the price He has payed for us,
to redeem all of us,
remember His Sacred Wounds,
and the two Hearts
You Yourself united in Love
and who suffered together,

54

this One of the Immaculate Conception
and Your Beloved Son,
O Father,
remember His Promise now
and send us the Advocate,
in full force,
the Holy Spirit of Truth, to remind
the world of the Truth
and of Your Son's docility,
humbleness, obedience and great Love,
Father,
the time has come,

55

when the reign of division cries out
for Peace and Unity,
the time has come
that Your Son's wounded Body
cries out for Righteousness,
that of which the world has not
known yet,
but through the Immaculate Heart
of Mary,
and the Sacred Heart of Jesus,
give us,
Precious Father,

56

this Peace in our hearts,
and fulfill the Scriptures
by fulfilling
Your Beloved Son's Prayer to You:
that we may all be one,
one in the Divine Holy Trinity,
so that we worship and praise You
all, around one single Tabernacle ♡
Amen
My daughter, love Me as I love you, love one
another as I love you ♡ be blessed, come ♡

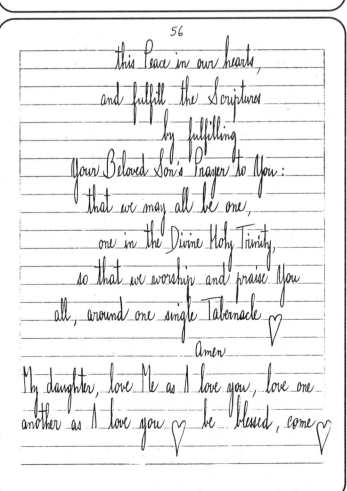

57

8.4.91

My Lord? I Am; little one Peace be with you, love Me and cling to Me, for you have not seen the last of Me*¹ I'm pleased and relieved! I shall not allow your strength to crumble, I shall give you My Food as I always did.; flower, My Message this time is a prayer for all nations a prayer for unity, come, write: "Praised be the Lord, for the Celestial Food*² you are giving us, and this is to fulfil Scriptures and to complete Your Work, You have given Your Knowledge to mere children and not to the learned, for this is what pleases You Lord;

*¹ Jesus means in this way, interiorly, and hearing Him in locutions. *² Spiritual Food

58

Praised be the Lord, to have laid open roads so that your people walk in them and come to You and fill Your House, for though You have sent Your Son into the world and the world plainly saw the Light, they have not all accepted the Light but turned instead towards darkness, falling in apostasy; the world has apostatized because they have refused the Truth and preferred to live under a Lie; yes, Lord, You so much love the world that You are to-day, in spite of our wickedness, sending us without reserve Your Holy Spirit to enliven us and

59

revive the world, renewing every creature, so that everyone sees Your Glory and believes and thus be converted; Praised be the Lord, for opening the doors of Heaven to pour out from Your Reserves this Hidden Manna*¹ reserved for our Times; no, it was not Moses who gave bread from Heaven, it was You, Father, who fed the true bread, and as Your Son, Jesus Christ, is the Bread of Life, the Holy Spirit too nourishes us, for all Bread that descends from Heaven is Life; it is written in Scriptures: they will all be taught by God*², and flesh and bone cannot

*¹ Ap. 2:17   *² Is. 54:13

60

reveal the Truth unless the Truth is given by the very One who established the Truth and imprinted It into our hearts ♡ Father, may Your Name be praised always and glorified again; let the world pass from Darkness to Light, from Lie to the complete Truth, from Lethargy to Fervour; Father, Creator of Heaven and Earth, the hour has come to show us the New Heavens and the New Earth where Your Holy Spirit will make His Home in us; most Tender Father, as You glorified Your Son and Your Son glorified You, let Your Holy Spirit of Truth

61

glorify again Your Son; in a short time, Father, according to Scriptures, the first heaven and the first earth shall disappear soon, to prove to the world that Your Word is something alive and active and that Jesus has indeed conquered the world ♡ when that day comes, Your Son's prayer to You will be also fulfilled, for we shall all be one in You as the Holy Trinity is One and the same; we shall not differentiate ourselves under Your Name anymore; Praised be the Lord and Glory to the Highest for sending us, in our

62

great apostasy Our Holy Mother, whose Heart You Yourself united ... in love with Jesus' and who suffered together; and it is together again, that the two Sacred Hearts will renew us and bring us back to life and in You; lost sheep will be found, wandering lambs shall be reminded of their true fold and their True Shepherd, this Shepherd who neither deserts his flock nor abandons the lost, but heals the wounded and supports the weary; Praised be the Lord ... in Whose Holy Spirit we receive baptism, indeed, fountains of living water

63

flow out and are given to the man who is thirsty, since they flow out freely from Your Holy Sanctuary*, this Sanctuary which You raised in three days, and from Your fulness we are receiving in these last days the Graces of Your Holy Spirit, to revive us, for this is Your Manna from Heaven, the Spiritual Food coming from the Spirit; let your people, Father, realize that the ban soon will be lifted and that the Lamb's and Your Throne will soon be in Its place and among us; prepare us, therefore, Righteous Father, for

* Jesus' Chest (Body)

64

this Glorious Day, when we can praise You and glorify You all around one Holy Tabernacle ♡ Father, I thank You for hearing my prayer and for having given me Your Words to indicate to the world "the Riches of Your Sacred Heart ♡ Amen" come now daughter, come now, ♡ little friend, do not stop loving Me; words of encouragement you will always hear from Me; so be confident and trust Me;

α☧ω

1

13. 4 . 91

Lord, our division, and I am now only talking the division between Orthodox and Catholics, is a real scandal! How is it possible that we, Christians, continue to be divided and not only a temporary division but a division that lasts, with deep roots, founded on conflicts that are so absurd! Each one being a rival to the other and some of us still holding anger and hatred, how is it possible to speak with integrity when an old quarrel is still unresolved in our hearts? Can we really face You and say that we are reconciled with our brothers and we can come to You with good conscience to offer You our offerings on Your altar? No, we cannot as long as we live, under Your Holy Name and are not reconciled we cannot claim to come to You with a clean conscience. Yet, we all know that Your greatest wish, dear Christ, is UNITY and yet we hold firmly on the barriers that separate us and we do not seem honest enough to say: "we are not inclined to bend since it is we who hold the real Faith and the Truth." Have we not understood how much more Beautiful Your Bride would look if

2

we unite? How much more Powerful the Church can become? How much more progress She can make? How many more Fruits She could produce? Now She's like stagnant. Can we honestly say She's progressing and earning souls in Her when we see daily in front of our eyes, soul after soul leaving Your Bride for a second-rate philosophy, yes, esoteric sects, like New Age, Jehova's Witnesses and others. Yet these people, I feel, are in search of You, so help them to find You ...

Ah, My dove, I have not been teaching you in vain ... they have not yet understood that I need their heart to unite them; I need their heart to rebuild inside it My Church into One; unity will be by the heart; look, I have commissioned you to bear witness to a people not

3

your own, but many of your own have not yet understood why Wisdom sent you to foreigners, your people believe that you have been yielding to foreigners, they have not realized that it is I, the Lord, who united your heart to theirs, double indeed is your cross on you My child, since you are whirled away too by some of the foreigners who challenge you without cease to become one of them; by remaining as you are I am teaching to both of them a lesson of how you should unite and what unity will be like; unity is not to differentiate yourselves under

4

My Holy Name, unity is to share Holy Communion and believe in My real Presence in the Holy Eucharist ♡ unity, My child, is to give to each other your riches;   " Lord, teach us, when we judge, to reflect on Your Kindness and when we are judged, to look for mercy." Wisdom 12:22

ah, My child, your race is not finished yet, but remember, in front of you I am, and at your side your Mother, to encourage you, and at your heels your guardian angel to protect you; hear Me, among brothers the leader of them deserves honour, so honour My Peter, this is only a

5

reminder of the Most High ♡ *Now I know that*
I shall never be deserted; You have directed my
soul towards You; I have stretched out my hands
to Heaven and You have lifted me; my soul
rejoices in You, oh that You do to my brothers too
what You have done to me!

not only will I lift into My Heart your brothers,
daughter, but even people who do not know Me
I will lift into My Heart; hence Mercy and
Grace shall come even to the heathens, for they
too are part of My creation ♡ daughter, I am
known to help the poor and the wretched ...
come now and caress Me again with your
gentle words that come out from your heart,

6

repeat them to Me ♡

Lord Jesus, use me to dry Your Tears,
Lord Jesus, use me to wipe Your Tears,
Sacred Heart, use me to console Your Heart,
Sacred Heart, use me to pluck the thorns
    encircling Your Head and Your Heart,
Lord Jesus, use me as Your Head-rest,
Sweet and Gentle Jesus, use me in every way
    to please You and console You;
    My desire is to bring to Your Lips a smile.

then I shall use you if you offer Me your
will too ♡ — *I offer You, Jesus, my will, my heart,*
my soul, my spirit, my body, everything.
Love then shall do His Will in you, and My
Peace shall reign in your heart, and My Image
shall reflect in your soul, and your spirit shall

7

worship Me in accordance with My Spirit, and
your body will reject all that is not holy since
I shall transfigure it and perfect it into My
Glorious Body, to become an altar for Me, your
God; you shall share My sufferings but also
My joy; I shall continue teaching you so that
you will bear witness not only to a crucified
Christ but also to a resurrected and victorious
Christ ♡ I shall remind everyone that wonders,
miracles and signs are also part of Me ♡
come, then ♡ αᛉω

8

10.4.91
Love loves you, love Me; without trials you
will not grow; My affection for you is manifest,
this is why Satan hates you all the more;
even if you feel you are under a constant threat
from My enemy, I am near you to support you,
realize that I have made *you* to be a
threat to him; anyone who snatches souls from
him is a threat to him, this is one of the
reasons why he never loses any occasion to aim
at you; very often he uses people for his purpose,
out of nothing at all he can produce an act
of accusation to utterly ruin the one he wants to

9

strike; but this is not all; one of his most malicious acts is to suggest in the sleeping soul all sorts of ideas that lead the soul into an agitation and a total unrest, wrenching out all peace within that soul; this is why you must stay awake, do not let him find you sleeping ♡

                                                                14. 4. 91
"Blessed be Yahweh, who performs marvels of love for me." Ps. 31 : 21

peace be with you; now, tell Me, pupil: are you happy to have Me as your Spiritual Director?

Yes Lord, more than happy... I am learning many things directly from Your Mouth, and others too!

10

would you like to write? I am ready to serve You my God, make me ready and open my ear to hear only Your Voice;

hear Me then:

- blessed are those who work for Peace, they shall prosper in My Peace and radiate My Sight for - ever and ever;
- blessed are the compassionate, they shall see Mercy in the Day of Judgment;
- blessed are the generous souls who share My Cup, they will be called heirs of My Salvation;
- blessed are those who espouse themselves to Me,

11

this same joy I feel as a Bridegroom, they too shall feel, the day they meet Me face to face;
- blessed are you who have not accepted any other testimony but the One and only Truth, I Myself have given you; I tell you: Come! come into My Kingdom and share everything I have with Me;
- blessed are those who do not differentiate themselves under My Holy Name, but show their unity through their humility and love; they shall be called Pillars and Foundation of God's Sanctuary;
- blessed are you, who believe without seeing,

12

rejoice for the Grace you received from My Father and pray for those who have not yet received this Grace;
- blessed are you who accept to be scourged, humiliated and nailed with Me to the Cross, and who bear the marks of My Body on yours; your room in Heaven will be opened to receive you and your compensation will be great;
- blessed are those who keep My Name Holy, when they call and ask in My Name, I shall listen;
- blessed are the small ones who praise and adore Me, in them I shall do great things;

13

- blessed are the faithful, who observe My Commandments and from Scriptures do not change
one stroke from what has been written, theirs
is the Kingdom of Heaven;
- blessed are you, My lambs who are chased like
game, for My sake, by ravenous wolves, because
I shared your meal side by side with you;
I tell you, all your sufferings are not in vain;
the Father sees all this and takes accounts of
everyone's deeds; it will not go as hard on
Sodom and Gomorrah as it will go on them
for having persecuted My Holy Spirit;

14

so stay awake, because no one knows the day
nor the hour of My coming; your King will
be coming soon; the One you have been waiting
for so long shall suddenly come upon you; so
courage, beloved ones; indeed, the devil's smoke
has penetrated into My Sanctuary, but what smoke
lasts forever? I shall, with the Breath of My
Holy Spirit, dissipate and blow away this smoke
and no authority nor any power from beneath will
be able to intervene ♡ I am coming to bring
Fire to the earth ♡ and purify nation after
nation ♡ be blessed; ΙΧΘΥΣ ⤳

15

15. 4. 91

Lord, come to us in full force with Your Holy
Spirit. For, most tender Abba, as You glorified
Your Son and Your Son glorified You, the hour
has come that Your Holy Spirit of Truth glorifies
Your Son. Prove to the world that Your Word is
something alive and active and not just printed
words on paper. Let Your Holy Spirit "turn the hearts
of fathers towards their children and the hearts of
children towards their fathers". Ml 3:24

peace be with you, Vassula, Scriptures never lie;
it has been said that in the last days to come,
people will keep up the outward appearance of
religion but will have rejected the inner power
of it;* ah! my beloved, will there be any faith
left on My Return? ...
the inner power of My Church is My Holy Spirit

* 2 Tm 3:5

16 -

in it, alive and active; like a heart in a body,
My Holy Spirit is the Heart of My Body which
is the Church;
- the inner power of My Church is My Holy Spirit
who gives freely and distributes its gifts and its
graces, so that the Church gets some benefit;
- the inner power of My Church is My Holy Spirit,
the Reminder of My Word, revealing nothing new,
but the same instructions given by the same Spirit;
- the inner power of My Church is My Holy Spirit,
that transfigures, uplifts and turns you into
real copies of Myself;

17

- the inner power of My Church is My Holy Spirit this Fire which enlivens you, purifies you and makes out of your spirit columns of fire, ardent braziers of love, living torches of light, to proclaim without fear My Word, becoming witnesses of the Most High and teaching others to look only for Heavenly things ♡

- the inner power of My Church is ♡ My Holy Spirit, the Life and the Breath that keeps you alive and makes your spirit desire Me, calling Me: Abba; if you refuse, My child, and suppress the gifts of My Holy Spirit, what services will you be able

18

to do and offer Me? do not be like corpses that keep up the outward appearance of religion but reject the inner power of it, with futile speculations thus limiting Me in My Divinity; do not stop those who come, as children, to Me, living a life of devotion to the Holy Spirit; it is I, who calls them to the wedding of My Holy Spirit; the secret of holiness is: devotion to Me your God, and you can do nothing of yourselves, unless My Spirit living in you guides you and teaches you Heavenly things; I tell you truly, whoever fears Me will accept My correction; so do not sleep

19

now, for these are the Times when one should be awake and vigilant, more than ever; these are the Times to open your ears and listen to My Spirit and not disregard it; do not play the sage at the wrong moment by pushing the Breath of My Holy Spirit aside and suppressing the inner power that activates My Church; you want to be prudent? open your eyes then; you want to be prudent? open your heart and your ears, My friend, not your mind; a prudent person never scorns a warning from the Spirit, only the proud do not know anything about fear;

20

the fear of the Lord is the beginning of Wisdom; you want to be prudent? look for the Truth that desperately leans over your misery to save you! look Who is bending towards your wretchedness and your wickedness to pull you to Him and lift you from your graves to breathe life into you again! O come! do not misunderstand Me, I am not forcing you nor am I trying to violate your liberty! I have taken pity on your generation; do not say that all I had to say has been said; why limit Me as yourself? I am the Reminder of My Word, yes, the inner power of

21

My Church and I am free to send you new portents and do fresh wonders; I am free to raise your generation and pour healing ointment on you from the Riches of My Sacred Heart, when I wish and on whom I wish; I am building, yes, re-building My Church that lies now in ruin, so do not let Me face you, generation, in the Day of Judgement and be obliged to tell you: you, you were one of My persecutors who pulled down while I used to build; Mercy is at your doors now and My Compassion knocks on your doors in your times of tribulations; you say yourselves

22

holy? prove yourselves holy by showing Me your adoration to Me; prove yourselves holy by showing Me the souls you are converting and bringing to Me, for My Kingdom consists not in spoken words, nor of an outward appearance of religion, but an Inner Power that only I can give you through My Holy Spirit, if you seek it; feel My Presence and My Love I have for each one of you; I, Jesus Christ, am present and bless you all out of the depths of My Sacred Heart, leaving My Sigh of Love on your forehead; be one; ecclesia shall revive ♡ ⳨ΙΧΘΥΣ

23

20. 4. 91

Lord, I thank You for making me Your Property and Your bride, teach those who do not understand that You do allow Your persecutors to attack me, because You can also be glorified in this way too. And You made it very clear that You will never allow them to hunt or touch my soul. Make them understand the difference, for a difference there is.

flower, My Cup tastes bitter, but do you still want to share It with Me? I want to share Your Cup with You. yes, prove your love for Me by offering your will, be eager to glorify Me, your God, by embracing My Cross; you have become My Property in which I draw My delights out of you; you have entrusted your life into My Hands; daughter listen: stay weak for in

24

your weakness I can do great things; be nothing for in your nothingness I can be Everything; stay silent and in this silence I shall find My repose; stay pliant so that I may shape you into a copy of My crucifix; stay limited, so that My Power will be seen in you; become a model of Myself by being docile, patient, pure, obedient, humble, faithful and in constant prayer, like I was with the Father; never sleep; never cut the bonds you have with the Father; My life on earth was an incessant prayer with the Father, at favourable and un-

25

favourable times; listen to the Father and do His Will, your food is given by Me, your Redeemer, all that you eat comes from Me to teach you to live the only True life in Me your God. I tell you truly, do not be afraid of those who kill the body but cannot kill the soul; fear him rather who can destroy both body and soul in hell;* remain in Me and I in you; I shall allow your mortal nature to be put to the test, so that you grow in your trials, but your soul shall not be touched; flesh and blood cannot inherit My

* Mt 10:28

26

Kingdom, so do not fear, through your trials I am glorified too ♡ abandoned you shall never be ♡

♡   ΙΧΘΥΣ ⟩═⟨

For Canada St-Georges 23.4.91

I come in your country to leave you a sign of My Great Love; I come, I your King, like a beggar, in rags, and bare-foot, to ask you to make peace with Me and ask you a little bit of your love. out of My Boundless Mercy, I bend all the way to you to take you out of your lethargy and your darkness so that you may taste My

27

Great love for you ♡

Chateauguay 24.4.91
Canada

please Me, daughter, and glorify Me; Help me Lord to proclaim Your Message of Love. I shall take over completely, so do not worry; I will be standing by you, so come ♡

25.4.91
Before the meeting I prayed again for the Lord to help me.

My Vassula, can I ever demand from you something beyond your capacity? daughter, the fulfilment of My Law is Love; Love is the Root of My Law and the other commandments cannot stand if love is not there; created

28

you are to glorify Me; listen, My Spirit shall invade you;*' give to Me the families of this nation; give Me, flower, the glory due to Me now; tell them:*² I am your Redeemer and I come not to condemn anyone, but to save with saving justice, so call on My Name, beloved children, Jesus means He Who Saves; I am at your very doors beloved ones; I bless all of you ♡

Message to someone   2.5.91

peace be with you; the coming of My reign on earth is at hand and My Will shall be

*' for the meeting *2 The Canadians at Chateauguay

29

done on earth as it is in Heaven* and in your hearts I shall rebuild the unity of My Church, I shall not wait any longer for human approval and My Bride shall once more be vested in glittering Glory; the ban of division shall be lifted and the Woman clothed in splendour in the sun, whom I am sending before Me to educate you will encourage you; I have given Her the power over every race and every land to open a broad pathway for Me ♡ the smoke that penetrated into the

* Jesus in saying this was looking up in Heaven. He said it very majestically.

30

heart of My Sanctuary, staining Chalice, Tabernacle and all that is holy shall dissipate with one blow of My Breath; the nations then shall speak one language and all of them shall worship Me around One Single Tabernacle, this One of the Sacrificial Lamb, this One of the Perpetual Sacrifice that My enemies are trying to abolish and replace by their disastrous abomination, very soon now, My friend, I shall be with you all again; and My priestly prayer to the Father shall be fulfilled: you shall be one like Us,

31

in the Holy Trinity; I still have hidden in My Sacred Heart, many things to divulge to you and show you, for the Treasures I have within Me are innumerable, but they would be too much for you to take now,* your soul will not be able to take in everything, but little by little I shall unfold to you the Treasures of My Sacred Heart and step by step I shall guide you into what looks like a Light-House: a Mystery of Unfathomable Riches that have been hidden for generations and centuries; I shall reveal to you, My

* Jesus was speaking with humor.

32

friend, the rich glory of Hope, Wisdom and Knowledge; be rooted in Me and you shall bear fruit; remain in Me and you shall live; I have told you, My friend, all this so that when trials come, you may not falter; Love is by your side ♡ Love Me ♡

3.5.91

Lord, drench me with Your Holy Spirit; come and invade me with Your Holy Spirit, so that the enemy finds no space within me, let Your Holy Spirit subside in the very depths of my soul to water it and load it with riches, these of which are not of the world. Blessed be God.

I Am is with you; have My Peace, I went

33

down into your room and befriended you; I
was then a stranger to you, but see? My Teachings lifted you in My Heart and today I have
turned your aridity into a fertile soil; My dove,
I delight in you, My little one, I live in you;
My head-rest I repose in you; glorify Me now
and restore My House; glorify your Father who
is in Heaven by treating Him as a King; ah,
My daughter, My Mouth is dry for lack of
love, I thirst for lack of love, dress My Wounds
with your love; pluck My thorns and console
Me, praise Me all the time from your heart,

34

speak to Me and do not wait until tomorrow,
delight Me and stay small; allow Me My
Vassula to use your little hand, offer Me your
time and I shall saturate you with My Fountain, and the Treasures I shall give you can
never be assessed, no man can fathom their
magnificence; I, the Lord, shall make Myself a
Throne in you to govern you; and I shall
allow Myself, since you have given Me your consent, to follow the passions of My Heart, I
am in My Domain and I have full authority over you now; praise Me often and bless

35

Me; Love is with you IXΘΥΣ 〜▷
6.5.91

Lord, my God, who could bring us salvation, but You? who could bring us back
home, but You? who could bring us happiness but You? Then: Maranatha!

daughter, the dead cannot praise Me, this
is why I shall descend with full force upon
you and raise you all to remind you of
My greatness, My splendour and My sovereignty;
come, write My Vassula: peace be with you;
My sons and daughters ♡ I have counted
My sheep and My Heart♡ is crushed with
sorrow, only a remnant are left today who

36

have not been raided by Apostasy; only a
handful have not lost their faith; only a
few are left who survived the perils of Rationalism, and I, from above have strained My
Eyes waiting for you to offer your heart and
your abandonment, but this generation's heart
is gross with foolishness; yet, even if you have
not observed My Law of Love but have turned
away your hearts and made your own law
and statutes, I shall not stand by and see
you stray more and more from My Commandments, I mean to rescue you, generation,

37

I mean to school you back to your senses and guide you with great love back into the path of Righteousness; I shall teach you to invoke My Name, I shall teach you to walk in My Presence, I shall teach you to live a life of prayer My child, I shall teach you to love Me with all your soul, I shall unbind your death's cords that bind your soul to all that My Soul abhors if you give Me your will, My child; look, look around you, My Holy Spirit comes to meet you and revive you all, dressed as a beggar with Tears of Blood streaming

38

down My Cheeks; I descend from My Throne leaning all the way to you to save your soul from disaster and from famine; for the sake of My Holy Name I shall demonstrate Myself through these very things you do not believe anymore; I shall demonstrate My Holy Spirit through marvels, through miracles; I shall demonstrate My Power through weakness and wretchedness as never before; I shall come with thousands of myriads of angels to pour on you, generation, My Celestial Manna, this hidden Manna* and fill your mouth with

* Ap. 2:17

39

My Food so that your mouth proclaims My Glory; Apostasy challenged My Mercy and Rationalism, this plague of your era, challenged My Power; I am sending, before Me, to educate you, the Woman clothed with the Sun, the second Eve, to school you and lead you step by step into Heaven; I am sending you My Holy Spirit in this Night to be your Companion and Consoler and remind you of My Word; I am sending you a mission of angels of hope to expel your fears; come and listen all you who

40

are starved; happy the man I invite to the Wedding of My Holy Spirit, he shall be filled with My Celestial Food and though their faults overpower them, My Holy Spirit shall blot them out in His rest in them ♡ understand, My beloved, that My visit on earth is not to condemn you, but to save you; who is going to see Me? who will take notice? who will recognize the Throne descending from the Heavens among you? do not resist My Holy Spirit of Grace; I am with you always; pray fervently for the

41

conversion of your era, open your hearts and speak to Me; will you offer Me your will? O House of Mine! come, come to Me and walk in My Light; yet, when I come in My Great Return, will I find any faith on earth? Today I am speaking in plain words, My little children, in a short time Love will return as love; I will come back to you and I tell you truly, if you recognized My Holy Spirit and have seen Him, it is because you belong to Me since the world can neither acknowledge Him, see Him, nor receive Him ♡

42

ah, My little ones what will I not do for you! I am longing to see you strengthened with the gifts I am pouring on you; *¹
<u>receive your strength</u>
<u>in prayer,</u>
<u>a constant prayer to Me</u>.
I bless each one of you; and <u>you</u>*² who came because your cross is crushing you, <u>lean on Me beloved</u> and offer Me your distress and your hardship; I love you; I shall come to your

*¹ Jesus had paused there. Then, majestically, straightening then not moving, said these words.
*² Jesus speaks specifically to one person in the group.

43

help; glorify Me by praising My Name; receive the Breath of My Holy Spirit on your foreheads and be one under My Holy Name ΙΧΘΥΣ ⋈

13. 5. 91

My child, allow Me to speak to My children by giving Me your consent to use your hand and your time ♡   I am bound to You out of love,

Lord, am I not Your Property? So use me fully and as You please My Lord, for this is my delight. Come Holy Spirit and invade me ...
City!* whom I came to visit to proclaim My love through you to all of you, and to heal

* God suddenly and unexpectedly changed tone and His Voice with great force cried out to me calling me City.

44

your sick inhabitants, I shall not let you perish in guilt nor will I wait to see you decay, I shall triumph over you; I am your King, I am the Perfect One, hear Me, and I intend to model you Generation into a reflection of My Divinity; the sinner's brood I shall consume by a roaring Fire, your Generation will have her wedding with My Holy Spirit,*¹ and I shall with My consuming Fire change the surface of this earth into a divine, prosperous and new Earth, and the world of today will be gone; I shall turn you all with My consuming

*¹ AP: 21:2

45

Flame as pure as gold and transparent as glass,*¹ because your hearts will be Mine and in Mine, I and My Father will be your Abode*² and you too will be Our abode; I intend to give you back your divinity creation, so that My radiant glory will be like a lighted torch *³ inside you; then like a sentinel guarding a gate I shall guard you too, from anything unclean which may want to come inside you*⁴; I shall make out of each one of you a radiant city, I shall renew you entirely for

*¹ Ap. 21:21   *² Alluding to: God Almighty and the Lamb were themselves the temple: Ap. (inside us, the "city")
*³ Ap. 21:23   *⁴ Ap. 21:27

46

this is the way I shall have you ready to wed My Holy Spirit; — My Holy Spirit will make His Home in you, transfiguring you to become His Holy City,*¹ His Domain and His Property; the world of the present shall be gone and My Will on earth shall be done as it is in Heaven; Love shall descend as love and I, the unseen God will become visible inside your heart; the hour is coming when you shall no longer grope your way in the dark, since your heart will be lit by My radiant

*¹ Read Ap. ch. 21: 1-3

47

glory; My glory will become visible in your hearts ♡ come, My child, hear My Mother now, remain ♡ near Me, we, us? Yes my Lord.

I am seduced by You, seduce others too ... intercede for them ♡ and I shall come and seek out and save what was lost,* read Isaiah 41: 17-20 Love loves you IΧΘΥΣ ><>

13. 5. 91

Our Holy Mother's Message for prayer groups.
children, I am calling each one of you today to examine your hearts ♡ let your tolerance be your witness; I implore you to re-examine

* Ap. 21:24   * Lk. 19: 10

48

your hearts; God's Message to you all is the proof of His Fidelity; God does not demonstrate Himself to judge you, God demonstrates Himself to show His Fidelity in your lack of fidelity; God is seeking your reconciliation; He is coming to take you out of the Power of Darkness and show His Reign on earth; the unseen God will become visible in His Glory in your hearts; and the Heavenly things will become visible in your hearts and the pale reflections of what you have taken as shadows before shall prove their reality; the Reign of God's Kingdom on earth

49

is very near you now; I implore you therefore
to be ready for this Day; if you say you
have died to yourselves and the principles of
this world, prohibit then your hearts from flutter-
ing into the world; live for God and
place Him as first; have no more to do with
quarrels, disputes and accusations, do not allow
your lips to condemn you, fear the Lord and
Wisdom shall soon come upon you like dawn,
the Lord seeks and desires an undivided heart.
I had asked you and am asking you again
to pray, pray, pray with your heart; a

50

simple conversation with your Father who is in
Heaven, because if I request from you today to
offer God an undivided heart, it is to teach
you to keep faithful to the principles I have
been teaching you; what is valuable to God
is the heart which honours Him by keeping itself exempt from all temptations that lead to
sin; if you have disciplined your bodies by
fasting, I request from you to discipline also
your lips to pronounce only prayers and praises
to the Lord, do not allow your lips to condemn you; set your heart, your mind,

51

your eyes and your lips on Jesus and be whole
and undivided; I invite you, dear children,
to put all these things into practice, nevertheless without leaving the other values of the Law
undone; and remember that the Heart of
the Law is Love ♡ I bless you all;

Fr Toulouse 18.5.91
Jesus? I Am; be in peace little one, there
will be more than one that I shall bring
back to Me; I have indeed called you here *
because this is where they need Me; I love you

* Jesus wanted me to go to Toulouse instead of Montpelier.

52

to passion, always remember this; I draw to Life,
I do not repel anyone, sinner or unjust, all
of you are My children; My Message is a Message
of Love, a call to your real foundations, a
reminder of My Word and of My Existence;
do not fear Me, fear only the one who pretends
he does not exist and draws you ever so mali-
ciously to Death; I am the Light; come,
tell them that this Message is not given to
them to draw sensation but to make them
realize the urgency, the graveness and the
importance of My Call; the urgency of

53

their conversion; the graveness of the condition of their soul; the importance to change their life and live holy, the importance of My Messages which are spiritual food, a nourishing supplement to their spirituality, a medicinal ointment to their wounds inflicted on them in this darkness by the evil one; I want My children to listen very carefully to all that I have to say. Let My Spirit of Truth guide you back to the Truth; let My Spirit of Knowledge remind you of the One and Only True Knowledge I Myself have given

54

you; I, your Lord and Saviour bless each one of you ΙΧΘΥΣ ><>

23.5.91

Yahweh my God, You are lavishing Your scents on me, praised be my Yahweh. You are mine and I am Yours. Give me Your Shoulder to lean upon, unworthy as I am, a puff of wind that passes unnoticed and does not return, a speck of dust washed away with the first drops of rain, allow me to be in the Presence of Your Splendour. Lead me through this wilderness with a sensitive hand Beloved.

Vassula, even in your wretchedness, I shall speak to the nations through you, to make your generation proclaim their praises to Me; — Generation I am going to pasture you; — daughter, I descend, everytime you call Me,

55

from My Throne to come all the way to you in your room and meet you; subject to misery, you have captured My Infinite Love, rejoice! rejoice that your King hears you everytime you open your mouth and call My Holy Spirit to come and assist you, invoke My Name, My child, and Love shall overshadow you entirely and keep you company ♡ delight your King now and let Him hear from His Poverty-Stricken child her vows once more ♡

I got up and repeated my vows to the Sacred-Heart of Jesus.

56

Vassula of My Sacred Heart I accept your consecration, your offerings pleased My Heart; honour Me, your Lord, by staying devout and loyal to Me, I, who am your Rewarder ♡

25. 5. 91

Jesus, I have been charmed by Your Perfection, I have been seduced by Your Beauty; Your Consuming Love besieged my frailty to consent and become the victim of Your Love, but how was I to retract upon seeing so much Beauty all at once? Your Graciousness mesmerizes me all day long; what spells lie in Your Love?

beloved of My Soul, your eyes have seen My glorious Majesty, your ears have heard My Song of Love and I Myself have put My Own light in you to make you forever Mine;

57

My Nails and My Thorned Crown I have given to you to show My closeness to you; your Spouse I have become making you My bride, to share My Cross as our matrimonial bed; My Passion will seize you to become a copy of Me your Spouse. I am your Comforter in days of sorrow; I have chosen you and not you Me, to show you My inexhaustible Riches;

Lord, what do You want me to do for You?

bring back My people to the real Faith based on love; pray that My Church be one, exempt from all evils; expiate, daughter, expiate for

58

the sins and iniquities of the world that so much offend My Sacred Heart .... My daughter and bride, look into your Saviour's Heart, look inside this Heart that saved you; take My Heart, console it by loving Me, I, Jesus, kiss you on your forehead; ΙΧΘΥΣ 🐟

1.6.91

daughter, let Me preach to you; it is I who have given you the Knowledge   pray that My Kingdom on earth becomes as it is in Heaven;

Here Jesus deciphers ch.21 of the Apocalypse   2.6.91
part of ch. 22 and Daniel ch. 11: 31-39
My Lord?

59

I Am; peace be with you; soon, very soon now I shall strip off your old behaviour, and your old self, creation, to vest you with My Divinity *¹ and remind you of the True Knowledge, so listen, My beloved ones to My Holy Spirit; allow Me to prepare you all so that you may be ready to receive My Kingdom; I the Lord invite everyone to share with Me and see My Glory; My Heart is sick with love for you generation ... alas! for those who would still be carrying their sin, coiled in-side them as with child when My Day comes! *²

pray that everyone may be ready when that day

*¹ Allusion to: New Heavens and New Earth. Ap.21:1

*² Allusion to: Matthew ch. 24:19

60

comes; ail for your brothers who still live in dark-ness and have flung My Glory for a worthless imitation, this very one that the prophet Daniel speaks of *; I shall speak to you in plain words considering the state of your soul and your lack of Knowledge, I do not come by force upon you with My Holy Spirit to violate your liberty, nor do I come to condemn you; I come to you out of Mercy to give you freely the fullest Knowledge of My Will; through My Perfect Wisdom I come to augment in you the Knowledge I Myself have

* To the unbelievers who do not believe any more in the Perpetual Sacrifice: Holy Communion. The Resurrection

61

given you; I do not come to add new things into that which has been given you already, but I come to place My Kingdom in the middle of your hearts, Citadels!* have you not yet understood? have you not yet understood that I, the Lord, live in you? have you not understood that you are My sanctuaries? when I speak to you about heavenly things are you ready to receive them? listen: Scripture says: "Zeal for Your house will devour Me"; indeed, today again My zeal has reached its zenith, and

* We are God's house, a citadel for God. God called out to us calling us 'Citadels': Daniel ch. 11: 31-39　　Look at:

62

from above Fire shall come down and devour My sanctuaries*¹ I shall transform you, Citadels, into a state of Grace in which you will no longer apprehend to desire My Glory, nor fear to admit My Divinity*²; the Plunderer*³ infiltrated like smoke in you, you who are the sanctuary of My Holy Spirit, the sanctuary citadel of My Divinity, Satan's smoke penetrated through hinges and holes invading you in your sleep, because you had not acknowledged Me in My Divinity but rather followed your own irrational ideas, I tell you

*¹ Us.
*² Here God means that the unconverted and the unbelievers who refuse the Holy Eucharist and deny the Real Presence of Christ in the Eucharist, God shall change with Grace.
*³ Satan

63

this: I shall fill your darkness with My Light because I intend to wed you, generation, with My Holy Spirit*¹; it has been said that by force the Rebel will feed you one day a portion of Rationalism and the other day a portion of Naturalism with the intention to abolish and extinguish the little light that is left in you, you who are My temple, the Invader has invaded many of My Citadels*³, forcing his disastrous

*¹ Ap. 21: 2　　Ap. 21: 9-11
*² Satan.
*³ Us. Allusion to: Dn. 11: 31 "Forces of his will come and profane the sanctuary citadel."

64

abomination*¹ inside you and abolishing My Perpetual Sacrifice*² from within you*³ to erect in its place a worthless imitation*⁴, an image of mortal man, which is an abomination in My Holiness*⁵

*¹ Sects like New Age etc; Materialism, rationalism that lead to atheism.
*² Once these people fall into these sects, or into atheism, they also stop receiving the Perpetual Sacrifice which is the Holy Eucharist. Dn. 11: 31
*³ Read Dn. 11: 31-39 + Ap. 13: 14-18 + Ap. 21: 1-27
*⁴ Sects: aping the Word of God
*⁵ Jesus was weeping.

1

you are My Holy City, *¹
and you, you who allowed My Holy Spirit to flow
in you like a River, *² you are My New Jerusalem, *³
the First-Fruits, *⁴ those very ones who had constancy
and faith *⁵; and like dew coming from My Mouth,
like raindrops on the grass, you shall put Hope
in many arid hearts, because all the radiant
Glory of My Heart shall reflect in you, making
you glitter like some precious jewel of crystal

* ¹ Jesus said this very majestically. Ap. 21:2
* ² Read Ezk. 47:1-12   Ap. 22:1-2
* ³ Ap. 21:2
* ⁴ Ap. 14:4
* ⁵ Ap. 13:10

2

clear diamond; *¹ I tell you solemnly, many of
you who are not born of the Spirit shall receive
from above by My Grace the Spirit of Truth;
the Spirit of Truth shall descend in all its
radiant Glory out of Heaven and make His
Home in you, My Holy Spirit shall wed you
to become His bride, *² embellishing you by His
Holiness, and suddenly the Heavenly things will
become visible in your hearts, and My Kingdom
unseen yet to the heart shall become visible
and crystal clear in all its Glory; beloved

* ¹ Ap. 21:11
* ² Ap. 21:2   Ap. 21:9

3

of My Soul, Citadels, blessed are you that will
be found blameless; *¹ (this *² is My way of teaching
you heavenly things; it is not without labour,
My child, but be reassured, all that I have
to say, shall be written and read, this is
Wisdom teaching you My Vassula, I love you
and My love for you is everlasting ♡)

Continuation from previous message. - 2.6.91
I shall let everyone marvel at My first-fruits,
and little by little the old world will vanish *³
and wear out like garment *⁴; only a little

* ¹ Allusion to: Mt. 24:19-20   *² Jesus speaks to me now.
* ³ Ap. 21:4   *⁴ Heb. 1:11

4

while now and all that had been covered shall
be uncovered and all that had been hidden shall
be unveiled in front of your very eyes; My New
Jerusalem! you, who are the first-fruits of My
Love, you whom My Holy Spirit seduced by My
New Hymn of Love, you whom I wed, go out
to the nations and sing to them My New Hymn
of Love *¹; work for Peace, sow the seeds I have
given you, be like trees growing by the banks
of the River of Life *², let your leaves be a
medicinal *³ balm for the wretched and let your

* ¹ Ap. 14:3   *² Ap. 22:1   *³ Ap. 22:2, Ezk. 47:12

5

branches bear fruit in holiness ♡ be My breech-
menders *¹, restorers of My ruined sanctuaries; give
to those who fell into Satan's impious nets and
were fed portions of Rationalism and Naturalism,
and My healing Water from My Breast, this
stream that flows out of My Sanctuary *² will
fill you and make you wholesome; no man
shall be able to arrest this rivulet; the stream
will keep on flowing profusely out of My Heart;
it shall flow everywhere, breaking into several
parts, separating into other and several rivulets

* ¹ Is. 58 : 12   *² Christs Body (Heart) Ezk. 47:12

6

going into all directions, and wherever this healing
Water flows, EVERYONE, sick, lame, blind
will be healed, even the dead shall come back
to life again; no one will be able to stop Me
from purifying you; Ah! beloved ones, from
rebels, I shall raise levitical priests, from dis-
honouring Me I shall turn you into pearls, radiant
cities of light to honour Me ♡ and I shall
live in you, because you shall be vested in
My Own Holiness; I, the Lord will be in the
land of the living, and those who stifle My
Holy Spirit and see everything as nonsense, I

7

tell you: I have things that go beyond your
minds, I shall demonstrate the power of My
Spirit and make your lips open and your
heart cry out to Me:

Abba!

Love shall perfect you; Wisdom shall teach
you to acknowledge My Holy Spirit, and I shall
make you join the saints too; I bless each one
of you leaving My Sigh of Love on your forehead;
be one under My Holy Name ♡ ΙΧΘΥΣ ⫸
and you, who are My chosen instrument to bring
My Love before pagans and rebels, continue

8

your journey with Me; allow Me to call you when
I wish; I Am is with you and loves you;
come ♡

6. 6. 91

When my spirit becomes cold and I fall in a
kind of lethargy, Lord, and when I become so
ill disposed to dialogue with You and meet
You in this special way, do I, like a leaf
wither and dry slowly before Your very Eyes?

I have been waiting for you .... I had been
speaking to you, soul, but all I heard
from you was, silence .... give Me your attention, soul, I have so much to say to
you and arouse your interest; lethargy?
then cry out to Me! I shall breathe

9

on you and the ice will melt; Lord, there are times when the Light You have given me seems to vanish behind obscure smoke.

child, your voice can carry as far as Heaven and all the way to My Throne, so, cry out to Me and like a flash in the clouds I shall answer: "here We* are, We shall hear your petition"; Then come now and rescue me, fill my lamp with oil, breathe on me to revive me, imbue me with Your fragrance of myrrh, perfect me in Your Presence, show Your Kindness on me ....

do not withhold your question; speak child!*²

*¹ The Holy Trinity. *² Jesus seemed eager to hear the rest of my sentence, which I knew He already knew.

10

What You do to me with so much Love, Faithfulness and Mercy, will You not do it to everyone of Your children, who are in the same need as I am?

be blessed*¹! I God shall come and rescue each one of you; I shall not allow My Church*² to pine away; generation, I mean to save you ... but not by menace or disaster, anger or blame; I mean to save you, generation, by enveloping My Love and Mercy around you to cover your nakedness; I am sending you My Holy Spirit lavishly upon you so that your

*¹ Jesus seemed very happy. *² We are the Church.

11

spirit filled with My Spirit cries out to Me: "Abba!"

today, tears of Blood flood My Eyes from the deafness of My creation; a most obstinate spirit has penetrated into My Domain*¹; their soul is fainting within them; I look into what was once My Faithful City*² to see her today become a harlot's! Lord! Your Reign, has it not yet begun? write this: "happy are those who are invited to the wedding feast of the Lamb"; (Ap. 19:9) My Reign has begun

*¹ God means: our soul. His Domain where He abides is to be found in the core of our soul, which belongs to God.
*² God means us here. He calls us "City".

12

in many hearts already; I have espoused these souls to Me making them new*, and I tell you: My Spirit of Truth will continue to swarm over My whole creation and besiege City after City*², and the obscenities, the iniquities and all the impurities to be found within them, I, with My Own Hand shall extirpate; I shall extirpate all that had been planted by Folly, with the Fire I will send from Heaven ♡ daughter, the first heaven and

* Allusion to Ap. 21:5: "Now I am making the whole of creation new."
*² God means: Soul after soul.

13

the first earth shall disappear (Ap. 21:1) and each one of you shall be renewed by the love of My Holy Spirit, I shall change the face of this world; *Is this what You mean by the renewal of Your Church, the renewal of ourselves, because we are the Church? The New Jerusalem?*

pupil, you have said well; you are all My Church, My Sanctuary citadel,* My Domain, My City, My Property, My Jerusalem ♡ I shall renew City after City*² with My ♡ Fire of Love; I mean to gather you from the four corners of the earth and cure you, I mean to burn

*¹ Dn. 11:31

*² Us

14

with My Fire the disastrous abomination *¹ installed inside My Temple;*² the disastrous abomination is : the spirit of Rebellion that claims to be My equal; it is the spirit of Evil that enthroned itself in My sanctuary*³ taking the place of My Perpetual Sacrifice*⁴, turning your generation Godless; it is the spirit of Rationalism and of Naturalism that led most of you into atheism; this is the spirit that makes you believe you are self-sufficient and that you can achieve

*¹ Dn. 11:31 , Dn 12:11   Mt. 24:15
*² The Temple is us.
*³ Sanctuary is us. *⁴ The Holy Eucharist, Holy Communion

15

everything by your own efforts and by your own strength; this disastrous abomination turned you into a waterless country of drought, a desert; My Perpetual Sacrifice you have abolished from within you because you have lost your faith, generation; how many of you are thirsty for Me? very few come to drink Me, and yet you can drink Me without money; who is hungry for Me? you can have Me free, at no cost at all; yet almost no one is hungry to eat Me; evil has warped your understanding, fascinating your spirit to absorb all

16

that is not Me, instead of absorbing My Light, Satan made you absorb his darkness, instead of becoming radiant and beautiful, you dulled, pining away, and like a withered branch you are now ready to be cut off and thrown on the fire to be burnt; do not be afraid of Me, I am the River of Life ♡ I am the Way to Heaven, I am the only Truth that leads you to share My Glory for Eternity Temple of God! daughter of Mine, walk with Me ♡ ΙΧΘΥΣ ⊱

17

12. 6. 91

Lord, You pursue my persecutors and overtake them — and they cannot touch me ; foreigners *[1] come wooing my favours but yet   when I go to my own *[2], like poverty at their elbow, like a beggar in want, to tell them of Your Wonders, it seems like their ears are sealed, so that they would not hear Your New Hymn of Love. Am I to trod the winepress alone and have not one of the men of my people with me ?

is My Own Arm not enough for you ? Are My Own Eyes that watch over you day and night not sufficient for you ? daughter, soon, I shall show My Holy Face to them, I will inundate your country *[3] with My Spirit , and Rivers shall flow over, pour out ; I shall

*[3] Greece .

1 * The R. Catholics
2 * The Orthodox

18

not hide My Face from them .... hope My Vassula, hope ... your King will abandon no one ♡ He shall come with healing ointment in His ♡ Hand and cure you one by one ; rejoice, My daughter, rejoice, I shall unseal their ears for My Glory ♡ come, the mysteries of the kingdom of ♡ heaven are revealed to you, pray that they may be revealed to them too ♡ ΙΧΘΥΣ ⠶⟩﹤

13. 6. 91

Message of our Holy Mother.

Vassula ? will you write down My Words to assuage this desert ? yes Holy Mother, Mother of

19

God, write My daughter, blessed of My Soul, beloved of My Heart, today I ask each one of you to apply your heart to walk with God ! God is your Strength, your life and your Happiness ; no man can live without God ; Jesus is the True Vine and you the branches ; a branch cut off from the Vine, dries and withers immediately ; it is then of no use but to be thrown on the fire ♡ walk with the Light and do not be afraid in abandoning yourselves entirely to Him ; give yourselves to God and your hearts shall be filled with Joy ; understand,

20

beloved children, that God, in these days is coming to save you and untangle you from Satan's nets and bring you back to His Sacred Heart, Our Two Hearts are united in spite of the arguments and the denials of the world for this Truth, for they have not all accepted this Truth but use this Truth instead to combat one another, Our Two Hearts are united and thirst together for your salvation, children ; come and hear Us this time : make Peace with God, be reconciled, lift your face to God and ask Him to fill your heart with His Light ; learn to love God as your

21

Father, He who loves you more than anyone can
imagine ♡ and without cease sends you from His
Heart His flowing Peace, like a River to assuage
the interiour desert of your soul; do not live out
of words only, act and live every word given to
you in the Gospels; do not be dead at the letter of
the Law, live it ♡ do not be afraid if anybody
mocks you or refuses to believe in the Wonders God
is giving you today, for I tell you: if anyone
reduces you to silence, the stones will cry out *
all the harder; only God can give you Peace

* Images of Jesus and Mary that pour out Tears of Blood are
a Divine manifestation when men try to suffocate the Holy Spirit.
(Lk. 19: 40)

22

and Happiness; I am praying for you without cease
so that from hard stones this generation's heart can
turn to God and be like a watered garden,
from an uninhabited desert a Holy City full of
God's Light, a Light coming from God, and not
by sun or moon *¹; after the storm will be over
and gone, flowers will spring up *², changing the
surface of this earth; *³ I, your Holy Mother, bless
each one of you ♡
                                              17.6.91
Message for Pistoia in Italy (m. Florence.)

peace be with you; I have come all the way

* Ap. 21:23   *² flowers: the first fruits: the newly converted.
              (Allusion to Ap.21: 1-3)

23

to you to tell you:
            I am here;
beloved, My Sacred Heart is on Fire, this is
why I descend from My Throne to come all the
way to you and offer you My Peace and My Love;
Mercy is at your doors; if there were two
knees to receive you with great love at your
birth and two arms to hug you with affection,
I tell you: I have done more than that,
I have laid down My Life for you; I
am the Source of Love; come, renounce all
that stains your soul and follow Me; do not

24

say: "Thy way of life is faultless;" you are
without beauty and without majesty so long as
your soul is stained and imperfect; come, I
can perfect your soul since I am offering you
free and at no cost My Blood and My Flesh;
surrender yourself to Me, I am the Life;
today I suddenly descend upon you, I look
around Me and My Heart is filled with grief;
I had once cultivated this earth and turned
it into a Garden, with the subtlest odours
from its flowers, I left behind Me 'levitical
priests' to keep it, I entrusted them with

25

My interests, but My Garden I find neglected, My flower-beds dry, I am surrounded by an endless desert, devastated, even the jackals have difficulties of surviving it; scorpions and vipers are the inhabitants which prosper in its treacherous dryness and if only a remnant of My lambs are alive it is because I had been sending you without cease, My angels, to snatch away My lambs from the viper's fangs and the scorpion's sting; I had been told that I would find all My sheepfold secure and untouched in My Return and My Garden kept and watered

26

but hardly had I gone, scarcely had I turned My back, than they turned My Garden into a haunt of the lizard and the spider ... O come! you who err still in this wilderness saying: I have sought My Redeemer but have not found Him; find Me, My beloved, in purity of heart, by loving Me without self-interest, find Me in holiness, in the abandonment I desire of you; find Me by observing My Commandments; find Me by replacing evil with love; find Me in simplicity of heart; sin no more; cease in doing evil; learn to do

27

good, search for justice, help the oppressed, let this wilderness and this aridity exult; let your tepidness enflame into an ardent flame; relinquish your apathy and replace it by fervour; do all these things so that you may be able to say: "I have sought My Redeemer and I have found Him; He was near Me all the time but in My darkness I failed to see Him; O Glory be to God! Blessed be our Lord! how could I have been so blind?" I shall then remind you to keep and treasure My Principles so that you may live ♡ I shall come like

28

a lightning, as a flash in the clouds with My Holy Spirit to wipe away the tears from every cheek, so courage, My beloved, Love shall return as love; I, the Sacred Heart bless you all leaving My Sigh of Love on your forehead; be one under My Holy Name ♡

ΙΧΘΥΣ 🐟

18.6.91

Sacred Heart, You are the Theme of my life. You are on my side and ever ready to help me. Now You have made me Your Property and Your Own Arms are my enclosure, what more can I ask; You have swept my accusers in a twinkling of an eye and the fire that was surrounding me is not there anymore!

Lord, You have given me a vision now again of Your Sacred Heart, I could hardly recognize that it was a

29

heart at all! Your Heart looked one big wound ... scarcely
had I lifted my head from my oppressors than I
found that another fire has been lit, yet another
wound on Your Heart, another big thorn in Your
Head, my Jesus ... this time I am going to bargain
with You, if You allow me; here is what I propose:
Take this big thorn off You and put it in me instead.
I shall keep it until the Father gives to this priest
the Grace and the Light he needs to be able to
understand his mistake, and that I belong to You.

Vassula, let it be so; let it be as you ask;
I accept your sacrifice, My child, be blessed;
I am not alone to swallow My Tears, your Holy
Mother is weeping too; come to Us in this
way by sharing; this storm too shall be calmed
♡ the Father sees everything, My child; I shall

30

overturn entire valleys and uproot mountains
were these too, to become a menace for My Love
Verses, Love Verses which are a Call for your
conversion; My Love Messages shall proceed; Satan's
grip is getting loose now and I shall soon put
a muzzle on his mouth ♡ Love is near you
all the time and He peers inside His room* now
and then to check that all is well, this room
where He takes His rest ♡

   I am Yahweh; flower, Saint Bede is by
your side; who is he?   Yahweh loves you;

* room: my heart, God's resting place.

31

                                                22.6.91
Ah, how Mercy and Love incessantly cover me and
bless me!   Wisdom is my personal Teacher and
She's instructing me and others; Your Holy Presence
ever so constant by my side reassures me and
gives me hope and courage. Ah, Yahweh my
Father, I long for You, how I long for You!
Yahweh my Abba, You have seduced me to the
marrow.

I preached to you My Knowledge ♡ learn from My
Mouth, free; you will one day, commit your spirit
into My Hands; Lord, as You have by Grace mez-

merized me, by Grace too, mesmerize the rest of
the world; for instance the pagans, the godless,
and especially those who claim to be gods, because
of their wisdom, and who claim to be Your equal.

I shall come to their help; now they lie helpless
trapped in Satan's net, but you have to pray

32

for your brothers so that I may reveal My Holy
Face to them too; ♡
                                                27. 6. 91
come, let us work; put your faith in
Me ♡ — it has been said that before My Great
Return there would be signs given to you; you
are to watch these signs preluding My Day of
Glory; one can, by reading the Scriptures carefully discover all these truths; how is it that
your minds are not opened to understand the
Scriptures? come now and understand, hear Me
now My child: your generation is thriving in
its rebellion; how they have apostatized!! for

33

My part, I increased My calls, My warnings, I beckoned to you day after day, I increased My Blessings; but I got no response; I said: "would I find anyone when I come?" why did no one answer when I called? but instead of a response to My supplication you turned your backs to Me," who does He think His Message is for?" is all I heard; how they rebel and how they blaspheme against My Divinity! but no man is able to push away the Appointed Time, nor the Hour; they shall come upon them, as sudden as a thunderclap; today, daughter,

---

34

the Antichrist is the spirit of Rebellion given by Satan, as Scriptures define him : the Rebel*¹, who is the disastrous abomination set up in My Temple of which the prophet Daniel spoke of — each one of you is My Temple ... the one Scriptures call Rebel and is defined as the disastrous abomination is one of the two preceding signs of the end of Times; the other sign is your great apostasy ♡ your era, My child, has defected from giving Me the adoration which is your due to Me but also your life; Satan's plan was to conquer this era and make you believe you

*¹ read 2Th. 2:1-12

35

can do without Me; so the spirit of Rebellion, which is the Antichrist entered into My Dwelling*¹; that is the spirit of Lawlessness, not to say more, and it has installed itself today in the very core of My Sanctuary*²; this spirit of Rebellion is the one that makes those ones who have it cry out: "I am a god!"*³ men have defected and in their defections Satan's way was opened to step inside them and lead all of these to a violent death; this spirit of Rebellion which devastates one's soul, one's mind and one's heart, is the Enemy of which

*¹ In our souls.   *² The core of our hearts.   *³ Ez. 28:2 ⎫
                                                    Is. 14:14 ⎬
                                                    2Th. 2:4 ⎭

36

the apostle Paul spoke of; the one who claims to be so much greater than all that men call 'god' so much greater than anything that is worshipped*¹ the one who says: "I will rival The Authority,"*² so they enthrone themselves in My place and promulgate their own law to make war on My Law and anything that comes from My Spirit; day after day, hour after hour they keep grieving Me and offending My Holy Spirit; O dust and ashes, you who removed My Perpetual Sacrifice from within you, do you want to die? why do

*³ allusion to Ez. 28:2 " I am sitting on the throne of God."
*² 2Th. 2:4   *¹ allusion to Is. 14:14: "I will rival the Most High."

37

you rival Me? why do you deny My Holy Spirit of Grace? anyone who denies Me is the Antichrist, for he is denying the Father, the Son and the Holy Spirit who are one and the same because all three of Us agree*; today, many of you are denying the outpouring of My Holy Spirit; the graces and the gifts My Holy Spirit is giving you out of My Infinite Generosity, are ignored and suppressed; these peoples deny and reject all the gifts of My Spirit; many go around keeping the outward appearance of religion but are rejecting the inner power of My Church,

* 1 Jn 5:8   * look at message 15.4.91, book 51

38

the inner power which is My Holy Spirit; they say: "I have kept My faith, all there is to come now is the trophy of My righteousness;" I ask you: have you done everything you can to present yourself in front of Me? I have been trying to awaken you and tell you that you are like a dried-up river, and that all you say is hollow; and while the sinner is being converted by My Holy Spirit, no sooner does he enter My House, no sooner does he discover the Treasures of My Heart reserved for all of you, than you come upon him like a gale

39

to tempt him back into godlessness ♡ he who has just escaped from rebellion, you tempt him back to rebel; in the Day of Judgement I shall tell you: you have not believed Me, but made Me out to be a liar, because you have not trusted the testimony I have given you about the Advocate, the Reminder of My Word, yes, My Holy Spirit of Truth, this very One you never ceased to ignore and persecute, never ceased to deny and suppress; instead of joining the saints who acclaim and praise with blessings and shouts of joy My Holy Spirit

40

you hound them and persecute them unceasingly, clinging to your illusion of piety; you are provoking Me with your constant denials ... how can I than not let the stones manifest My grief? you prohibit My first-fruits to acclaim My Holy Spirit, this is why I tell you: if these keep silence the stones will cry out* My grief*²; what I once said to Jerusalem I tell it to you now with sorrow: "if you in your turn had only understood the Splendour of My Message of Peace! but, alas, it is hidden

* Lk 19:39   *² Divine manifestations of images and statues of Jesus and Mary shedding tears.

41

from your eyes!" if you in your turn had only grasped the Splendour of My Holy Spirit, bestowing blessing upon blessing on all of you ... but, alas, you neither see nor hear the Advocate, the Holy Spirit, whom the Father sends in My Name, teaching you and reminding you of all the truths I have given you ♡ because the prince of this world is using your freedom for your own downfall;   Lord, show

Your Mercy to these too, and like You made me hear You, let them hear too; and like You showed Your Beauty to me leaving me dazzled, show them Your Perfection too.   they are not listening, they are

42

listening only to their voice, even while My Tears flow before them there is no reply; I have gone in all directions to find a way of breaking through their deafness and tell them to come to Me and base their strength on Me, so that I in My turn lead them to holiness and allow them to inherit My Light; I am the Holy One they are so wickedly betraying and I am the first to forgive them, had they one moment of regret ... but as long as they maintain their stand of self-sufficiency they shall not hear Me nor will they be able to see how today

43

I am revealing entirely and as never before My Holy Face to all the world*¹; I, the Lord, shall keep on shining on you, creation, and I shall spread across the face of this earth My Light; the sun that has darkened and the moon that lost its brightness*² in your era, leading you in your darkness to apostatize, soon, your distress shall be over; I intend to turn your marshlands*³ into a garden, the night into day, your cities*⁴ which are only a rubble now into cities of Light, your broken altars*⁵ will be

*¹ allusion to Joël 3:1   *² allusion to Mt 24:29   *³⁴⁵ us.

44

rebuilt and of your temples*¹, I, with My Own Hand shall lay the foundation ♡ I shall make the whole creation new*²; I shall renew you all with My Holy Spirit; come, Vassula, My lamb, all shall be written and as I want everything to be written; Love is by your side;

ΙΧΘΥΣ ⊃Ð   6.7.91

Lord, heal me.

if you listen carefully and bring no objections to Me, no rivals and no doubts, if you come and admit you are a sinner and show no hesitation to repentance, I shall heal you

*¹ us.   *² Ap. 21:5

45

you belong to Me and I have given you My
Heart, this is why I want you to crucify all
that is you, let the only marks on your body
be those I have on Mine; if you see footprints
that do not belong to Me, do not follow
them; My Footprints are stained with Blood
and perfumed with myrrh. were you to hear
something from someone clothed in splendid
robes, let it die with him and give no heed
to what he says; I, your Saviour, am clad
in rags made out of sackcloth,* and walk
barefoot; My cloak is soaked in Blood

* Ap. 11 : 3

46

and My Heart is covered with flames of Fire;
My Lips are parched for lack of Love, .
Lord, heal everyone, everyone !
fill My Heart with joy and pray for all
those who's hearts are shut to reason and
to My Wisdom; For this reason Lord, draw
us close to You, we are so weary walking in this
exile ...
My Dew from My Mouth will relieve your
heart; I shall deliver you from your sorrow;
My Eyes look down at the world; they
scan each one of you; should I descend now

47

I would only find a handfull with My Sign
on their forehead; the Heavens I have Opened
with the price of My Life, so that they are
yours too; . . I ask you : what man clings
on death and not to Life ? yet how much
longer will you not reason? for ever? how
much longer must your reject My Love, disown
and offend your Anointed ? Righteousness and
Justice are sitting on the Throne that is coming
among you from Heaven, to tell you that
the way to your room in Heaven, the Home
of the Light, is through Me; if you abandon

48

yourselves to Me, I shall show you the way
Home, if you rely on My Love, I shall bring
you to the Room of She who conceived Me,
to nurse you back to health; I am not tying
a rope round your liberty, I am only binding
you with wreaths of Love ♡ I love you with
an everlasting Love and My ♡ Tenderness for you
is an Inexhaustible Source; listen daughter,
tell this to the foreigners and to your own, tell
them how My Heart aches for lack of love;

ΙΧΘΥΣ ⊂≻

Jesus is sending me to a USA. prison, to witness.

49

8. 7. 91

To be read for Kansas City Prison; to the prisoners.

behold, it is I, Jesus of Nazareth that come upon you speaking through this weak instrument; I tell you : the world has not yet fully known the Peace I bequeathed to you, because the world rejected My Ways of Righteousness; I have said, that in the world you will have trouble, but you are not alone, NEVER, I am with you every minute of your life; I am ever so present, beloved of My Soul; to-day I am sending you this instrument of Mine all the way to your doorstep; she has not

50

come to you because she chose to, no, I chose to send her to you; and therefore what she reads to you is what I say to you; − My little children, My Return is imminent, I will come back to you; Love shall return as Love; ... I have told you this now before it happens so that when you see the evidence of My Words, you may believe; come to Me, as you are, do not wait to be saints to fall into your Saviour's Arms, come to Me as you are, and I shall forgive you your sins that bind your soul; ... Ah, creation, Mercy bends

51

all the way to you; approach Me, do not fear Me, a man can have no greater love than to have given His life for his friends, you are My friends; do not say: " what can I say? how can I speak? from dawn to night and from night to dawn I cry aloud, yet no one hears my supplications, who will ever hear me?" but yet, I tell you, I, I the living God, heard you; it is I who come into your room to tell you with My Heart in My Hand : I love you, My child and I bring to you My Blessings

52

to flower in your heart ♥ My son, take My Sacred Heart, it is all Yours; take this Heart that loves you, do not refuse It; I am He who loves you most; look My child, when you see footprints that are not Mine, do not place your feet into them, for they will only lead you to your death; My Footprints, My child, are showing I am barefoot, they are stained with My Blood and perfumed with myrrh; My child, the Five Wounds on My Body are wide open again and My Cloak is soaked in Blood; I am clad in sackcloth

53

and in rags because of the iniquities and the sins of this generation, My lips are dryer than parchment for lack of love; love is missing; since this generation heap one betrayal on another and lead Me unceasingly back to the Cross to be recrucified; it is you whom My Heart seeks — it is you who can console Me; it is you who can be a balm and soothe My Wounds; it is for you, My beloved, My Heart cries out to reach you, come, I, Jesus, shall bear you on My Shoulders and lead you into My House which is your House

54

too; befriend Me, befriend Me and I shall become your Holy Companion every single day of your life; I, the Lord shall deprive no one of My Mercy nor of My Graces; I bless you all from the core of My Sacred Heart; I, God am with you ♡ ΙΧΘΥΣ ⋊⋌

12.7.91

My Lord? I Am; peace be with you; let Me rejoice and let Me feel you have your ear opened for Me; soul, feel My Presence; I Am is with you every minute of your life; Vassula tell Me, are you happy to be

55

with Me in this way? yes my Lord and I bless you. delight Me and try to follow My lips when I speak to you, when I bend over you, when I look at you; do not pretend I am not there; lift your head, flower, towards Me and absorb My Light; I will embellish you, I will revive your stem; peace, My Peace I give to you; allow Me to use you as My tablet for just a little while longer, then.... then I, your Saviour shall pluck you and transplant you in My Garden forever and ever; I your Redeemer shall resurrect

56

many hearts to worship Me; pray without cease; dialogue with Me, bless Me often for all that I am giving you; tested, you shall always be; this, My beloved, is for your growth; I desire to stimulate your desire for Me, your thirst for Me and ah.... what will I not do for your soul to perfect it! had I to make you suffer a hundred scourges bringing you near to death for the perfection of your soul, I would do it without hesitation, to save you; Lord, this might bring a soul perhaps close enough to give

57

up everything! are you doubting of My Wisdom?
No, but maybe some souls might not be able
to take all this.
I know each soul's capacity, so trust Me;
remember one more thing, you want to
glorify Me? yes. to glorify Me you must
go through My Crucifixion; I need victim
souls more than ever; pray more often and
bend to My requests; abandon yourself to Me
and offer Me your will so that I accomplish
My Divine Works in you; carry My Cross
when I am weary and console My Heart

58

that aches for lack of love; Abba is near
you all the time, delight Me and bless Me ♡
a✗w
My Lord? I Am, little one do not get
discouraged in this exile; I am by your side
to help you carry this burden; come and rest
in My Sacred Heart; make it your Oasis
while you are crossing this desert; I shall not
abandon you nor will I neglect you; I am
your Hope and your toil does not go in vain;
dearest soul, I offer you My Patience; satu-
rated by My Love, oh what will I not do

16. 7. 91

59

for you .... out of the path you were to tread
on, I layed out for you a bed of roses;
I shall not conceal how I, your Saviour,
love you; I am today revealing to all humanity My Jealous Love; I am revealing you
all My Holy Face to remind you to be holy
and live holy; you belong to Me, created
from the Source of My Sublime Love, meant
to have eternal foundations in Me and be
an image of My Divine Nature, Death was
never meant for you, but you have accepted
the powers from below, generation; - daughter,

60

I, the Most High, had foreseen the betrayal of
My Church and the inflictions My Body would
receive; today, the sun does not give you
daylight nor does the moon shine on you;
Satan has covered the entire earth with his
smoke; you have apostatized .... you have
made out of My Perpetual Sacrifice a mockery,
a worthless imitation, a disastrous abomination;
you are concealing the Truth with a lie;
you are guilty for blasphemy .... My Holy
Presence in My Tabernacle disturbs you so
you made out your own law, forcing Me

61

out of My Throne*; have you asked My consent
before doing so? but these are the signs of
the Times; your great apostasy and the
spirit of Rebellion, which is the Antichrist in
your days and the abomination of the desolation; ah, Vassula, practise all that I
have given you and share My child My
agony, all I want is love, faithfulness and
mercy; (Jesus' lips trembled holding back His Tears)

*Theresa, remember me
telling you what I thought the next step to follow
would
be
here*
* Jesus here, means, the new system of putting the
Holy Tabernacle at the side of the Church or even
in a side room with the pretext that Jesus is
in a safer and more quiet place.

62

I feel betrayed as when Judas betrayed Me;
Come Lord and rest in the hearts that love You.
flower, I tell you; I am revealing My
Holy Spirit to mankind in this way to
save you and to remind you of My
Word; the Holy Spirit of Truth is My
Witness; the Holy Spirit brings nothing new
but gives you the fundamental truths
that I Myself have given you ♡

Feast of our Lady of Carmel - 1.15 a.m.   18.7.91
New York. Meeting with Conchita of Garabandal.

My Lord, I thank You for all that You have
done to me. I shall never be able to praise

63

Your Holy Name enough!
Love is near you; Love rests on you; Love
shall accomplish one thing after the other in
its own time; do not fear; your Saviour
is like a watchman; guarding you without
cease ♡ the Most High will not abandon
you, hear Me, long ago I prepared this,
before you were even born I planned it
and now I carry it out; see? I am sending you to My children so that you give
them your news, and to encourage them
thoroughly; have faith in Me; trust Me;

64

I know your hardships and your misery,
but soon, very soon now I shall come
and overturn the rebel and reign in
your hearts, generation; the Kingdom
of God is soon with you ♡ I bless
My dear children of Garabandal;
    learn that I Am is by your side;

        ΙΧΘΥΣ   ⤳◁

Our Holy Mother asked me to read to
everybody 2 Cor. 1:10-11

1

Greece - Rhodos 23.7.91.

"For your Creator is your Husband, Yahweh Sabaoth is His Name." Isaiah 54:5

Yahweh my Father whom I adore and long for, You who led me out of the countries underneath the earth and who lifted my soul entering it, consuming it with Your Fire and leaving me in total rapture for You; Yahweh, Your Majesty and King of Kings, You who lead me by this marvellous road, keep me free from sin and from falling; I am a sinner and am more apt to sin than do good; fortify your city....

be in peace, I the Lord love you; take My Hand and follow Me; pray My Vassula for there is still a long way to go for your perfection; you are not exempt from sin nor from falling and falls you will have, but I am near you to help you up and

2

press you on My Heart so that you may feel My Love and how I cherish you; come, we shall pray together:

Father, come to our help,
and guide our steps to perfection,
bring back our divinity
and make us the perfect
dwelling of Your Holiness;
Amen ♡

Jesus? I Am;

My Holy Spirit, My Vassula shall go to the very ends of the earth and seek

3

even the least amongst you to save you from the disastrous abomination that dwells within many of you now .... the Heavens soon shall deluge at My Coming upon you; I, the Lord have done many wonders for you and shall do more these coming days;*

pray My child, pray for those who offend My Holiness and blaspheme My Holy Spirit calling My Spirit foolish; have I not said: "... everyone who says a word against the Son of man will be forgiven, but no one

* The fall of Communism in Russia after the 3 day Poutch

4

who blasphemes against the Holy Spirit will be forgiven;" (Lk. 12:10) for the Spirit is not opposed to the Son nor is the Father to the Spirit, since all three of Us agree;*¹ many of you are condemning My Celestial manifestations and persecuting those whom My Spirit speaks through them because you do not believe they come from Me; daughter, look at the Wounds of My Body....*² I have little time left now before My Father's Hand strikes this generation; listen to your Father

*¹ 1 Jn. 5:8

*² Jesus' garment was soaked in His Own Blood, His ankles which I could see had blood with wounds like stripes

5

from whom you are sprung; listen to His
Voice :   I went all ways, seeking to gather
you and remind you to live holy since I
am Holy, but only a remnant of you pay
attention when I speak; I have spoken
through those you call contemptible; I have
spoken through weakness and poverty, but you
have made a cult in persecuting My Holy
Spirit that guides them, to the point of
frenzy !! I have been sending you through
them the spirit of Elijah and the spirit of

6

Moses, those two witnesses dressed in sackcloth,*¹
to prophesy and remind you of My Law, before
My great Return; they are to speak to you in
My Name and bring you back to the Truth
and back to your senses; but over you spread
a heavy darkness and your claims to your
knowledge became a battlefield to My Knowledge:
the lie was and is persecuting the Truth,
but Scriptures never lie; it was said that
"the beast*² that comes out of the Abyss

*¹ Ap. 11 : 3   *² In this context God made me under-
stand that beast meant: lie.

7

is going to make war on them and overcome
them and kill them";*¹ indeed your battlefield is drenched now with innocent blood,
because My Holy Spirit of prophecy has become a plague to those who belong to the
world;*² their frenzied persecutions and total
rejection they have for My mouthpieces are
similar to those of Sodom; their stubbornness
to open their heart and comply, their refusal
to open their ear and listen to My Voice

*¹ Ap. 11 : 7
*² God is alluding to Ap. 11 : 10 : '... because these two
prophets have been a plague to the people of the world.

8

today, have gone beyond the stubbornness of
Pharaoh in Egypt;*¹ today I am giving you
"things that no eye has seen and no ear
has heard, things beyond the mind of man,*²
all these things that lift your spirit to
call Me Abba; My Holy Spirit is calling
you all to true devotion and to a better
knowledge of God Himself, that is why
I am continually repeating the same truths

*¹ God is alluding to Ap. 11 : 8 ... their corpses will
lie in the main street of the Great City known by
the symbolic names Sodom and Egypt (...)
*² 1 Cor. 2 : 9

9

given to you; I shall continue calling you
until I break through your deafness, generation,
I shall not stop calling you in agony, not
until I hear from you the word:

Abba !

the new heavens and new earth are soon

upon you; ΙΧΘΥΣ ⊶

Rhodos   24.7.91

Message for the Rhodos' prayer group.

My eagerness to preach to them is beyond
human understanding and that is why
Wisdom is at the door of their heart; no

10

one is worthy of My Wisdom, nevertheless,
the Father out of His Infinite Graciousness
is willing to give Wisdom to mere children;
ah .... My beloved, you are all My offspring,
wretched you have become and still are,
yet, what Father would ignore his child in
his misery and send him away to continue
his immorality until Death overcomes him?
would he not intervene and quickly rescue him?
Now that I have lifted you from the pit,
lift your gaze on Me; your eyes shall behold Perfection; allow Me to keep house with

11

you, you shall not regret it .... I the Lord
bless each one of you; be a vessel of light
for the others who walk around like tainted
vessels, unable to tell their left hand from
their right and bring them to Me; I shall
give you My Strength, do not fear, the
human race grieves Me to the point of death
and My Heart lacerates to watch such iniquity
and sin into the world; you, you have
heard My laments, because I came near you;
you have heard My Voice, rejoice! rejoice
and be glad that I healed your eyes that

12

were dim, your heart that was sick with
lawlessness; I made you come back to Me
through My Mercy and now allow Me to use
you all for My Divine Plan, young and old
alike; pray and ask for My guidance; you
are very precious to Me; pray without cease for
this shall be your nourishment ♡ ΙΧΘΥΣ ⊶

27.7.91

Lord, perfect us in Your Beauty.

little one I give you My Peace, ask always
and it shall be given unto you; pray
frequently, fervently, and while the sinner

13

still continues his wickedness without remorse, you shall continue to sacrifice, love and pray for all those who have turned their backs to Me; lend Me an ear and I shall accomplish all that has to be accomplished; I, Jesus, will continue to help you and do all the work I have asked from you; My little pupil, stay near Me and love Me; I the Lord love you and bless you; have My Peace; come, Love is by your side IXΘΥΣ ⋆

14   Rhodos   29.7.91

My Lord, Your Name is an oil poured out,⋆¹ like those the icons pour out. It is your signature, my Lord. — "A spreading olive tree so fair, so sturdy, was Yahweh's Name for you..." Jr 11:16

My daughter, you are my Creator? I Am ....⋆²

ah My child, I came not only for you in this way but for all My other children too, to ask you to live holy and turn away from your evil ways of living; let Me fill your hope; I intend to come and visit every kind of misery on this earth and break you free from sin; I Am is My Name and I am Holy so I want you to live holy; sanctify your lives and turn into

⋆¹ Sg 1:3   ⋆² I sighed filled with joy but languishly desiring to be with Him.

15

My direction ♡ the Evil one has no hold over those who stay awake and pray without cease; open your hearts so that I enter in you and make My home in you; have My Peace ♡

30.7.91

My Vassula, let nothing stand between Me and you; like the moon and the sun are steady and follow faithfully their course of nature and do not simply vanish from the sky, I too am steadfast and by your side; yet even if these become unsteady, I shall never be unsteady; I am, I was, and will

16

always be steadfast by your side; when I reveal Myself, in fact when I reveal My entire Self to you and tell you that I shall never abandon you nor withdraw My gift from you or strip you of My Jewels, believe Me, and do not have the slightest shadow of doubt ♡ I have raised you up to be with Me and follow Me; so pupil of Mine, follow your Master, let your thoughts settle on Me; you were dead because you never knew Me, but the Word came to your ear and with a blessing, raised you, and with the Breath of His Holy Spirit

17

revived you and opened your eyes, then, with a Kiss from His Mouth made you His bride;

‒ I shall save you all in this way ‒

do not be afraid when I come with My Cross, My Thorned Crown and My Nails and offer them to you, because these priceless Jewels that I will be offering you, are those very ones I embraced ardently with love; they are the Instruments of your Redemption; ‒ allow Me to use you Vassula, so that through you in writing and orally I can pour out My Heart on this generation ♡ hope in Me, desire Me, do not

18

feel downcast; I Am is ever so near you, am I not worthy for more joy? O yes Lord! but let me feel You more! have I been with you all this time, and you still do not feel or notice My Presence? I have been preaching to you a considerable number of years and you still do not feel Me? I want more of You. I want to be drenched completely and litterally invaded by Your Holy Spirit.

come to Me and eat Me .... drink Me and at no cost at all! eat Me and you will hunger for more, drink Me and you will thirst for

19

more! receive Me with joy and let Me rejoice; learn how My Heart palpates and rejoices everytime I and you become one, united in love; come and get sanctified by eating My Body and drinking My Blood; ‒ yes, I thirst for You my Lord. hope in Me, thirst for Me and soon, very soon, your Holy One shall come and fetch you and take you to His Home which is your Home too; I bless you My daughter; I bless

You my God. ΙΧΘΥΣ ⤳

‒ For the Greek prayer group - Rhodos 2. 8. 91
Jesus, my Lord, blessed be Your Name. May Your Holy Name stand in Glory for ever and ever.

20

My Holy Name stands and will always stand in all its Glory ♡

May Your Hand guide us to the Truth and the only One Truth. Let nothing part me from this Truth You Yourself have given us.

you came empty to Me and departed full; I never stood in awe of greatness nor of strength; I Myself have filled your mouth with My Wisdom so that you may learn and not fall into error ♡ I have given you My instructions so that you may find your defence in them; listen now and understand:

set Our Two Sacred Hearts like a Seal on

21

your heart — the Sacred Heart of your Mother shall be your defence and My Own Sacred Heart your Home; with this Sign sealed on your heart, the foxes that make havoc of My Vineyards that are now in fruit, shall be caught; you, My little ones are : Our Vineyard* of Our Two Sacred Hearts; come, My little children and listen : who among you delights in Eternal Life? — adore Me then in the splendour of My Holiness; be constant with your prayers; — Satan will be chained by

* The prayer group is being named : "Prayer group of the Two Sacred Hearts."

22

the Rosary; — be constant in your confessions, little children, to be able to come and receive Me in the Holy Eucharist as often as you can; fast on bread and water two days a week, to make reparations and sacrifice; do not look to your left nor to your right, look in front of you where I Am; wherever I go you shall go, wherever I live you shall live; these, My beloved, are My Principles; My Word should be taken in like your daily food, it is your Heavenly Bread, it is your Life; come often to Me and consecrate yourselves to My

23

Sacred Heart and I shall breathe on you and make you Mine to spread My Word to the four corners of this earth, and remember, let your thoughts be My Thoughts, your desires My Desires, — imitate Me — blessed are you who do not see Me and yet believe; I leave My Sigh of Love on your forehead; bless Me and love Me; — tell them My Vassula, how I honour the Room* in which I was conceived;

ΙΧΘΥΣ 🐟

Our Blessed Mother's Message for the same group.
Blessed children, let your heart be like a

* Heart : Mary's Heart.

24

garden, agreeable to the Lord, a resting place to your King; allow Him to enter your heart so that even when He finds it arid and desolate, He would transform it into a garden of delights; allow Him to breathe in your heart to revive it; His Breath is of the subtlest fragrance, then, with His Blood, like morning dew, will wash away your stains to perfect you, My little ones; ah .... how I love you... come and listen to your God, His conversation is sweetness itself, compassion in its fulness, pray, My beloved ones, pray without cease;

25

your answer to your problems can be found in
a constant prayer; let this be your weapon,
pray with your heart, dialogue with God in
this way — Satan flees everytime you invoke
God with love, so today, tomorrow and always,
I will say to you: pray, pray, pray;
My Love for you is great, do not allow
Satan to tempt you to cut Me off from your
sight — be on your guard — I, your Holy
Mother bless you all, —

Yes my Jesus? (Jesus called me.)
Vassula, let your prayer groups be called:

26

Prayer group of the Two Sacred Hearts ♡♡
since Our Hearts are united in love and one,
— I Am by your side, love is near you;

Later on late in the evening I asked Jesus to explain
to me what happens to me when I'm living the Passion.

we are united as in one single body, then ....
I hold you, I seize you entirely, since you are
My property and I arrest your spirit; like a
kernel covered by the flesh of its fruit, I too
cover you in a similar way, your spirit becomes embodied in My Spirit, in Me, your
Christ ♡ love Me, adore Me and pray, I am

27

inseparable from you; O come, come, let your
love be an inexhaustible fire; I Am an Inexhaustible Fire that consumes souls; so imitate Me
your God, this is My desire for everyone;
have My Peace ♡

Rhodes 4.8.91

Lord, when the time comes for Your visitation
will we be ready? No one knows the hidden things
You have, yet, how many will continue to press their
persecutions on Your message? They twist what You
say, all they think of is how to prove to the world
that these messages are diabolical, New Age (sect),
or from an evil spirit; but my Yahweh whom I
adore, I intend, with Your Strength to "pay You my
thank-offerings, for You have rescued me from
Death to walk in Your presence"... Ps. 56: 12-13

fragrance of Mine, lean on Me; hear Me: shout!

28

shout to the nations without fear: repent!
for the Time of Mercy is almost over; change your
lives and live holy, sacrifice and amend your
lives before the Coming of the Lord; pray,
pray for those who suppress My Spirit, pray
for those who speak of unity but stretch a
net for those who practice it; I shall ask
their accounts in the day of Judgement, because
I have called and no one would answer; I
have spoken openly, yet no one listened; the
House I am rebuilding with the price of My
martyr saints' blood, they keep tearing

29

down; pray for the Peace of My House, peace between brothers, sincerity in the heart, lowliness and love, then.... unity will blossom in each heart ... and My Holy City, Jerusalem, will in one united whole, glorify Me ♡ Ah, Vassula, nothing is in vain, My Work that keeps you up late at nights will not go in waste; My word shall reach the ends of this world; be reassured My child; I, Jesus Christ, your Mother, the saints and your guardian angel are all beside you, do not fear, your Abba is your Strength and your Shelter; you are very precious

30

to Me My child; α ω

Rhodos   5.8.91

Lord, I feel like a boat without oars! My spirit is far from Yours, help me!

My wretched bride, who is taking care of you? who is taking care of your needs? You my Lord.

say: You, My Spouse; I have spoken through your confessor's mouth; I am your Spouse ♡ happy are you who received this grace; Heaven is your home ♡ we, us? Yes Lord forever.

My Lord and my God, I bless You, praised be Your Name! Glory be to God.

come, rest your head on My Heart, feel this Love I have for you; feel Heaven in you and rejoice,

31

rejoice My little one for your Saviour is with you and it is He who guides you and it is He who forms you to resemble Him ♡ ah..... be thirsty for Me and desire to drink from the Living Waters of Life, I the Lord shall provide your soul with this Water forever; alone you are not, NEVER!

... caress Me with your love, your thoughts, your heart, your good actions; daughter and bride of Mine, I shall help you ΙΧΘΥΣ ⟨⟩←

6.8.91

Save us all, Jesus! wait my Lord for all Your children to convert before Your Day comes! Your Throne is soon to descend among us, but are we all ready? Allow Your River whose streams refresh arid cities to flow in us Lord, drench us. Invade

32

us; besiege us, and once You are in us, Your cities can never fall! Sanctify Your dwelling; divinize us.

the Anointed One blesses you and urges you to pray; do not despair;* I am giving you enough time to reform, but will your generation understand? will they be willing to change their lives? you have to take in consideration, My child, the daily offences that are committed against Me; for, how long must your Anointed One be offended?.... have you got anything to tell Me; daughter? .... I hear nothing from you, grace! we need

* I had felt that somehow my prayers would not be enough nor of those others who prayed, because we are so few ...

33

grace to come back to You, just like me. I did not know anything about You and of how much I offended You my Lord, not until You came by grace to me.

keep praying for your brothers then, I said: it will not go as hard on Sodom as on this generation; do you remember Nineveh? they were at the verge of a great disaster, but they listened to Jonah, My mouthpiece, and from the highest to the least ... all, fasted, repented and vowed to change their life and live holy; "*† put yourselves on the ways of long ago, enquire about the ancient paths", seek the Truth; daughter,

* Jr 6 : 16

34

happy the man who will follow My advice; let Me tell you one more thing ♡ I, the Anointed One will engulf you all with My Fire and consume you to give your soul a new life; I have little time left now; these Times of Mercy and Grace are almost over; I am not concealing My Plans, nor am I hiding My Face, I am revealing as never before My Face; and you, My beloved ones, your duty is to go and spread these Messages of the Second Pentecost, and what the Spirit teaches; ΙΧΘΥΣ ><>

35

— Rhodos —
6. 8. 91

My Spirit is with your spirit; I fill you; ah, Vassula of My Sacred Heart, always remember these words:

The Way to My Cross is marked with My Blood;

and everyone who willingly takes this road, I bless and anoint; — you are hounded for My Sake, do not fear, I am near you and by your side to encourage you; — you are condemned, but it is only by the world; — for My Sake you are disgraced by human lip, rejoice! for I was too! have I not said

36

that no man is greater than His Master? you are the jest of your people,* but so was I, your King; when they scourge you on the Way to Calvary your blood will mingle with Mine, what better favour can I offer you than making out of you another live crucifix for My Glory? when I see your feet on the point of stumbling, I lift you and place you on My Shoulders, like a lamb; come; with Me you will always be safe ♡ Jesus, You are my Hope, My Strength, my Joy and my Song. I will always take refuge in Your Sacred Heart.

* many Greek orthodox theologians and monks mock me.

37

Rhodos 10. 8. 91

I Am asks you to abandon yourselves daily to Me; seek Me and you shall find Me, I and your Holy Mother tell you : pray, pray, pray and keep praying; Satan comes when you sleep, so do not give Satan a foothold; pray, for prayer _is_ your weapon against Satan; Love loves you, ΙΧΘΥΣ ><>

11. 8. 91

To the young prayer group of Athens and Rhodos.

I have said : you are My children of Light and I shall add to this : and your Dwelling is My Sacred Heart, remember, My Love for you all is Great; never, never ever forget this; ΙΧΘΥΣ ><>

38

(Jesus then asked us to read Col. 3 : 5-17.)
– For the group. –   Rhodos 12. 8. 91
My Lord and my God?

I Am; I shall speak freely to My lambs : all I ask from you is love; love Me without restrain; I am the Source of Sublime Love; come to Me and draw from Me and fill your hearts to be able to give this love to others; I am Present wherever you are, so never ever forget that where you are I Am; I the Lord bless you; ♡ care for your brothers and sisters and lead them to Me, let them too see My Holy Face ♡ I, My little children, have created you out of Love to

39

love Me, to console Me, to praise Me; – you want to Glorify Me? then love Me and adore Me, the door to Heaven are your prayers to Me; I want prayers from your heart; so I tell you, pray, pray, pray; – remember that your Mother's Heart and Mine are united in Love; so _you_, you whom My Heart loves, come to both of Us and I shall offer you your nest in My Sacred Heart and protection will be offered in your Mother's Heart; – I am the Resurrection and I shall re-surrect many more of you as I resurrected you; I am Mercy and out of My Boundless Mercy I let

40

My Heart be touched; Love and Mercy _is_ at your very doors, _now_! ΙΧΘΥΣ ><>

Rhodos 13. 8. 91
O Yahweh my God and Father, smile on us.
Lord? I Am; it is I, Yahweh, your Abba;

O God, have mercy on our wretchedness.

flower, I, Yahweh your God am most Merciful; I Am an endless Ocean of Mercy, Compassion and Tenderness ♡ I have given you My Law but it is not enough to say you know My Law, you have to practice My Law; it is not enough either to say you believe I Am, I desire you to love and adore Me; even the

41

demons believe that I Am but they do not love Me nor do they adore Me; they listen to My Voice but they do not love Me; be loyal to Me and you, you who are My seed, come to Me your Abba, and console Me; I - Am - weary - and you are only a remnant who can console Me; you are the smallest of the flock and My Eyes are upon you; your Abba, from His Throne tells you: I love you all with an eternal Love - be blessed a✝w

42

13. 8. 91

Lord, forgive us, for we have really failed to appreciate Your Great Love, we failed to appreciate Your Great Sacrifice, we failed to love and stay united; we keep repeating our errors continuously. O Lord Jesus we need desperately Your help to come back to our senses. Come and rescue us, the garland of divinity has fallen from our heads; look on us and see our wretchedness, our pitiful degradation, our atrophy to what is holy. Make us come back to You, by coming to visit each one of us, as You have visited me, visit the rest of Your children and show them Your Heart.

I want My Vassula to hear from every lip:
" Jesus, I love You, save my soul and save the souls of others too " ♡ so pray for the conversion of these poor souls, pray novenas and I shall listen; I can change

43

stubbornness to comply, so pray to My Sacred Heart and I shall do the rest; ♡

18. 8. 91.

O Lord, I am so troubled, to the point of death. It is my Gethsemane today; my soul is battered and distressed. Satan has definitely made me a target to dash me to pieces. Pitiless, he pierces me through and through ... I am the butt of my persecutors, where then is my hope?

In My Sacred Heart My dove; your cote is My Sacred Heart; turn to Me and My Spirit will console you; offer Me your troubles and I shall thrust them in My Heart, I shall make good use of them, I shall liberate souls from purgatory .... then forget your troubles of these days

44

and rest in Me your God; I am an Ocean of Peace; give Me, daughter all your tribulations and My Peace shall annihilate them; have My Peace My lamb, - I love you; - I offer Peace; rest in Me; go now in Peace; ΙΧΘΥΣ ><>

19. 8. 91

Lord, when peacemakers* work for peace, sowing seeds which bear good fruit, guided by the Holy Spirit, why are they told to keep quiet, why are they hounded, why are they disbelieved?

because they*² are bought like expensive material by merchants; Rationalism blurs their spirit, dulls their sense of discernment and kills their

* Peacemakers: those who evangelise the Word of God to bring the world back to God and reconcile with God.
*² The disbelievers

45

humility ; like Sodom and Egypt they are rejecting all that comes from the inner part of the Church, the inner power, which is :

My Holy Spirit

nevertheless, I shall give you My Strength to proceed for this is My Will ☧

20.8.91

How delightful it will be for all christians to live together like brothers. How much greater Your Glory would be to see us humble, around one single Tabernacle and Altar, praising You with one heart, one mind, and one voice... yet when I follow Your orders and I witness of unity, I am not understood nor believed. Like a millstone they smash me on the ground.

My child, the Anointed One is your shepherd and

46

He shepherds you by opening your path ; clothed in My Blessings all I ask from you is to pass on the Love I have given you to the nations ; allow Me to use you little soul ; Abba has you in His Arms ; I Am is with you ; — look at Me, what will I not do for you .... and you, can you utter the same words? Yes Lord — arise then and continue to witness ; your race is not yet over, but do not lose heart, by your side I am to encourage your little heart ; your ankles are bonded to Mine, and My lips are stuck to your ear to whisper

47

to you and remind you that you are not greater than your Divine Master, you who are just My pupil will they not induce on you the same marks as your Master, the Prime Martyr ? My daughter, love Me and I shall continue to pour out to you the Riches of My Sacred Heart, all this Wealth that had been reserved for your Times ♡ I had once said that from My Sacred Heart I will perform at the End of Times, works as never before, works that will marvel you, to show the radiant glory of My Sacred Heart ; I had promised that I would

48

expose My Sacred Heart entirely and wholeheartedly to entice hearts because My words are sweeter than honey, ♡ everything shall be accomplished in time, ♡ trust Me ; let no one deceive you My child, My Gift has already proved itself ; — I bless you ; — Wisdom shall continue Her Good Works with you ♡ ☧

30. 8. 91

My Lord and my Life.

I Am ; silence is the best weapon after prayer ; — I will trample on My enemy soon ♡ Vassula, hear Me : your Holy One ♡

49

is resurrecting Russia to be a noble nation; Russia will be perfected in the Arms of her Spouse ♡ I the Lord shall perfect her; have I not said to you My child, that I have My Hand on her cold heart warming it?* and the day My bride will open her eyes and see Me her Spouse standing beside her, she shall see and understand what My Hands have done in her midst and from thereon, Russia, My bride shall openly hold My Name Holy; and all erring evil spirits

* See prophetic message on Russia of 11.03.1988

50

within her will flee; I had told you all these things before they happen so that you may believe that it is I, the Almighty, who is guiding you; hear Me: I shall not conceal My Plans; if men are tempted to conceal My Plans, I, with My Own Hand shall unveil everything to you all before they happen the Holy One has been warning you, I ♡ had not been menacing anyone of you ♡ — a Ray of Light from Heaven shall come in the midst of My Body* and change the

* Church

51

face of this earth and bring peace among brothers*; this will be the reward of the martyr saints' prayers, sacrifices, penances, constancy and faith; — do not be afraid when the hour of great distress comes if you were constant and kept your faith, for this Hour has to come to change the face of this earth; thus everything said at Fatima will be accomplished; — the Father loves you all and He judges no one; already

* Here I understood that the Lord was alluding to the UNITY of the Churches.

52

The Reaper is at work ♡ the Father's Works will astonish you all; — and to you, My child, look back into My Messages, had I not said that I, the Lord, have done many wonders for you and shall do more these coming days?* see how My predictions come true? and now I am telling you that the Heavens soon shall deluge with My Coming upon you; My Fire shall be hurled on this earth to burn up her crimes;

* God refers to His message of the 23.7.91, that in the coming days He shall do more wonders. Prediction alluding to the fall of communism in Russia.

53

I will not restrain My Hand ♡ My Holy Name is daily profaned and My observances are scorned; this is to fulfill the words said in Scriptures; (write): "Immediately, there was a violent earthquake, and a tenth of the city collapsed; seven thousand persons*¹ were killed in the earthquake, and the survivors, overcome with fear, could only praise the God of Heaven;" (Ap. 11:13)*² there is very little time left now; forgive your

*¹ That is, a great number of all classes.
*² Read also: Mt 24:22 + Mt 24:29-30

54

neighbour while you have still time; make reparations, fast; if you are a sinner who sows trouble between friends, repent, for the sake of My Holy Name return to Me; you are master of your will but not of My Plans, and I urge you to surrender quickly; Satan is sending his adepts untiringly to all of you, so be on your guard more than ever;

his reign is near its end; this is why he will just for one last time vomit on this earth hoping to sweep away as many souls as he could; ♡ this is why there

55

must be constancy and faith in you, because you can avoid and even stop Satan from vomiting on this earth ♡ — courage, daughter, lift your head and lean on Me; I shall continue helping you ΙΧΘΥΣ 🐟

Lord all Merciful, let those who say:
"We will go our own way;" return to You; and those Christians who say to the Pope:
"We will go our own way;" return and obey the Pope. Let their human pride lower its eyes and their arrogance humbled. Amen.

                                    3.9.91
Lord, Father and Master of our lives, do not abandon us now nor in the days of distress.
Lord, Father and Master of our lives, help Russia to grow in Your Spirit. You have pierced the Red Dragon through, that had besieged her.

56

Lord, Father and Master of our lives, rescue us from the Rebel that still remains among us.
ah, My child, I shall teach you all by My Purifying Fire, wait and you shall see ♡ Hear Me now and write, My child:
not long ago most of the nations of the world never believed that the enemy, the Red Dragon would lose its power, in Russia, so suddenly; Vassula, if your sister Russia rebelled against Me, it came through the sins of the world and its crimes; tyranny comes from below; But how did her children feel, those martyrs who belonged to You?

57

how can I describe what her children suffered, to what can I compare them, daughter? all Heaven mourned for her children; her sons layed helpless, but who was there around them to mourn for them? was there anyone strong enough among them to pierce the Dragon through? not when their skins were shrunken against their bones; her children went begging for Bread, oppressed by the enemy, they collapsed under their burden; if they left in secrecy to take refuge in My Arms, they would be punished severely; they were not allowed to show their

58

zeal for Me; their pursuers were swifter than vipers eyeing each step they took, and had they any suspicions that The Book of Life would be hidden under their mattress, My children would be harassed, tracked, then captured, ah, daughter, My Eyes wept ceaselessly to see this nation reduced to silence by the sword; priests and prophets were made prisoners and were forced to dwell in darkness; many of them were slaughtered pitilessly before My very Eyes; - this nation who at one time honoured Me and praised Me openly, radiant as a sapphire,

59

a Citadel of delights, was reduced into a waterless country of drought, by the sins and crimes of the world; I tell you, daughter, Russia, your sister, has not yet shown you what she will accomplish in My Name ♡:

the Day of Festival has yet to

come and how I wish it were

here already!

pray, pray for this Glorious Day ♡ -

9. 9. 91

My Jesus?

I Am; love Me Vassula, it appeases the

60

Father's wrath on this generation; -

I have prayed for you, My little one, to the Father to liberate you of "the thorn" you took from Me* ...   Lord, confirm please what

I've come to hear from You by giving me a passage from Scriptures. (I open at random the Holy Bible and my finger goes on to Lk 22:42) It reads :

      Father, he said, if you are willing take this cup away from me. Nevertheless, let Your will be done, not mine. "

be blessed I shall guide you; ΙΧΘΥΣ ⋈⊙

* I had offered Jesus to take upon me this "thorn" from Him (18.6.91) It meant one thorn less on Jesus. "The thorn" that Jesus talks about is referred in a message dated 18.6.91. - This thorn was given to Jesus by a loved one who actively persecutes the Message. Satan confused him and now uses him.

61

11. 9. 91

Lord, I look up at the heavens and search for heavenly things; I search Your Holy Face to feel Peace and be able to rejoice; I search for Your Holy Face to be able to contemplate.

And I for My part My Eyes look down at the world of today, searching nation after nation, scanning soul after soul for some warmth, for some generosity and for some love, but very, very few enjoy My favour; very few bother to live a holy life; and the days are fleeing and the hours are now counted before the great retribution ♡ My cities* have become a harlot's! pitiless ♡!

* cities here is used by God for the word: "souls"

62

they have become a citadel for the demons! all corrupt from within, eaten up by worm! a refuge for the viper and the scorpion! how can I not breathe on these renegades My Purifying Fire? ..... (Jesus suddenly changed tone and after waiting a few seconds, with a a tone very grave that left me in awe said:)

___ the earth will shiver and shake ___ and every evil built into Towers* will collapse into a heap of rubble and be buried in the dust of sin! above, the Heavens will shake and the foundations of the earth will rock! pray

* Like the Tower of Babel

63

that the Father's Hand will not come down in winter; the islands, the sea and the continents will be visited by Me unexpectedly, with thunder and by Flame; listen closely to My last words of warning, listen now that there is still time; read Our Messages*, and stop being scornful or deaf when Heaven speaks, lower your voices and you will hear Ours; think twice before you judge; think more than twice before you condemn the Works of the Holy Spirit; I shall not spare anyone who mocks

* Jesus' and Mary's, those Two Witnesses.

64

the Holy Spirit blaspheming Him outright; Justice will send them down to the underworld ♡ lift all of you your faces and search the Heavens for My Holy Face to contemplate! lift your eyes towards Heaven and you shall not perish; repent! and ask the Father to relent; soon, very soon now, the Heavens will open and I shall make you see

The Judge

α ✠ ω

Order Form

Quantity	Title	Price	Amount
	"True Life in God" Volume 1	$9.95	
	"True Life in God" Volume 2	$9.95	
	"True Life in God" Volume 3	$9.95	
	"True Life in God" Volume 4	$9.95	
		Sub-total	
	Tax for Missouri Residents 5.975%		
	Shipping and Handling @ $2 per book		
		Total	

Please type or print clearly

Name _____

Address _____

City _____

State _____ Zip _____ Phone _____

❑ Check   ❑ MasterCard   ❑ Visa

Account # _____

Expiration Date _____

Signature _____

Trinitas™ *P.O. Box 475, Independence, MO 64051, USA* • *Phone Orders:* (816) 254-4489

Order Form

Quantity	Title	Price	Amount
	"True Life in God" Volume 1	$9.95	
	"True Life in God" Volume 2	$9.95	
	"True Life in God" Volume 3	$9.95	
	"True Life in God" Volume 4	$9.95	
		Sub-total	
	Tax for Missouri Residents 5.975%		
	Shipping and Handling @ $2 per book		
		Total	

Please type or print clearly

Name _____

Address _____

City _____

State _____ Zip _____ Phone _____

❑ Check   ❑ MasterCard   ❑ Visa

Account # _____

Expiration Date _____

Signature _____

Trinitas™ *P.O. Box 475, Independence, MO 64051, USA* • *Phone Orders:* (816) 254-4489